...IN SEARCH OF

THE
HEALING
PLACE

AFGHANISTAN... & OTHER STORIES

D D MURRAY MCGAVIN MD
MBE MD(Hons) FRCSEd FRCOphth

WESTBOW
PRESS®
A DIVISION OF THOMAS NELSON
& ZONDERVAN

WestBow Press books may be ordered through booksellers or by contacting:

WestBow Press
A Division of Thomas Nelson & Zondervan
1663 Liberty Drive
Bloomington, IN 47403
www.westbowpress.com
844-714-3454

Graphic design of Book Covers by Don and Ellie Watson

ISBN: 979-8-3850-2413-1 (sc)
ISBN: 979-8-3850-2415-5 (e)

Library of Congress Control Number: 2024908138

Print information available on the last page.

WestBow Press rev. date: 8/2/2024

REVIEW BY ALISTAIR PETRIE

What a timely publication—especially when the global arena is crying out for hope and clarity in the midst of many pressing challenges!

Murray is clearly a champion of, and for people—irrespective of their status and nation. In this publication we find a treasure of medical skill combined with the testimony of extraordinary breakthroughs, mixed with personal and humorous anecdotes. While focused upon Afghanistan, the principles and content of this publication are for all people in all nations—so appropriate for such a time as this.

Well-presented and easily understood, these pages offer the reader a lifetime of personal experience and transparency, mixed with reality and a deep faith.

I am very aware of the timeliness of this publication since it is not only about the subject of physical sight but also contains a compelling wake-up call for spiritual insight.

Be prepared to be informed—challenged—and deeply encouraged as you read the testimony and insight of a living blueprint of and for life. I strongly recommend *In Search of the Healing Place* for all people—all leaders, and all readers—and would hope this blueprint for life reaches into many nations.

Murray lives out this inspiring reminder—'But one thing I do: Forgetting what is behind and straining toward what is ahead, I press on toward the goal to win the prize for which God has called me heavenward in Christ Jesus' (Philippians 3:13b–14 NIV).

Rev Dr Alistair P. Petrie
Pastor—Author—Executive Director, Partnership Ministries

REVIEW BY SANDY MILLAR

This is no ordinary biography!

At one level it is a fascinating and inspiring account of one man, his family, and a life lived to the full. It is by turns extremely interesting and informative, covering his wide interests and experiences with humour and humility.

Murray is one of a long line of Scots, whose ancestry and rugged faith—steeped in a love of rugby, a sense of fun, and a real call to sacrificial service in many lands—has led to a life full of interest. Our increasing admiration is maintained as the story unfolds.

The medically minded will be inspired by Murray's long service as a senior ophthalmologist in Afghanistan. His insights and infectious love of all things relating to that country, even in dangerous situations, are gripping!

At a deeper level, it becomes clear that Murray's whole life and approach to every situation springs from his lifelong Christian faith, shared with Ruth and their family, David, Andrew, and Carrie.

Their love for God and confidence in His provision saw them through great joys in professional and family life—and later, in the deepest tragedy when David was killed, aged 28. Some of the most moving passages in this book cover their experiences of God's love with unsentimental and profound honesty—not just in the laughter, but also supremely in the tears, that make up the Christian life.

A book very hard to put down. I wholeheartedly commend it!

Bishop Sandy Millar
Former Vicar of Holy Trinity Brompton, London

REVIEW BY MARTIN FAIR

This is a book which would be worth reading at any time, but the recent events unfolding in Afghanistan have made it all the more relevant.

The first thing to say is that it's a wonderfully easy read—not because it's an 'easy' subject but because Murray has a style which allows you to flip effortlessly through the pages in something of a roller coaster ride. And on top of that, the account is thoroughly personal. Murray invites you to journey with him and his family, and the intimacy of the narrative keeps it from ever becoming dry or distant.

In this volume, you'll find vivid geographical and topographical descriptions of the land of Afghanistan; you'll find careful analysis of the sociopolitical circumstances; and, of course, you'll find an exhilarating account of God at work in the most dramatic of ways. Something of that 'God at work' is seen in Murray's own life. He speaks of a prophetic word being spoken over him and of the immediate difference it made in his life. He speaks of being 'free, released and liberated' and of that being a pivotal moment in his life. The authenticity of Murray's recollection of those moments is clear, and his excitement comes rushing off the page—here as in so many other places throughout the book.

As someone who loves mountains, I read extensively of the early European exploration of the Everest region—and without fail, I'm left feeling somewhat jealous, with a sense of 'I wish I had been there!' This book had exactly the same effect on me. It draws you in and leaves you with such a vivid picture of the times and places and people being described that you can't help but picture yourself among them.

And, throughout, that is the quality of Murray's writing: evocative, detailed, engaging. Very occasionally, I'll give up on a book. Try as I might, I just can't get into it and reluctantly decide not to devote any more time to it. *In Search of the Healing Place* is at exactly the other end of the spectrum! As you read, very fittingly given the subject matter, your eyes are opened. God at work indeed.

The Very Rev Dr Martin Fair
Former Moderator, General Assembly of the Church of Scotland (2020–2021)

For my dear family, this is offered as an attempted history, initially on my side of the family. Ruth has written her own parents' story some years ago.

To Ruth: 'Who can find a virtuous woman? Her worth is far above rubies.' (Proverbs 31:10).

To David (1972—2000), Andrew, and *Caroline:* I trust that what is written reflects in some way our love for them and theirs for us.

CONTENTS

ACKNOWLEDGEMENTS

Some family members and friends have encouraged me to write and present these stories in book form.

My dear wife of over 50 years, Ruth, has been her usual encouraging self and, indeed, has contributed to a number of the stories offered. How many times have Ruth and I said to each other, 'It's not been boring!'

My sister, Margery, has been a vital and always available adviser, particularly on the early days and years in China, when my appreciation of events was non-existent, as a brand-new baby, about whom the Chinese were very concerned, as I was completely bald!

The stimulus to write was certainly enhanced by my cousin, Elizabeth, with her husband, Sanda. Elizabeth and Sanda very kindly set up a housing arrangement for us to settle in Arbroath, Scotland. At the time of that arrangement, they encouraged me to write. A letter, dated 24 January 2017, included the following handwritten note:

> We still feel you have a wonderful story to write.
> Just get on with it!

Why Arbroath? The draw to Arbroath on Scotland's east coast was especially because my best man of many years ago, Rev Alistair Keddie, and his wife, Elizabeth, lived there. Alistair, Elizabeth, and I had been together in Theological College (BTI, Glasgow).

In the early stages of writing, Craig and Anne Stocks, leaders of our Church Fellowship in Dundee, kindly provided an office in The Friary so that I could file my papers in some semblance of order.

Two readers with considerable experience, wisdom, and insight have read the early texts and given sound advice and suggestions.

I am so grateful to Peter Horrobin, Founder of Ellel Ministries. My thanks also to the Reverend Dr Martin Fair, minister of St Andrews Church, Arbroath, and also Moderator of the Church of Scotland (2020 – 2021), for 'early' advice and encouragement. More recently, Dr Fair has kindly written a Review.

Bishop Sandy Millar, formerly Vicar of Holy Trinity Brompton, London, where our son David was a member, has written a generous report, with personal insight and understanding of our family.

The Reverend Dr Alistair P. Petrie, BC, Canada, has written a kind endorsement, a timely and refreshing boost for an author bringing a manuscript towards final copy.

Chris Mungeam has been a wonderful resource person, with vast experience of publishing and publishers. His guidance has been invaluable.

Richard Fairhead provided expert advice and practical support on the layout of the manuscript after the umpteenth proofread and adjustments to the text.

Jonathan Lee, an expert on Afghanistan and its people, kindly advised on Farsi texts, where I have attempted to record the colloquial language we learned.

The discipline of writing needs conducive environments and a well-maintained laptop to see words actually appearing in print. Darren in The Cold Room, Arbroath, has been the excellent go-to man for all laptop problems and needs, as well as advising regarding the idiosyncrasies of my printer.

My thanks to Marco and his team at The Old Boatyard

Restaurant, Arbroath Harbour, who have always provided a cheerful welcome and an excellent cappuccino when I arrived with my laptop and printed text in hand.

Finally, I want to acknowledge the family members and friends who have enriched our lives and yet may not have been written about in this story. Some, of course, may be quite content to have been omitted. But for the glaring omissions, please forgive me.

INTRODUCTION

It all began in Shanghai.

In the years that followed, two invasions and two civil wars, in China, as a boy and later, in Afghanistan, as a doctor, who had specialized in ophthalmology.

Japan had invaded China. In the late 1930s, our family watched Japanese fighter planes bombing Shanghai.

Later, in 1949, Mao Tse-tung marched south with his communist People's Liberation Army, defeating the Nationalist Army of Chiang Kai-shek.

The coup d'etat of April 1978, in Afghanistan, was quite another story, an experience we shall never forget! Our home in Kabul was suddenly shaken by thundering shells and rockets, with the sound of gunfire and tanks rumbling down our road a few yards away. Jet fighters dive-bombed the palace in Kabul, and when a tank shell screamed past our boys' bedroom window, we took the family downstairs at speed, under the dining room table!

At the end of 1979, Soviet forces invaded Afghanistan.

From an early age, I felt the call of God to serve Him, as a doctor, probably in a country distant to the UK. The country that captured my interest and affection was Afghanistan. By this time, I had specialised in eyes (ophthalmology). I was introduced to NOOR, a fine eye-care programme in Afghanistan.

Prayer has been a vital part of my daily walk with God. This has included, at times, prayer 'in the name of Jesus' for healing, even in the medical context.

Let me now share some of these experiences while in search of the healing place.

Angus, Scotland
January, 2024

Part One

EARLY YEARS IN CHINA AND PREPARATION

PARENTS AND GRANDPARENTS

MY FATHER, DAVID

My father did not have the early privileges of my mother. Born in Glasgow in 1901, his much-loved mother died after a sinus operation during one of the awful Glasgow fogs. Dad was just 14. At the same time, the Great War was slaughtering the best young men in Europe. His older brother, William, who was in the Highland Light Infantry (HLI), was killed in France. His was an unknown grave, of which there were so many.

Dad's father, my grandfather, married again, but it seemed that his wife was not so concerned about the young David. A family in my father's church, The Tabernacle, near Charing Cross, Glasgow, took David in and cared for him.

My father's mother was musical, and Dad inherited her gift. He was an organist, playing regularly in churches from a young age. But an even more striking gift was his singing. He had a rich and dramatic tenor voice with a wide range, singing the tenor solos in Handel's *Messiah* and in other oratorios.

Aged 17, my father stood in for the usual organist in a big church in Glasgow. The young minister kept on apologizing to a visiting and well-known preacher that it wasn't the usual organist. Eventually, the 'great preacher' said he was sure the young man would do fine. Now, my father had been told by a patronizing critic that he could really play the organ if he played the 'Wedding March' by Mendelssohn. At the end of the service, he launched into the postlude, and the congregation left the church to the glorious music of Mendelssohn's 'Wedding March'!

He had a high sense of duty and responsibility, one could say characteristic of the Presbyterian work ethic. His writing was neat, but with a symmetrical flow.

One lesson for me was his response to my delight that I was only a halfpenny out when I was dealing with cash for our Bible class. 'Oh dear, Murray! Where could that halfpenny have gone?'

After two years' training in architecture and studies at Theological College, God called him to China.

My father returned home from China in the 1920s, when he was still single. He was expected to do 'deputation', which meant visiting many churches and speaking at meetings about the work in China. Of course, he was happy to do this. My father was an easy storyteller and a very good mimic. He would relate many stories, whether informally, often with humour, or in the pulpits of different churches. However, after months of moving around, living out of a suitcase became quite wearisome. Then an apologetic request was made.

'David, we're so very sorry to ask you, but would you consider going back to China earlier than planned?' The plan had been to be in Scotland for nine months. 'There is a real need for you go back and sort out issues that have arisen. We're so sorry to make this request.'

My father apparently replied quickly and easily that he would be absolutely delighted to go back to China immediately.

ERIC LIDDELL

In China, my father shared a bachelor home with three other men. One was a surgeon. Another was Eric Liddell, the famous Scottish sprinter who refused to run on a Sunday at the Paris Olympics in 1924.

Liddell was offered an alternative place in the heats of the 400 metres, which he had seldom run before. He was into the final but was in the least favoured outside lane, with a staggered start. Just before the race, Liddell was given a note by a member of the British support team. It included the words from the Bible 'Those who honour Me, I will honour' (1 Samuel 2:30).

As we will know if we have seen the film *Chariots of Fire*, Eric Liddell won the gold medal and beat the Olympic and World records for the 400 metres!

My father once asked Eric Liddell if he prayed to win a race. Liddell replied, 'I pray that the best runner will win!' That story has often been repeated when stories have been shared about Eric Liddell.

It certainly sounds like a Christian response. It very definitely influenced how I would pray and also how my children have prayed when playing in different sports over the years.

SAILING OUT TO CHINA

So far as I know, there was no discussion between my future father and mother about marriage before he sailed to China, probably for his second tour of duty in the late 1920s. They would have met at different church meetings and informal gatherings, particularly as my mother's parents had previously been in China. However, my father apparently did suggest that they might write to each other.

In those days, the way you travelled to far-off lands was by sea. After 30 years of service in China, my father had sailed around the world six times. He would say that in all his travels, visiting many countries, the most beautiful country in the world ... is Scotland. Clearly, there was absolutely no bias in this statement of fact!

In later years my parents said how much they appreciated the three weeks sailing out to China and the return journey, perhaps via the United States and Canada, because they were able to relax and be refreshed before arrival at their destination. In modern-day travel, of course, you reach your destination within a matter of hours, with very little respite.

THE MONGOLIAN TRANSLATOR

My father's stories of the effect and power of the Word of God (The Bible) in people's lives never ceased to move me.

One story he related was about a Mongolian man whom the Bible Society in China asked to help them translate the New Testament into a Mongolian dialect. The man agreed, but on one condition: they should not try to convince him about the truth of the gospel. It was agreed they would simply translate the words before them.

It seems that they were progressing through the gospels of Matthew, Mark, Luke, and John. They reached the words of Jesus, spoken when He was at the point of death on the cross: 'Father, forgive them, for they know not what they do' (Luke 23:34 KJV).

I have always pictured the group around a table with Bibles open in front of them. The Mongolian translator had spoken the words from Luke's gospel. Then he repeated the words: 'Father, forgive them, for they know not what they do.'

The way he said the words once, then twice, captured the group's attention, and each one must have been looking at him. The Mongolian looked at his new colleagues and friends in translation. He said, 'I see it now. It was for me He died!'

MY MOTHER, MARGARET

My mother, Margaret, had altogether more advantages in her early life. She was born in Edinburgh but lived in Glasgow, where she attended Park School for Girls. Her parents were in various businesses, particularly in the Glasgow area. One of their business interests was the famous Murray's Diary, which had provided train time tables since the early 1840s and continued for over a century until the 1960s. My mother's parents, with their family business interests, were able to raise their own financial support in travelling to China.

So it was that God called my grandparents, James and Elizabeth Murray, to China. They were there, in China, in 1900 and at the time of the anti-imperial, anti-colonial, and anti-Christian Boxer Rebellion.

The stories of my grandfather travelling on horseback, carrying the Scriptures over considerable distances, are recorded in airmail letters that he wrote and sent back to Scotland. Each letter had fine line drawings illustrating the texts.

One day, my grandfather was on horseback, guiding Old Rascal along a mountain path. Old Rascal slipped and stumbled, then, tragically, was unable to recover and fell over the cliff edge! My grandfather just managed to hang on and survived, but, sadly, Old Rascal was lost.

Another letter home to Scotland described the occasion when the only place available for my grandfather to sleep as he travelled was an opium den! The line drawings show men lying about in a large room, smoking tobacco mixed with opium.

James and Elizabeth Murray had four children: Alexander, Margaret, Thomas, and William.

In the early 1980s, my Uncle Tom expanded on a previously drafted Murray family tree. The family tree has the usual mix of the famous and the infamous! Suffice to say (and I'm a wee bit proud of this) the family tree goes back to Robert the Bruce, King of Scotland, victor at the Battle of Bannockburn in 1314.

All three brothers were good rugby players, each one in the Glasgow Academy 1st XV. My mother was a respected field hockey player, tipped to play for Scotland. She said she had to join her three brothers to play rugby and make it two-a-side! Of course, no girl played rugby in those days.

My mother and her brother Tom both studied Medicine. Younger brother, Bill, became an accountant. The oldest, Alexander (Alec), went straight from the cadets in his school, Glasgow Academy, commissioned as a Second Lieutenant in the Highland Light Infantry, to the war in France. So very sadly, he was killed leading his men out of the trenches, near Beaumont Hamel. It was on the 18th of November, 1916, on the last day of the Battle of the Somme. He was 18 years old.

Uncle Alec, who was born in China in 1897, wanted to become a doctor and serve God somewhere overseas. He wrote about this in a letter before the battle. God would protect him if his life's work was still ahead of him. At the front of his Bible, he had written words referring to the Christian's battle in life and its ending:

> And when the fight is ended,
> By Him so well begun,
> What joy for me, His face to see
> and hear Him say, 'Well done!'
> Lord help me ere I finish
> And lay my armour down,
> To win for Thee the victory
> And gain from Thee the crown.

A booklet was written about Uncle Alec, called *In Memoriam*. Many contributed to the content of the book. One of my favourite tributes was by a schoolboy contemporary of Alec, recorded by the Reverend John A Hutton, Minister of Belhaven United Free Church: 'Alec Murray looks fierce at football (rugby), and yet he is the decentest fellow you could ever meet!'

A poignant and special memory for me, in playing rugby, was the comment by an older friend of the family who was watching me play. He had known my Uncle Alec as a boy, and he said that my mannerisms and style of play were my Uncle Alec all over again! I was born more than 20 years after Alec's untimely death at the Somme.

The loss of my Uncle must have had such a profound and shattering effect on the Murray family. We have visited their home, Wilmore, off Byres Road in Glasgow's west end. I imagined my grandmother receiving the much dreaded black-rimmed telegram at the front door.

My mother described the heartbreak of families who attended the nearby Belhaven United Free Church during the 1914–1918 Great War. She said that hardly a Sunday went by without a family losing a son. One family lost three sons!

In describing both sides of my family, I am sad that I never knew any of my four grandparents. This being so, I prayed early on that our three children would know their grandparents. The prayer was answered, because David, Andrew, and Caroline knew and remembered all four grandparents, even if Caroline was only a very small child when she describes my father, before he died, standing near to the baby grand piano in my parents' flat in Kelvin Court, Anniesland, Glasgow.

A ROMANTIC LONG-DISTANCE PROPOSAL

My father-to-be sent a letter to my mother-to-be from China, proposing marriage. The year was 1930. Probably, he asked her to reply by telegram, which she did, with just the answer he was hoping for!

My mother, who in the 1920s had been practising Medicine

in Glasgow, had previously planned to go to China, but one of her parents became unwell and so she deferred going overseas. Sometime later, Dad's letter arrived!

In 1931, my mother sailed out to China. On the ship with her were her brother, Dr Tom Murray, and sister-in-law, Cathie, who had been a medallist nurse at the Western Infirmary, Glasgow.

Many years later, when we lived in Bedford, UK, my mother was visiting, aged 86. We had discovered that a fellow traveller out to China lived near to Bedford, and so we arranged a meeting. George Aldis presented my mother with a most historic photo. It was of my father meeting my mother on the quay when she disembarked at Shanghai, having sailed out to China to be married. Taken from the ship, at the dockside, there was a barrier still between them, and my father had a new trilby hat for the occasion.

My mother had no knowledge of this photo, seeing it for the first time 55 years after it was taken!

My sister, Margery, was born in Tientsin, China in 1933. There was a gap of five years before I came on the scene in Shanghai. The year, for me, was 1938.

Much was to happen in the following years to every family, including ours. The world was at war!

In 1931, Japan had invaded Manchuria, north-east China. From 1931 to 1937, China and Japan continued the conflict, mainly with smaller confrontations, described as 'incidents'. Some consider the Second Sino-Japanese War as stretching from 1937 to 1945, but, inevitably, that War was absorbed into the worldwide conflict that was World War II. This was especially so when the Pacific war erupted after Japan attacked Pearl Harbor, Hawaii, in 1941.

It was to be five years after I was born before we reached the United Kingdom, in 1943. First China; then Australia; after that, Canada; followed by Portugal and, finally, Great Britain.

EARLY YEARS IN CHINA AND SECOND WORLD WAR: 1939–1945

Japan had invaded China in 1931. With its powerful imperialist army, it soon controlled the Chinese provinces in the north-east, the region of Manchuria.

The relative impasse in the conflict was disturbed by renewed Japanese aggression during 1937 and 1938. Shanghai and Nanjing were captured by the Japanese in 1937.

I was born in Shanghai in 1938. Being rather small, I have no memory of events of those days and had always thought that we sailed from Shanghai 'on the last ship' *before* the Japanese took over Shanghai. But my sister, Margery, corrected my understanding of the sequence of events.

THE JAPANESE ATTACK SHANGHAI

In 1937, Japanese forces attacked the Chinese defences in and around Shanghai. My sister describes watching the fighting from the roof of a building. Our father allowed Margery to see Japanese planes flying over the 'Chinese areas' of Shanghai, which, of course, was most of Shanghai. The Japanese pilots were certainly instructed to avoid hitting the recognized French and British Concessions and the International Settlement, where many foreigners lived. Our family had a home in the French Concession—1292 Avenue Joffre.

The Japanese occupied Shanghai.

Margery has filled in some details. 'Murray, I remember riding in a rickshaw to school in Shanghai through Japanese military checkpoints.' The distance travelled each school day, one way, was about a mile.

She relates a rather poignant story concerning a certain Japanese soldier who was on duty at a particular checkpoint. He seemed to appreciate my sister coming through the checkpoint in the early morning and had a ready smile. One morning, he took a photo from his pocket and showed it to Margery. The photo was of his own daughter, who was about Margery's age.

On 3 September 1941, our family left for routine leave, deciding to go to Australia for what was called, in those days, our 'furlough'. I suppose there was no immediate prospect of travelling back to the United Kingdom for leave, with the world in such increasing turmoil.

As events unfolded, we certainly had no opportunity of returning to China. Many of our friends and colleagues, including the Scottish runner Eric Liddell, were detained in internment camps.

FLYING CHINESE CARPETS

A story that came to light after the War concerned one large and two smaller Chinese carpets. It was 1947. I had sailed out to China with my mother. My father had gone ahead of us. Margery stayed in Scotland for her secondary schooling, a very difficult decision. A family living in Shanghai, expats like ourselves, appeared at our house with three absolutely filthy Chinese carpets. 'These are your carpets. We turned over the corner of a carpet and saw your name very clearly indicating ownership!'

Apparently, the Japanese had used our carpets in their offices right through the war years, but they had lasted the test of time and found their way to the home of our friends.

The 'flying' carpets found their way to our home in Glasgow, Scotland.

EN ROUTE TO AUSTRALIA

Our British ship took us to Java, Indonesia, where the heat was almost unbearable. Dad arranged for us to go up into the mountains, by train, to beyond Bandung, near to the volcano Tangkuban Perahu. The landscape around had many terraced rice fields. We were there for two weeks. It was a fabulous hotel. Each family had its own self-contained bungalow, and breakfast was brought to us each morning on our personal terrace.

A Dutch ship carried us all the way south to Sydney. The Dutch crew were so friendly and particularly good with children. We had a one-night stopover in Surabaya, staying with friends. It was the end of September, and so Margery had a birthday, for which the friendly crew made her a birthday cake. The only other one-day stopover was in Brisbane, where the jacaranda trees were in full bloom.

We arrived in Sydney in November 1941. For some weeks, we were housed in a hostel, before renting a bungalow in Clifton Gardens, overlooking Sydney Harbour.

I was just three. It was here that my first memories of life are reasonably vivid. Nothing too dramatic. Simply 'painting' a green garage wall at the nursery, using a paintbrush dipped in a bucket of water.

PEARL HARBOR

But the War in the Pacific was escalating, and the United States' entry into the conflict was violent and sudden! Five weeks after our arrival in Sydney, on 7 December 1941, the Imperial Japanese Navy Air Service attacked the United States Naval Base at Pearl Harbor, Hawaii. The War in the Pacific was exploding on all fronts!

At the same time, the Japanese in China took over the International Settlement and other Concessions in Shanghai. British and American nationals were interned.

These were difficult days in which to make decisions. Should my father leave us as a family and even try to get back into China? The problem was resolved when my father was asked to return to Scotland, whenever possible, to assist with the work on the home front. Dad responded positively, but it took nine months before a sailing across the Pacific became available.

Still in Australia, and living in the choice location of Clifton Gardens, an astonishing attack took place. Three midget Japanese submarines came right into Sydney Harbour!

It was the night of 29 May 1942, and five large Japanese submarines had positioned themselves a few kilometres off Sydney Heads. The next day, the mother ships released the three midget submarines. There was loss of life on both sides. One submarine escaped, and two were destroyed by Australian armed forces. A reconstruct of a midget submarine was made and is still in the Australian War Memorial in the capital, Canberra.

We moved after some months to Epping, a suburb of Sydney. Memories begin to appear. My mother trying to teach me to ride a bicycle. One other memory is very clear. There had been a plague of flies. I remember walking into church and counting (or someone did) over 50 flies on the back of the woman in front of us! Of course, I was told that flies are not clean. Later, when out visiting, I was given a piece of sultana cake. So far so good; I like sultana cake. But on this occasion, I was observed picking out the sultanas from the cake, muttering, 'Dirty fly! Dirty fly!'

SINGING OUR WAY HOME

The more serious matter of our living and, for my parents— particularly my father—generating income in some reasonable way must have weighed heavily on them during those early weeks, during which we had been made most welcome in

Australia. In fact, my father had said, at some point in our early travels from China to Australia, 'We have nothing to worry about, because we have nothing!'

There has been reference previously to my father's singing voice. He had sung many times as tenor soloist in oratorios such as *The Messiah* (Handel), *The Creation* (Haydn), *Elijah* (Mendelssohn) and *The Crucifixion* (Stainer).

There had been many opportunities and requests to sing in China, particularly in the expat community, and also in the United Kingdom.

An invitation was extended by the Australian Broadcasting Corporation, with a mandate 'To Whom It May Concern' that our father was to be engaged in 'Work of National Importance'. My father's work was singing!

During the many months in Sydney, our father sang in *The Song of Hiawatha* (Longfellow; music by Coleridge-Taylor) with the outstanding tenor Heddle Nash. They were the male soloists in *Hiawatha*, sung in the original Sydney Opera House.

Years later, in Scotland, I would listen to Heddle Nash singing the tenor solos in Handel's *Messiah* while studying for my Highers.

We sailed from Sydney on 7 January 1943, in a Norwegian ship. At night, the ship was blacked out. The status of the ship was interesting. The Nazis had already occupied Norway, on the other side of the world. We crossed the Pacific without stopping, reaching San Francisco, thence to Seattle, and on to Vancouver.

Margery describes our meeting with Mrs Ronald Coleman, wife of the well-known actor, on board ship. Apparently, Mrs Coleman had a beauty spot somewhere on her face.

'Why does Mrs Coleman have a dirty mark on her face, Daddy?' she asked. 'That's a beauty spot!' replied our father. It was far too difficult to work this out. 'Can't she put it somewhere else?' Margery suggested.

Again, Margery asked a question, this time in Seattle. 'Why can't we go home, Mum and Dad?' 'We don't have a home!' was the sad reply.

CANADA

In Vancouver, the next part of our journey was over the magnificent Canadian Rocky Mountains, courtesy of Canadian Pacific Railways. It was unforgettable for a little boy. These mighty trains surge through and over the mountain passes, from Vancouver to Calgary and beyond.

Our progress took us on from Calgary into the heart of the Prairies, to Minto, Saskatchewan, where my father's cousin and his wife had set up home. One month in Minto was enjoyed, despite the intense cold. The temperature outside was as low as minus 30 degrees Celsius.

Margery attended the local school for four weeks or so. It was Valentine's Day and, clearly with kind and thoughtful prompting, all twenty-eight of her fellow pupils sent her a card!

My own troublesome memory was of my father clipping the front gate while backing out of the drive in our host's car. There were some scratches and a dent on the side of the car, and a little boy reckoned that these could never be repaired and would remain forever, adorning the car. Nothing could be retrieved or restored. How very embarrassing!

Onward across Canada, travelling huge distances eastwards, again with Canadian Pacific Railways. Our destination and final stop was Toronto, where we were initially in a guest house, then a rented property. During one breakfast, Margery and I had to share a slice of toast.

NEW YORK

Our little family moved south, into the United States and New York. We visited famous landmarks and places of great interest, which included going inside the Statue of Liberty and way up to the highest accessible floor of the Empire State Building.

Family outings to Central Park were enjoyed, apart from one day when a 4-year-old boy had a painful experience which brought tears. The sun had been beating down all morning. I decided to slide down the metal slide in my very little boyish shorts. By halfway down, the hot silver slide was frying my bare skin! I couldn't stop, and a howling and inconsolable little boy arrived at the end of the slide in a crumpled heap, with red and blistering thighs and bottom!

THE ATLANTIC, AND A STORM!

The plan was to make our way, by whatever means, back to the United Kingdom. A Portuguese ship found berths for the family.

It was an eventful Atlantic crossing. We encountered a terrific hurricane! The captain made the decision that we would run with the wind and storm, so much so that we were at least 1,000 miles off course. Three times the ship rolled dangerously! Even the crew feared that our ship might turn turtle.

During the storm, Margery and I found ourselves in the children's dining room. The fixed tables and chairs were wrenched from their positions and were crashing down, breaking, and slithering here and there. Margery and I were on the floor, partly under a table. Crisps had tipped from the table tops and spread over the floor. My distinct memory was of sitting on the floor, under a table, munching crisps while the storm raged!

The storm abated. We sailed to the Azores and Madeira. But there was one further drama for the crew and passengers to handle. The captain sighted a German U-boat! There was a stand-off, no doubt with considerable tension for an hour or two. But nothing happened. We were allowed to proceed.

However, the same ship, on its next voyage, in the same direction across the Atlantic, again sighted a U-boat, or the U-boat sighted them! This time, the U-boat commander instructed the passengers and crew to disembark into the ship's lifeboats, which, of course, they had to do. Thankfully, after some time, the shivering passengers and crew were allowed to reboard their ship and proceed on their way.

PORTUGAL—RESCUE FROM THE SEA

It was September 1943. We arrived in Lisbon. After some days, we were transferred to accommodation in Estoril, along the coast. Estoril was a seaside resort with sandy beaches and an esplanade a few feet higher than the beach. Every so often, along the beach, there were stone steps going up to the paved esplanade.

I was playing with a couple of older boys on the beach. We were making our way along the sand, in a north-westerly direction. Our parents and friends were walking along the esplanade above us, in the same direction.

The tide was coming in. But the waves were coming in at an angle, with huge waves beating against the esplanade ahead of us. Each wave receded after hitting the stonework of the solid walkway above us. This meant that when an angled wave receded, it 'opened up' a flight of steps before us boys ... for a few seconds. A wave receded ... steps appeared ... the bigger boys decided to run for the steps. After hesitating, the much younger boy decided to run for the same steps.

A huge wave gathered strength and thundered in over the

beach. The older boys made it up the steps, just! The younger boy didn't!

The wave swept into me and lifted me bodily on its crest, up to the height of the esplanade. As it peaked and began to recede, a man on the esplanade bent quickly down, stretched out his arms, and grabbed me. He lifted me onto the walkway, and safety!

A SUNDERLAND BOMBER AND A BOEING SEAPLANE

After a month in Portugal, my father was asked if he would supervise the transport of a planeload of children, taking them in a converted Sunderland bomber to Poole in Dorset, via Shannon in Ireland. The detour to Shannon might have been to avoid the greater danger of direct flights. Three months earlier, a plane from Lisbon had been shot down because the Germans thought Winston Churchill was on board. He was not, but the British actor Leslie Howard was on the flight and died.

It was a difficult decision for my father. He didn't want to leave Mum, Margery, and myself. However, he agreed and went on ahead of us. The seating was typical of a converted bomber, with seats against the fuselage on each side. There, the children in our father's care sat and huddled together. One little boy seemed to be paying attention to something in his pocket. My father watched with interest. The object was alive—a mouse!

Our mother, Margery, and I followed some days later, this time in a Boeing seaplane. It was relative luxury. We flew to Shannon for refuelling, had breakfast there, and then flew on to Poole Harbour.

LONDON AND A FEAST OF MARZIPAN

Dad joined us. We had set out from Sydney, Australia, on 7 January 1943 and arrived in London, England, on 3 November 1943.

We were to stay with 'The Cousins', maiden ladies who were the children of our mother's great uncle. We knew them as 'Cousin Elsie' and 'Cousin Lottie'. Their home was in Streatham, south London. It was a large Edwardian House. They welcomed the family travellers warmly.

Routine air-raids had largely stopped, although there were 'nuisance' raids and sirens regularly in the evenings at around 6pm. The destructive threat of V1 rockets (buzz bombs) and V2 rockets aimed at London and other British cities was to come later, in mid-1944.

One memorable evening, we were invited to the home of a lady for an evening meal. At least, it was not so much dinner, in the conventional sense, but an unusual high tea. Our hostess, it seemed, had made everything on the table with marzipan. I'm told that it was wartime marzipan; that is, not all the ingredients were freely available. This little boy had a wonderful time biting into marzipan medieval soldiers, horses, houses ... ad nauseam! The consumed marzipan was unpleasantly deposited on the step of the bus on our way home!

ARRIVAL IN SCOTLAND

We travelled on to Scotland and Balfron, north of Glasgow, where my Uncle Tom and Aunt Cathie (Dr and Mrs T. R. Murray) had their very pleasant and large home. We rented a property nearby soon after this, for about two years.

In 1946, after the so welcome end of the World War, we moved into Glasgow, to 4 Varna Road, Jordanhill.

BALFRON—SWINGING ON A GATE

One memory was swinging on the front gate of my Uncle and Aunt's home with my new friend, John McConkey. John asked me, 'What team do you support?'

'What do you mean "What team do you support?"' I asked.

It turned out that John supported Glasgow Rangers. I said that was fine with me. (Dear reader, you will find that there are very positive references in this treatise to the three major Glasgow football/soccer teams: Rangers, Celtic, and Partick Thistle).

My father was a wee bit proud of my accent, it seemed. You see, we had been in the expat community in China, then we had been a year in Australia, followed by many months in Canada. He would tell a story about his son, with weary resignation.

Again I was swinging on the same gate with my pal, John McConkey. My father came to the front door of the house and called to me, 'Murray, tea is ready.' (This was probably high tea, which is a little 'lower' than dinner). My father describes his son turning to pal John and saying, 'I have to go in for my—' I stopped abruptly, in mid-sentence. 'A'm jist gawin' in fur ma tea the noo!' My father's anguish was almost audible!

Schools in Glasgow

Relocating into the big city after the end of World War II, our new home was in Jordanhill, Glasgow. My sister, Margery, was enrolled in Laurel Bank School, and the question must have been, 'Where should Murray go to school?'

The beginnings of my schooling in Glasgow were not overly auspicious!

My three uncles all attended Glasgow Academy, where they excelled in many ways, including—and particularly—in sport! My two cousins, Bill and Douglas, also went to Glasgow Academy. I have a very dim memory of going with my parents to an interview for entry into Glasgow Academy. Frankly, my memories of the occasion are very vague. I didn't fully understand the significance of what was happening. In short, Glasgow Academy declined my parents' offer of their son's entry into this famous Glasgow institution.

The next interview, at Kelvinside Academy, also in Glasgow, was successful.

In 1947, after two years in the Junior School of Kelvinside, I accompanied my parents out to China.

Footnote: Years later, I was playing rugby for Kelvinside Academicals against Glasgow Academicals. By this time, I was a second-year medical student. It was our annual match between these two teams, played on Christmas Day. During the game, playing at centre three-quarter, I attempted a side-step and dummy, which worked, and passed the ball to our winger, Archie Campbell, who raced over for a good try! My Uncle Tom Murray, who had played for Glasgow Academicals in the 1920s, was in the stand with his friends, watching the match. He told me later that he turned to his peers and said, '… and we turned him down at Glasgow Academy!'

You can see and hear the importance of sport in our wider family. A question of priorities!

SHANGHAI AND HONG KONG: 1947—1949

My parents decided that Margery, my sister and five years older, would stay in Scotland when we went out to China in 1947. It was a decision I believe they regretted. As a teenager, there was the issue for Margery of secondary schooling.

In much of this writing, particularly about the early years in China, then Australia, Canada, with Pacific and Atlantic crossings by ship, followed by early years in the United Kingdom, my 'big sister' Margery has been a constant source of accurate and helpful information, often correcting my small boy impressions.

I should mention that many years later, a remarkable little Scottish lady, whom we called 'Aunt Nettie', a Quaker, who also served in China, made this revealing comment when she was in her early 90s: 'Murray, you've done well, but Margery has a better brain!'

My mother and I sailed from Liverpool on 20 November 1947. Dad had gone ahead of us some weeks earlier. On the very same day that we sailed, 20 November, the wedding of Princess Elizabeth to Philip Mountbatten took place in Westminster Abbey, London.

Our ship, the *Lancashire*, was a troop ship which sailed through the Bay of Biscay to Gibraltar, the Mediterranean Sea, Port Said, the Suez Canal, the Red Sea, Aden, the Indian Ocean, Ceylon (which later became Sri Lanka), Singapore, Hong Kong, Shanghai …

The whole journey took about three weeks and was relatively uneventful. Deck games like quoits were enjoyed. A couple of sorties to the deck below, to watch the soldiers boxing, were fun, particularly when the soldiers let me have a shot. One soldier was playfully sparring with me and was very good about the fact that my straight left—or was it a right hook?—drew blood from his nose and mouth!

For a small boy in the harbour at Port Said, watching boys not much older than myself diving to retrieve coins deep in the water from boats beside our ship was fascinating.

'VERY GOOD BABY!'

We arrived in Shanghai. A day or two after we arrived, we were visited by a little Chinese lady. When this lady saw me, a nine-year old boy, she launched herself towards me with a look of sheer delight and joy lighting up her face. She hugged me and hugged me! Were there tears of joy?

My memory of those moments when a 'bundle of Chinese lady' made me very special was explained later. For two to three years, this important woman had been my Amah, my nanny. I had been *her* baby and little boy, and now I was restored to her!

One story told about my Amah went like this: My Amah said, 'Very good baby! Very good baby! Three weeks he no wet!'

Apparently, she would hover over me, and if I showed the slightest sign of impending physiological activities, she would sweep me up and place me promptly on the potty! (Note: there were no polythene pants in those days.)

BOXING WITH BILLY TINGLE

I was enrolled in the Shanghai British School. There are no particular memories of schoolwork, but different sports were beginning to emerge and were enjoyed. Our gym teacher was an Australian, Mr Billy Tingle. Billy Tingle had been lightweight boxing champion of Australia. There was a boxing class for the boys.

Another boy, who also happened to be Scottish, dreaded, with me, the prospect of our fighting each other. But Billy Tingle usually seemed to single, or 'double', us out for a bout in front of our classmates. On one occasion, the two of us were belting each other, blow after blow, it seemed without mercy, when ...

Now, we were just of an age when it was required to be tough and manly in front of both boys and girls! We were giving it big licks, and yes, we were probably the best in our class. But we couldn't get the better of each other.

Our macho images were lost when, without warning, we simultaneously dropped our gloves, both of us utterly spent, and the tears streamed down our faces!

We remained good friends—or perhaps it was respect?

THE UNION CHURCH

My father played the organ in the Union Church, just off The Bund in Shanghai. He would go to the church early on a Sunday morning to practise and would take me with him. We would go to a cafe in the swimming baths, opposite the church, for a breakfast of French toast.

There, in the church, I was introduced to singing in a church choir and sang my first solo as a treble. Actually, it was my only solo as a treble!

AMETHYST AND THE YANGTZE INCIDENT

It has been important for me to realize, and I never understood this as a child, that in 1947, when we arrived back in Shanghai, it was only two years after the ending of World War II—in Europe, in May, 1945; in Asia, in September, 1945.

In 1949, Mao Tse-tung and his People's Liberation Army were approaching Shanghai. Two vivid memories were impressed on this 10-year-old British boy. One is fairly trivial, if unpleasant, the other much more significant and consequential.

My parents and I were walking along The Bund in Shanghai after church. The Bund was a broad stretch of road and buildings in the waterfront area of central Shanghai.

Suddenly, a Chinese man spat directly at us! He certainly didn't seem pleased to see us.

'Why would that man do that, Dad?'

I'm sure my father and mother tried to explain that Mao Tse-tung, a new Chinese communist leader, with many soldiers, was fighting against General Chiang Kai-shek and the Nationalist Army. Because Mao was advancing towards Shanghai, those who liked Mao were emboldened in their dislike of foreigners, telling them to get out of China.

The second memory involved a British warship, HMS *Amethyst*. If a British warship docked at Shanghai, which was situated on the Huangpu River, the pupils of the Shanghai British School might be shown over the ship.

But HMS *Amethyst* was a much-damaged warship. It was unforgettable, as a young British boy, to see this huge glistening and silver ship which had limped into Shanghai harbour. I remember thinking, again as a young and naïve British boy, 'How would anyone dare to do that to a British ship? Anyone who has done that is in for big trouble!'

In fact, *Amethyst* had run the gauntlet of the communist guns lining the banks of the Yangtze River, a huge river, many miles north of Shanghai. This river, nearly 4,000 miles long, originating on the plateau of Tibet, pours into the East China Sea. HMS *Amethyst* had been cut off upriver. Attempts to escape were thwarted initially, even with the attempted help of other British ships and a flying boat which was carrying medical personnel. There was much loss of life, and many were wounded. *Amethyst* was forced to retire upriver. But all was not entirely lost.

The daring of the captain and crew in racing downriver to escape is immortalized in the black-and-white film *Yangtze Incident*. *Amethyst* made it into the East China Sea and then entered the estuary of the Huangpu River, reaching the waterfront of Shanghai, there to be seen by a young British boy.

With the approach of Mao, it was decided that the printing office should be moved from Shanghai to Hong Kong. This was my father's responsibility. The family moved to Hong Kong in April 1949, just two weeks before Mao and his communists entered Shanghai.

HIJACKED!

As we sailed from Shanghai to Hong Kong, my one memory was of playing with the children of another 'foreign' family on deck. We said our goodbyes on arrival in Hong Kong. The next news of this family was tragic!

They had flown from Hong Kong to Portuguese Macau, a short flight. The plane was hijacked! Apparently, it might have been the first ever plane hijacking. The year was 1949.

The plane crashed into the sea. The only survivor was one of the hijackers, and he had a leg bitten off by a shark!

HONG KONG AND A SING-SONG

For us, the arrival in Hong Kong, at least from a 10-year-old boy's perspective, was fairly routine. We were to stay for about six months, and our home was the Soldiers' and Sailors' Home on Hong Kong Island. Folk like us were on the top, third floor.

On Sunday evenings there would be a sing-song, perhaps

with my father playing the piano. I remember a large sailor with a typical bushy beard who would always choose the rousing hymn:

> Will your anchor hold in the storms of life,
> When the clouds unfold their wings of strife?
> When the strong tides lift, and the cables strain,
> Will your anchor drift or firm remain?

Chorus:

> We have an Anchor that keeps the soul
> Steadfast and sure while the billows roll
> Fastened to the Rock which cannot move,
> Grounded firm and deep in the Saviour's love.

Our bearded matelot would always sing with gusto and conviction! It was an inspiration for a wee fella who was being grounded in the faith.

KING GEORGE V SCHOOL

My new School was King George V School, Kowloon, on the mainland. It meant a short boat trip of 15 minutes or so from Hong Kong Island. I was put on the Star Ferry each morning (it still exists) and returned on the same Ferry in the afternoon. My parents couldn't understand why their 10-year-old son would arrive back at the Soldiers' and Sailors' Home each day with a rather dirty smudge on the end of his nose. I also had no idea.

Then some detective work, considering the process of travel each day, provided an answer. The Star Ferry had a ramp at the bow which was lowered on arrival at dockside, to allow passengers to stream off, and for new passengers to flock onto the boat for the return journey.

A typical wee boy who wanted to get off the boat in the first group would press forward against the ramp which was about to be lowered onto the dock, like a drawbridge. The crowd pushed forward, even mildly crushing those in front against the vertically raised ramp before it was lowered. The crush was such that the most prominent part of my face more than touched the ramp on which many shoes had walked or run!

Voila! The smudge and its cause had been identified.

Our six months or so in Hong Kong were enjoyable with a merciful lack of anything too dramatic. I was enjoying playing football (soccer) at my new School, with the only mishap a greenstick fracture of my clavicle (collarbone) after landing heavily on my left shoulder.

Swimming in Repulse Bay on the other side of Hong Kong Island was a pleasure, the only complication being severe sunburn with skin blistering!

It would be 40 years before I was back in Shanghai and Hong Kong. That visit was partly to celebrate our 20th wedding anniversary. Ruth had said 'Let's go to China to celebrate; 20 years of marriage is china!' (15 years' marriage is 'crystal'; 20 is 'china'; 25 is 'silver', and so on.)

GOD HAS NO GRANDCHILDREN

Corrie Ten Boom, an outstanding Dutch Christian, who was sent by the Nazis to Ravensbruck concentration camp, but survived, said, 'God has no grandchildren!'

I had the privilege of being born into a Christian family. But when did I actually become a Christian? What does being a Christian really mean? Absolutely fair questions.

If I go on to describe experiences and occasions where I and we saw clear evidence of the power and presence of God, when did it all begin in personal experience? Some Christians are able to describe a dramatic conversion experience and they 'know' that a transformation has taken place. Probably, their relatives and friends recognize this change also. Often, for these ones, there is radical change, perhaps from a life which may have been far from the teachings of Jesus Christ.

But Jesus said, 'You must be born again' (John 3:7).

For those of us who have the advantage of hearing the word of God from our early years, it may be difficult to fix on a particular day or time. It is certainly true that a number of times I asked the Lord to come into my life, forgive my sins, and tell me what He wanted me to do. Even as a young boy, these were times of recommitment.

At the age of twelve, at a Scripture Union camp on the Mull of Kintyre, Scotland, I have a vivid memory of going outside our tent (the camp was under canvas) in the late evening. The sun was setting in the West, the sky was all reds and gold, with the darkness behind me. It was wonderful!

I raised my hands in worship and said out loud, 'The glory of God!'

It was then, as a twelve-year old boy, that I believe God told me that I was to be a doctor and go overseas to serve Him, the Almighty God. A young boy's experience, and life-changing! The awareness of God Himself and His overwhelming love. Understanding the sacrifice of Jesus for each one of us. The presence of the Holy Spirit, the Comforter.

SECONDARY SCHOOL IN SCOTLAND: 1949—1956

Returning from China in 1949, it was expected that I would resume schooling at Kelvinside Academy, Glasgow. So it was that I was placed in Remove B at Kelvinside.

CHING FU

Walking into the classroom, some of the boys there exclaimed, 'It's Murray McG, after two years! Where have you been?' But a few boys in the class, who had come to the School while I had been away, somehow were put out that I was not actually 'new' to the School. At the very first playtime / recess, one of these boys positively sneered, 'Here comes Ching Fu!' The name stuck, with some friends, for years.

That particular boy was not pleasant to me for some weeks. In fact, I recall very accurately the spot in the playground where I 'sorted him out!' How 'Christian' that was has always been a question ... but, you know, that guy was decidedly cautious and more pleasant with me thereafter.

These were happy years, although my academic efforts were not at all impressive while progressing through the Senior School. Art was my best subject, with a disciplined art master, Major Forbes, who was a veteran of the Burma campaign in the Second World War. His military bearing, suit, and tie, with a handkerchief in his breast pocket, made him the right military man to take over the Combined Cadet Force in place of Major Wise (French).

RUGBY AT KELVINSIDE ACADEMY

The very first competitive rugby match I saw was Shanghai versus Hong Kong, played in Shanghai. I was 10 years old. My father took me to the game, which would have been between expats, mostly British and French.

When we arrived back in Glasgow from Hong Kong in 1949, I returned to Kelvinside Academy and was reintroduced to rugby at the 'grass roots'.

With three rugby-playing uncles on my mother's side of the family, there was a delightful inevitability that rugby would become a passion during school years and beyond.

Of course, it was a great thrill to travel through to Edinburgh to watch Scotland playing at Murrayfield, the national stadium. On one occasion, in 1951, we young schoolboys were seated in the enclosure, with our royal blue caps on and near to the pitch. Scotland were playing Wales. A Welsh supporter behind us in the crowd told us that if Wales lost, he would eat his large leek, which was made of some kind of canvas. Scotland won 19—0, and a group of schoolboys swivelled in their seats, in great glee, and stared at our crestfallen Welsh supporter. Fair game! He attempted a large and ineffectual bite of his enormous leek!

We had a good Under-11½ team, beating Glasgow Academy 31—0, and tries in those days only counted as 3 points. Quite a few of us in the Under-14½ team were in the Kelvinside Academy 1st XV in the following year.

In our final year, under the excellent leadership of Shade Munro, we won 14 of our 17 games. Four of us were in the Glasgow Schools XV against the Edinburgh Schools XV.

AND CRICKET TOO!

Cricket was also a much-enjoyed sport. Two of us Kelvinside Academy boys, J. C. C. 'Johnnie' Walker and I were chosen for the Glasgow Schools team, to play against Western Union Juniors.

The previous year, in the same fixture, I had been given 'out' lbw (leg before wicket) third ball. As I trudged up the pavilion steps into the clubhouse, one of the Glasgow team selectors said, 'Didn't you see it, Murray?' I replied, ruefully, 'I thought I did!'

Playing in the same match the following year, Glasgow Schools versus Western Union Juniors, Johnnie and I (Kelvinside Academy) had to score 90 runs. I'm writing this because we just made it (Murray 52; Johnnie 43 not out)!

COMBINED CADET FORCE

A real interest and involvement was the Combined Cadet Force (CCF). We were affiliated to The Cameronians, Scottish Rifles. When we became more senior boys in School, our Company Sergeant Major was the excellent Jimmy Martin (hooker in the KA 1st XV), and I was appointed Senior Sergeant. Our Master in Charge was the aforementioned Burma veteran of the Second World War, every inch the military man, Major Forbes. Our uniforms were necessarily immaculate, and the shine on our boots reflected light impressively.

It was at a CCF camp at Cultybraggan, near Crieff, in Perthshire, that the senior NCOs (Non-Commissioned Officers) were required to interrogate the whole Company, individually. While on manoeuvres, one cadet had left an empty milk bottle at a farm site, after we discontinued our field exercises, for rations. Major Forbes was furious!

Three of us senior cadets set up a table with chairs in one of the Nissen huts. A Nissen hut has a curved metal roof and walls, with concrete flooring. It can be a very noisy place, especially when the bagpipes played reveille!

Each cadet marched in to stand at attention in front of the three of us seated behind the table. 'Where were you when the milk bottle was left at the farm?'

The dignity of the proceedings was destroyed when one cadet, marching in briskly and, snapping to attention, lost his footing and skidded under the table, ending up amongst the six feet of the interrogators, who were finding it very difficult to stifle their spontaneous laughter!

But were lessons being learned?

CATCH US IF YOU CAN!

Two of us, at Kelvinside Academy, ran a lunchtime Scripture Union group once each week. My friend Bill Crawford later was godfather to our son Andrew. Bill stands well over 6 feet tall, much loftier than I. I might have been 5' 8" plus on a good day! We were both in the Kelvinside Academy rugby 1st XV.

In our final year at School, for a few weeks, Bill and I went out to the playground to tell the boys that it was time for the Scripture Union, often with a visiting speaker.

A 'game' developed. Boys scattered; Bill and I grabbed them, threw them over our shoulders, and carried them in to the meeting!

Amazingly, the numbers increased, and the boys seemed to enjoy the game!

ENTRY INTO MEDICINE, UNIVERSITY OF GLASGOW: 1956

My acceptance and entry into the Faculty of Medicine at Glasgow was far from a foregone conclusion.

An outstanding seat of learning, with great traditions and history, Glasgow University was founded in the year 1451, some years after St Andrew's University (1413), followed by the Universities of Aberdeen (1495) and Edinburgh (1582).

Only Oxford and Cambridge preceded these four Scottish Universities.

These six Universities are the oldest Universities in the English-speaking world.

My own studies as a pupil at Kelvinside Academy, Glasgow, were not at all outstanding. I was so much more involved and interested in sport. Mr A. R. Forrester, Deputy Rector, who happened to be my mother's cousin, wrote, 'Unless Murray begins to do what he is capable of doing, any possibility of academic success is entirely out of the question!'

Many years later, I mentioned this in my address during the Kelvinside Academy Prize-Giving in the Bute Hall, Glasgow University, when Ruth and I were asked to give out prizes.

Armed with the basic requirements for University entrance— three Highers (English, Maths and Science) and two Lowers (French and History)—I applied for Medicine at Glasgow.

There was one interview with a distinctly professorial type, an older gentleman with a mop of white hair. 'I see you have an impressive extra-academic curriculum!' said the benign Professor.

What was that? I had no idea what the Professor meant by this statement. Then it slowly dawned. 'He must be referring to rugby, cricket, the Combined Cadet Force, and perhaps even the Scripture Union?' I remember two things from that interview: the reference to extra-academic activities and the Professor's final word to me. In fact, the interview was over, and I was leaving the room. The Professor called to me as I opened the door to go out.

'Yes sir?'

'I know your mother!'

Anyone who knew my mother would think well of her son. Thanks, Mum!

MEDICAL SCHOOL IN GLASGOW: 1956–1962

My mother graduated in Medicine from Glasgow in 1924, followed by her brother, Thomas, also from Glasgow, later in the 1920s. My own generation studied over six years (1956 to 1962) before graduating MBChB (Bachelor of Medicine, Bachelor of Surgery).

It is an interesting phenomenon that medical students the world over are recognized as relatively irresponsible, with a propensity to enjoy much fun and games during the student years. However, when they qualify as a doctor, overnight they are required to become fine examples of gravitas and responsibility. And rightly so!

A VOICE FROM THE MORTUARY

One story told by my Uncle Tom concerned a fellow medical student in the 1920s who allowed himself to be locked inside the mortuary of the Western Infirmary, Glasgow. How long he was incarcerated there is in question, but exactly on the midnight hour, he phoned the porters' station.

The porters on duty would have followed their nightly routine around the hospital, checking all was as it should be: doors closed, locked as appropriate—including, of course, the mortuary. The porter on duty at the porters' station looked at the telephone board in front of him and was shocked to discover that the incoming call was from inside the mortuary! With a trembling hand, the porter lifted his telephone. A sonorous voice at the other end uttered the words 'I'm not dead!'

I understand the student was not expelled for his escapade. Perhaps the powers that be remembered their own student days?

STUDENT DAYS

In 1956, we entered into the ancient portals of the University of Glasgow for six years of study. After qualification, two residencies/internships of six months each would be required, one in Medicine and one in Surgery, before formal registration which qualified us to practise with an element of independence. However, a junior doctor must always be under strict supervision.

It would be eighteen years after leaving secondary school before I had completed all examinations and a research doctorate. Of course, we should always be students throughout our careers in Medicine.

It was usual and necessary to consider a speciality. For myself, in the end, it was to be Ophthalmology.

Let's return to the years as a student. Our first year required study in Chemistry, Physics, Zoology, and Botany. We looked forward to the years following, when subjects nearer to our hearts would be addressed.

In the second and third years, we were getting closer to our real interest in Medicine, the basic sciences of Anatomy, Physiology, and Biochemistry. Exams in these subjects, at the end of five terms, were called the 'second professionals'. It was said that before you passed these exams, it was 'if you became a doctor', while after you passed these exams, it was 'when you became a doctor'! They were the big ones, only surpassed by the final exams at the end of six years.

Pathology and Medical Jurisprudence in fourth year continued to lay the groundwork of the learning process.

THE LADIES HAVE IT!

Professor Glaister, whose father before him had also been Professor of Medical Jurisprudence, was a man of dignified presence and some flamboyance! For example, after our exam results in his subject had been listed, the Professor announced to the class (about 150 of us), 'Despite the fact that the female cranium is smaller than the male cranium (he gave the dimensions), I have to inform you that the first four places in this class have been taken by the ladies!'

These were enjoyable years, studying the subjects which interested us immensely and gaining experience in the wards, operating rooms, accident and emergency, and outpatient clinics.

INTRODUCTION TO SURGERY—
AND A GOOD CATCH!

My first time in an operating room as a medical student provided an early lesson for me. It was an abdominal operation, and a scalpel was resting (unwisely) on the drapes covering the abdominal area. It seemed that only I noticed that the scalpel was moving and sliding towards the edge of the sterile area. It gathered pace and went over the 'cliff' edge, plummeting towards the floor!

I leapt forward and with my right hand made a frankly brilliant catch of the blade, just above floor level. On the cricket field, it would have been a sensational catch!

But not in the operating room. All members of the surgical team, the anaesthetist, et al., were staring at me over their masks. Any thoughts of approval were clearly misplaced; disapproval was etched on every expression. Their heads were shaking slowly from side to side!

'When a surgical blade is falling to the floor, you let it fall!'

LIFELONG FRIENDSHIPS

We were forming friendships that would last for our lifetimes. Many names should be mentioned, but a special few follow.

Gordon MacBain, a keen golfer and very musical, became Senior General Surgeon in the Southern General Hospital, Glasgow. Gordon married Margaret Wilson, who was from an accomplished family. Years later, in 1974, I was capped at a graduation ceremony by Sir Charles Wilson, Margaret's uncle and Principal of the University of Glasgow. The ceremony in the Bute Hall was made pleasantly personal as I knelt to be capped by Sir Charles, when he murmured, 'Well done, Murray!'

David McNair, whose medical parents had practised in China, and with whom I shared a competitive interest in rugby, specialized in Radiology and, with his wife, Chris, settled in Ontario, Canada. I was best man for both Gordon and David.

David Lawson, CBE, became an eminent Professor of Medicine and Therapeutics at the University of Glasgow, with many international accolades. Gordon MacBain and David Lawson had both attended Glasgow High School. One of David's particular interests was ornithology.

On one occasion, Gordon and I were sitting in the cafeteria in the Royal Infirmary, both of us silent and a wee bit glum. Scotland had been beaten the night before at football. David came cheerfully towards us, took one look at the miserable pair, and muttered, 'Oh no! Not another national disaster!' He turned on his heel and disappeared, deciding to return at a more opportune time.

Andy Motherwell had been a pupil at Loretto School, Musselburgh, near Edinburgh. Andy shared our love of sport and was easily the best skier of the bunch. He married Joan, a Canadian girl, then travelled to practise Medicine in Perth, Western Australia.

Alistair MacMillan became Senior Physiologist to the Royal Air Force. He contributed much to the safety of pilots when flying fast jets. After the sad loss of life of some US astronauts, the USA authorities sought Alistair's advice in this vital area of expertise.

When Ruth came on the scene in 1969, she so appreciated the warmth and welcome of these special friends and their ladies. These things you remember, they mean so much.

FINALS!

The build-up in our final year, towards our final examinations, was intense. The combination of accumulating practical experience in the wards, clinics, and operating theatres, covering all the medical fields, reading manuals and often very large tomes, became a basic routine of life.

The final exams themselves were spread over two and a half weeks, beginning with written papers in all the major disciplines: Medicine, Surgery, Obstetrics and Gynaecology, and Paediatrics. There followed clinical exams, most often in the wards of a particular discipline.

The finals always provide dramatic stories—some great, some not so great!

One vivid memory I have of the clinical final exam in general surgery was when I was examined in the surgical wards of the Royal Infirmary, Glasgow, by the eminent Professor Arthur Mackey. The patient I was to examine was a late middle-aged man who, by his appearance, had been involved in some form of hard physical work.

'Good morning, Mr Kerr! May I ask some questions and examine you? It's part of the exam process.' The patient nodded his acceptance.

'What's wrong with you?' My first question was direct and to the point. If Mr Kerr had told me that he had recurrent cholecystitis and gallstones, with the gall bladder due to be removed, that would have been excellent. I would have been well on the way to forming a good clinical assessment to present to the Professor.

Of course, one should never assume that the patient has understood or is accurate in their own diagnosis. I had one patient, for example, who informed me that he had a 'peltic ulster'—instead of 'peptic ulcer'!

Mr Kerr responded to my question with a blank 'Don't know!' He had no idea why he was in hospital and what was to be done. I groaned inwardly!

Now, apply your training, begin at the beginning, ask the appropriate questions, carry out a clinical examination, assess the patient's general health, all with the purpose of presenting your findings to Professor Mackey.

It turned out that Mr Kerr had a right inguinal hernia and was due to go for surgery the next morning. So far so good! But as I examined the patient, I discovered that he had evidence of heart failure, with marked sacral oedema. Fluid had accumulated at the base of the spine, above the buttocks, in the sacral region. There was also some evidence of dyspnoea (breathlessness).

Professor Mackey, an imposing figure, arrived quietly by the bedside. 'Now then, would you tell me about your patient, his particular problem, and what you plan to do about it?'

I went through my report on the patient, being careful to present Mr Kerr as an individual with a need, bringing him into the discussion as appropriate.

Should I give a direct opinion to the Professor? I decided to go for it! 'I don't think Mr Kerr should go to theatre tomorrow, Professor Mackey!'

'Really!' There was real surprise and concern in his tone. 'Why is that, may I ask?'

'May I demonstrate, sir?' I showed the Professor the sacral and 'pitting' oedema at the base of the spine.

This particular exam was over. The Professor had released me and was talking to the Sister-in-Charge at the entrance to the ward, just as I passed by on my way out to freedom. The Professor was saying, 'Sister, Mr Kerr should not go to theatre in the morning.' Professor Mackey then saw me passing by and nodded in my direction. 'As the *Doctor* has just advised!'

For a few minutes, I had wings to my feet and a light heart!

After the written and clinical exams in various disciplines, we were subjected to the trauma of oral exams, examined by professors and senior consultants, usually three eminent men and women who sat behind a suitable desk, ready to fire questions. Some, possibly most, were kind; a few were not!

It was a Wednesday afternoon. Our first oral exam was in General Medicine. It was to begin at 2pm. Six of us sat waiting, three facing three. It was tense, and we readily agreed with one of the girls who said spontaneously, 'This is terrible!'

The very first question I was asked went like this: 'Tell me the causes of the nephrotic syndrome.'

A surge of hope coursed through me. I actually had a mnemonic for that. *Take your time!*

1. 'Type 2 nephritis.' 'Good!' said the examiner
2. 'Kimmelstiel-Wilson disease (diabetic kidney).' 'Yes!'
3. 'Systemic lupus erythematosus.' 'Right!'
4. 'Amyloidosis.' 'Yes!'
5. 'Multiple myeloma kidney.' 'Correct!'

I went on, slowly. I had eight causes of the nephrotic syndrome. The minutes were passing. The rest of that oral exam is a blur. Over the years, I've used that personal experience in a lecture I would give on 'How to Pass Exams'. If you manage to get onto a subject you are comfortable with, don't rush it! Certainly, don't let the examiner think you have a little list. Waste time fairly! The examiner is more relaxed. You are more relaxed. And time passes!

RUGBY AND CRICKET: STUDENT DAYS AND BEYOND

Many years after my playing days, when driving in Scotland with my family and passing Greenyards, the ground of the famous Melrose rugby club (where seven-a-side rugby was first played), I began to point out the corner of the playing field where I scored a try (the equivalent of a touchdown, for our American friends) playing for Glasgow against South of Scotland. Was it the second time passing by that my kids said, 'Yes, Dad, we know you scored a try there!'?

PLAYING IN THE SCOTTISH BORDERS

In the 1957–1958 season, aged 19, there was the thrill of being selected for the representative Glasgow XV, which was chosen from teams in the west of Scotland.

We played at the same Greenyards, in the town of Melrose. A close match, we eventually lost 9–12. In those days, a try counted as three points.

GET THAT WEE MAN!

An amusing incident in that game, in retrospect, was a little cameo involving a famous Scotland prop forward, Hughie McLeod. McLeod was stocky and very strong, although not a big man. He came from the Hawick rugby club, which over the years provided many Scotland players.

I found myself in possession of the rugby ball, right in front of the grandstand and the pressing crowds, standing very near to the touchline. It was one of those brief moments when everything seemed to stand still. I was deciding how to dodge out of the impasse. Facing me, directly, was the immensely strong and focused Hughie McLeod.

A voice from the crowd, clear as could be, shouted from a distance of a few feet, 'Get that wee man!'

Hughie McLeod obliged!

SCOTTISH TRIALS AT MURRAYFIELD

There were other games for Glasgow, playing against Edinburgh and against the North and Midlands. These were matches where the Scottish selectors would be watching. Effectively, they were the first round of trials for the Scottish international team.

In December 1959, when I was 21, the letter arrived advising that I had been chosen as a reserve for the first Scottish trial at Murrayfield, the national stadium.

My cousin, Bill Murray, drove me through to the game in his father's sports car. A white saloon car raced past us as we drove east along the three-laned A8 from Glasgow to Edinburgh. Both Bill and I expressed concern at such dangerous driving!

We followed a gentle curve in the road and came across a scene of utter devastation! There had been a head-on collision involving the white saloon, with dust still rising from the impact! Three cars, six people—three of whom died. One of the six, a soldier, was standing unsteadily on his feet, having been thrown through a windscreen.

I was in fourth-year medicine, in the middle of training. Bill and I did what we could until the ambulances arrived. These ambulance men and women do a tremendous job, so often in such trying circumstances. As I gathered experience of the various types of trauma that present in Accident and Emergency, I began to realize how different it is to treat and care for a traumatized patient who arrives in A & E, compared with the emergency care and interventions required at the actual scene of an accident.

It's fair to say that this was not the ideal preparation for a rugby trial for Scotland, but it did give some perspective and did not seem to affect my play, I think. At half-time in the game, I was called onto the field and there was some opportunity to be involved in a couple of good passages of play. J. A. P. Shackleton (London Scottish), my fellow centre three-quarter, who already had caps for Scotland, kindly said 'Well played, Murray!'

Some days later, another letter arrived. Chosen to play at centre three-quarter for the Rest of Scotland versus Scotland, also at Murrayfield, in the Final Scottish Trial before the game against France.

Sadly, it did not work out. I was not invited to any further Scottish trials.

GLASGOW AND EDINBURGH XV VERSUS SOUTH AFRICA

The next season, 1960–1961, South Africa was touring Great Britain and Ireland. They would play over 20 games, including matches against the 'home' nations: England, Wales, Ireland, and Scotland. The South Africans were recognized as a powerful rugby nation with a huge degree of physicality in their game.

First, I was called into the Cities (Glasgow and Edinburgh) XV against Paris, in France. It was a boring game with a very unusual result in rugby: 0–0.

Now for the big one—at least the big one before the full international match: Glasgow and Edinburgh versus South Africa! South Africa came to that match undefeated.

It was a tremendous match! We were winning 11–8 with

only ten minutes to go to full time. Then three of our players had to go off injured. I have a photo of myself and a South African player, also a medical student, tending my stricken captain, whose ear had been ripped horrendously! D. B. Edwards (Heriots FP) went off, then returned with his head swathed in bandages.

In those last ten minutes, three of our players were injured and off the field, each for a few minutes, and in those days, there were *no substitutes or replacements!*

We lost 11–16. But what a game!

SCOTTISH UNIVERSITIES RUGBY

We were moving into our final year as medical students. The captain of the Glasgow University 1st XV was Campbell Stalker, a fellow final-year medical student. Campbell, a very fine full-back, asked me to play for the University in our final year. I moved across to play there during the season, 1961–1962.

Five of us from Glasgow University were selected to play for the Scottish Universities against the Irish Universities (all Ireland) at Ravenhill, Belfast, and against the English Universities at Headingley, Leeds.

Irish Universities' rugby was very strong! There were two full internationals and seven Irish trialists in their team. It was a good game, which we lost, 3–9.

The English Universities team was drawn from the great many English Universities, while the Scottish team came from the four 'older' Universities: Glasgow, Edinburgh, Aberdeen, and St Andrews.

We won 17–3. English newspapers praised the flowing rugby and free running of the Scottish three-quarters.

THE CASE OF THE RUSTY SPIKE

It was always going to be difficult to play good rugby during our early years of medical commitments in the residency programmes.

I recall one game, West of Scotland versus Kelvinside Academicals, the night before which I had about three hours' sleep. That was when I was a Resident in Obstetrics. Actually, the game seemed to go well. I just about survived, but the next day it all caught up with me!

When we occasionally compared our injury problems with other rugby players, usually years later, my 'piece de resistance' involved a game against Edinburgh Academicals at Raeburn Place. I received a 'hospital pass'—that is, the ball at the same time as the tackler was hitting me!

I went down! My shoulder hurt, but surely a dislocation must be worse than this? I got to my feet and looked at my right shoulder. There was a thick, rusty metal spike sticking into my axilla (armpit), having penetrated through my tough jersey! The spike must have been lying in the grass.

I went up to the referee, holding my arm aloft. The referee looked shocked and pale! He suggested I left the field of play. As I walked off, I pulled the spike out and became a little breathless. I had just qualified in Medicine and knew the anatomy of the region. The hospital in Edinburgh took an X-ray and said all seemed fine.

That evening, back in Glasgow and feeling lousy, our neighbour, Dr Mike Telfer, said that he would take me in to the Royal Infirmary for a further check. Another X-ray was taken and an antibiotic prescribed. The X-ray showed a right apical pneumothorax. The lung had been punctured by the rusty spike!

After a miserable couple of days, the official radiologist's report from Edinburgh (the X-ray was taken in A & E at the weekend) described the apical pneumothorax and advised another X-ray. This third X-ray, four days after the injury, showed that the lung had re-expanded and so healing was already happening.

We certainly don't want to dwell on injuries. But it is so important that the different Rugby Unions are taking the issue of head injuries very seriously. They need to! The huge impacts that occur in modern-day rugby are a real concern.

I recall playing in a match and kicking a penalty goal after I had lost half my field of vision following a head knock. Later, I was very sick, then slowly recovered over some hours, during which I was mildly disorientated.

MY FRIEND, RONNIE KEITH

Ronnie Keith had been an excellent cricketer. We had played together in the Kelvinside Academy 1st X1. After school days, Ronnie was obliged to go for two years of national service in the army. I missed national service because I left school later than Ronnie and went straight to Glasgow University to study Medicine.

Ronnie had a tough time in the army. He was tall and quite thin, but the problem was that his condition, which was becoming more evident, had not been diagnosed. He had early but progressive multiple sclerosis.

Some years later, I would take Ronnie to cricket matches when I was playing for Kelvinside Academicals. His folded wheelchair would jam in to the boot of my little blue mini. Ronnie would squeeze into the passenger seat.

On a particular Saturday, we were playing against a team in south-east Glasgow. As usual, Ronnie was with me. That evening, Scotland were playing Brazil at Hampden Park,

Glasgow. It would be a pack-out in the stadium, as Brazilian football was so outstanding.

I had an inspiration! 'Ronnie, why don't you and I drive to Hampden Park? If we go now, we should arrive about half-time in the game.' Ronnie agreed.

We arrived at Hampden Park. I drove the mini directly to the back of the main stand. Someone, who looked to be an official, was standing at the main entrance. I explained the situation. Could I take my friend, in his wheelchair, down to the running track beside the pitch and watch the game from there?

The official nodded in the direction of another official who was standing by a fairly small gate. 'Ask him!' was the advice. I approached the official and guard at the gate indicated. This man clearly had enormous power and authority in relation to the small gate. Again, I explained.

The man listened attentively. He made an executive decision with great warmth and understanding. 'No problem, Doctor!' The gate was opened and Ronnie, his chair, and I went down a ramp, under one of the enormous stands, on to the running track beside the pitch.

So-called invalid chairs and buggies were concentrated at the halfway line of the pitch, but on the far side from our entrance point. We sallied forth, with Ronnie in his chair and with me pushing, going the circuitous route on the running track, around the east-end goalposts. It was half-time in the game. The crowd, which numbered well over 70,000, were pausing and preparing themselves for the second half. As I began the task of shunting Ronnie around the track, some of the crowd noticed us and cheered! Ronnie, being Ronnie, raised his right hand towards the many thousands and, with his fingers crooked, began what can only be described as a 'papal blessing'!

The crowd responded. Probably 10,000 at a time, the crowd

roared their approval! It was like a slow Mexican wave as we moved steadily on our way, thousands cheering us—or at least Ronnie—and his ongoing, dignified papal blessing throughout our triumphant progress. There were even occasional voices yelling through the din, 'Hi Ronnie!' Ronnie was in his element. The enthusiastic affection of it all was heart-warming.

By the by, Scotland drew 1–1 with a strong Brazil that evening, including the renowned footballer, Pele. A good result!

ENCOUNTER WITH
THE HOLY SPIRIT

When I and my medical student colleagues moved into our sixth and final year in Medicine, I was asked if I would be President of the Student Christian Medical Fellowship. I felt quite inadequate for the task, and so I prayed.

My cousin, Ian Murray, was very much the older brother I never had. Ian and his family were back from Thailand and were staying in the home of Dr Jack and Eileen Kelly on the south side of Glasgow. Jack was a Cardiologist in the nearby Victoria Infirmary.

Ian contacted me, saying that he wanted to share with me his experiences of the Holy Spirit. I readily responded, first because I so respected Ian and second because we could share many of the 'deep things' of life. Apart from that, we had great fun together! Ian had polio as a child and walked with a slight limp but was very strong and a fine swimmer.

The plan was that I would come to the Kellys' home, early one morning in the summer of 1961. But I was going to our rugby club captain's wedding, and so I arrived in my kilt.

Ian took me through the Scriptures outlining the person and the ministry of the Holy Spirit. It was fascinating. My own spirit was stirred. 'Ian, this is great! I want to hear more. But I'll need to get away or I'll be late for the wedding.'

Ian understood and said that he would pray. I remember being grateful that Ian's prayer was so brief. I thought I would also pray, but very briefly, to conclude the special time. My thoughts were to get away to the wedding and bring the time of discussion to a close, for now.

Suddenly it happened. I trembled and shook as the tears began streaming down my face. This went on for a few minutes. Surprised by joy!

Later, when singing hymns in church, this joy welled up inside me again. I look back at that experience when my thoughts and emotions were initially elsewhere, but God had His own plans. Clearly, He was somehow preparing me for the future.

For those of my readers who are 'in the know' and have their own theological views about this encounter with the Holy Spirit, a few further words.

In sharing about this experience, usually I have simply told what happened. Also, I have emphasized that the Scripture uses the present continuous. 'Be filled with the Spirit' means 'keep on being filled with the Holy Spirit' (Ephesians 5:18).

For example, speaking at a Men's Breakfast in Cyprus, I told the men that I was only going to describe what had actually happened and not 'label' this wonderful experience. They could use their own label. However, I added to the story.

I described how I had travelled from Glasgow to London for meetings in Central Halls, Westminster, to find out more about what was happening to a group of us, seven young men, all in our twenties, who would meet in the Kellys' home on Thursday evenings to pray.

During the London meetings, I sat beside a distinguished-looking gentleman, the Reverend Henry Brash Bonsall. Of course, he suggested that I should come to his College in Birmingham. He pointed out a lady who was sitting about four seats away (not sure why she was four seats away) and said, 'Remarkable woman that!' 'Oh, yes?' I enquired.

'My wife! Fasted for 30 days for me to come into these experiences of the Holy Spirit.' I have to say that I was very much impressed with this amazing couple.

Several years later, I met Ruth, their daughter, and the Reverend and Mrs Henry Brash Bonsall became my in-laws. But I digress, even if enjoyably!

The speakers at the conference reported their visit with the Reverend Dr Martyn Lloyd-Jones, who was minister at Westminster Chapel in London. Dr Lloyd-Jones, who was also a highly qualified and eminent physician, had become an evangelical theologian and mighty preacher, a man held in great respect worldwide.

The speakers reported that Dr Lloyd-Jones had received them warmly and agreed with their theology about the Holy Spirit. This made an enormous impact on me personally. I resolved to write to the so busy Dr Lloyd-Jones. I received a long typed letter, almost by return of post, from 'The Doctor'.

> Dear Murray ... I rejoice with you in your experience! This is precisely what I believe, that the baptism in the Holy Spirit is distinct from salvation, although it may occur soon afterwards.

There followed some wise words about the gifts of the Holy Spirit. I still have that letter.

Looking back, I wonder if there were smiles in the heavenlies as a young Scot was baptized in the Holy Spirit, wearing his kilt!

A JUNIOR DOCTOR
IN SCOTLAND

We were now qualified to practise our chosen profession. Our required residencies/internships were in Medicine and in Surgery, each for six months. Thereafter, we made hugely significant decisions as we anticipated what the future might hold for us.

INFECTIOUS DISEASES

Ruchill Hospital, Glasgow, was an Infectious Diseases Hospital. This was my medical residency and absolutely ideal, as I looked forward to practising Medicine overseas, preferably in a developing country.

A ward specifically for infants with meningitis provided care for children who usually presented as an emergency. Such a distressing condition, meningitis may be caused by a number of different infecting organisms. Most of these tiny patients recovered if the infection had been recognized early and suitable antibiotics were given. We learned how to carry out lumbar punctures on infants, necessarily a very delicate intervention, with the withdrawn cerebrospinal fluid sent for laboratory examination.

THE RANGERS SUPPORTER AND
THE HORSE THAT 'LOST IT'

It was a Wednesday evening in Glasgow. I was on resident duty in Accident and Emergency at the Southern General Hospital. Glasgow Rangers were playing Dundee at the nearby Ibrox football stadium. I reckoned that a few scrapes and injuries might appear after the game, as possibly around 30,000 football supporters would be watching the match.

About half-time in the game, I estimated, a wee Glaswegian appeared in Accident and Emergency. He had on his blue Rangers 'bunnet' (cap), Rangers scarf, and his Rangers socks when he sat down.

'What are you doing here at this time ... it must be about half-time in the game?' I asked, as there was no apparent injury to be seen.

'Haw, Doctor! I never seen the match at all. I wis just goin' in the gate, when wan o' they big polis' horses bit me on the heid!'

After this brilliant description, duly recorded in his Casualty notes, our supporter lifted his cap, and there was a nasty laceration of his scalp. By the time he had revealed his wound, I was already trying to suppress my inner chuckles. Clearly, and reassuringly, the wee Glaswegian himself had this fantastic Glasgow sense of humour even in a time of distress.

The patient, who was sitting and looking up at the young doctor in his white coat, decided not to be offended by my smiling expression, but cheerfully added, 'Hey, Doctor, I think the horse thought it was grass!' Actually, his hair was red.

It took me a few moments to recover my composure. Then I and the nurse cleaned the wound, and I placed the appropriate number of sutures after local anaesthetic injections.

Those wonderful police horses which 'policed' football matches were so disciplined, but this particular horse 'lost it' for a brief moment. In fact, a newspaper the next morning described our supporter actually being lifted off the ground. Ouch!

Yet the patient found genuine humour in describing his plight. Well done, Glasgow!

IN THE LABOUR WARD

Robroyston Hospital, north of Glasgow, specialized in Obstetrics and Gynaecology. Six months in Obstetrics seemed common sense, as I thought I would be practising abroad in situations where all the different medical or surgical specialities would be required.

It is presumptuous on my part, as a then young male doctor, to write anything about two women who were in labour. The experience of childbirth must be quite extraordinary and so utterly demanding, yet often achieved with such fortitude and, at times, even humour.

Two contrasting experiences involved two women in the labour ward of Robroyston Hospital, Glasgow. One 'pulled my leg' so effectively and with such humorous composure; the other was the only woman I witnessed who was 'beside herself' before calm was realized by most unorthodox means.

It should be said that the nursing staff in the labour ward were mainly experienced midwives, most of whom had given birth to their own babies and then come back to nursing after maternity leave. These midwives were ideal in bringing reassurance and confidence to individual patients.

One mother was pregnant with her third child. Immediately after the birth, there is usually a very special moment when the mother is presented with the brand-new baby, most often by the attending midwife. It is almost invariably a truly joyful time.

On this occasion, unusually, it fell to me to hold the newborn child and present the baby to his mother. 'You have a lovely little boy, Mrs McKenzie!'

Her face fell! A look of sheer disappointment clouded her expression. I had never seen this reaction. Lamely, I asked, 'Did you want a little girl, Mrs McKenzie?'

She positively twinkled. 'No! No, Doctor! It's my other little boy, he wanted an Alsatian!' She burst out laughing at me! It was so well done.

The second mother was very much in labour and quite far on but was in considerable distress. It was the middle of the night, and I was asleep in my room. The phone rang. 'Doctor, would you come over to the labour ward and help us with this girl who is quite hysterical? We can't calm her.'

'Of course, I'll be with you in a few minutes.' I pulled on some trousers, left my pyjama top in place, and put on my long white coat. Over to the labour ward …

Apparently, when I came in, I asked, 'Where is the patient?' Quite unnecessary; it was very obvious. I went over to the bed where the woman was rolling around and screaming. My usual 'technique' was to go to the patient, take her hand, and say that all was fine because I was here!

I bent down to speak quietly to the very distressed girl. My hand sought hers. Her hand shot past mine, grabbed the edge of my white coat, part of my pyjama top, the hairs on my chest, the skin, and the subcutaneous tissues. She twisted all of these quite viciously! The pain was excruciating! It seemed to bounce off the inside of my skull!

The nurses told me that my method of speaking to the patient was not the way I usually acted. When I bent down to whisper quietly to her, the pain of twisted skin and hair brought an involuntary yell beside her right ear!

She settled down immediately. She was calm and cooperative. Labour proceeded normally to a happy conclusion.

FIRST-CLASS TRAVEL

After we had completed our six months in Obstetrics and Gynaecology, three of us decided to sit the examination for the Diploma in Obstetrics from the Royal College of Obstetricians and Gynaecologists (DObstRCOG).

We boarded a plane in Glasgow to fly to London. As we pressed into 'economy', it was immediately obvious that there were only two remaining seats. My two pals leapt forward and deposited themselves into the two seats, grinning hugely at my dilemma.

'Is anything the matter, sir?' enquired the air hostess. 'There doesn't seem to be a seat for me' I replied. 'Just follow me, sir.' The air hostess swept aside the curtain between economy and first class and indicated a plush first-class seat where I should sit. The curtain was still drawn and so a little wave of triumph in the direction of my friends seemed very much in order.

Into our flight of only an hour or so, a tray with a delightful meal was placed in front of me. I murmured to the kind air hostess, 'I shouldn't really be having this.' The reply was very clear. 'Sir, you enjoy the meal; after all, you're in first class!'

Another wave in the direction of my two medical colleagues was entirely appropriate!

Six Months in Paediatrics

A Senior House Officer position became available in Paediatrics, which would broaden my experience across the different disciplines. This appointment was at Seafield Hospital, Ayr, about an hour's drive south of Glasgow.

The hospital had been a stately home owned by the engineer who had designed the Forth Road Bridge, north of Edinburgh.

Paediatrics can be so rewarding, particularly with the wonderful powers of recovery from illness that children can demonstrate. At the same time, the loss of a child is such a heartbreak, after which words of comfort are quite inadequate. Our role was to provide all the support and care we could, with appropriate medical and surgical interventions where indicated.

During that time, I carried out around 25 appendicectomies ('appendectomies' in the USA).

The work was fulfilling, if demanding. But the heavy workload was hugely compounded when my co-resident, a Pakistani lady doctor who clearly was not at all well, was taken to another hospital for various investigations. This meant that I was the sole receiving medical and surgical officer at the hospital, with a catchment area of the whole of Ayrshire. (There were other hospitals in the county.)

For close on three weeks I was on duty day and night, without any break whatsoever. It was possible, of course, to go to bed and sleep most nights, but always on duty. The worst two or three days involved beginning a day with the ward round at 8.30 a.m., working through the day, not getting to bed at all through the following night, being on the ward round the next day at 8.30 a.m., and working through the day, eventually getting to bed at midnight on the second night!

The Matron of Seafield spoke to me after about three weeks. 'Doctor, I shouldn't suggest this, but why don't you go out of the hospital for an hour? I will cover for you.'

I drove to the Heads of Ayr down the coast and gazed out over the Irish Sea. It was an extraordinary feeling of release, even for an hour! I wondered how those in prisoner-of-war camps must have felt at their moment of release.

SPECIALIZING IN EYES

A position became available in the Tennant Institute, Western Infirmary, Glasgow. Professor Wallace S. Foulds was a very hard worker. We were obliged to follow his example, but with such benefit to ourselves, both in our knowledge of Ophthalmology and in our pursuit of higher qualifications in our chosen subject.

Those of us who were juniors were expected to study for these higher qualifications, and this we wanted to do. A full-time job and much studying, we were encouraged to push our frontiers of knowledge, keeping abreast of the relevant medical literature and research.

FIRST RESEARCH PAPER

The first research paper that I wrote followed a significant meeting and conversation in the ground-floor corridor of the Tennant Institute.

A Consultant Anaesthetist, Dr Mike Telfer, was our near neighbour in Carse View Drive, Bearsden, north-west of Glasgow. In our conversation, I was discussing an eye drop called Phospholine Iodide. These eye drops were used in treating open-angle glaucoma.

He said to me, 'You should look at an enzyme in the blood of these patients. The enzyme is a cholinesterase, and the level of this enzyme may be reduced when exposed to organophosphates.'

But why should an anaesthetist have this knowledge? He explained. 'The muscle relaxant we use in anaesthesia, called succinylcholine (scoline, suxamethonium), effectively paralyzes the muscles, including muscles used for breathing, so that a patient needs to be ventilated (helped to breathe) by the anaesthetist during surgery. The enzyme in the blood that breaks down succinylcholine is a cholinesterase. If its level is low, or if the enzyme is abnormal, the effect of succinylcholine persists, even when the patient comes round after anaesthesia. This is described as scoline apnoea. The anaesthetist has to keep ventilating the patient until the lower level of cholinesterase takes effect.'

This was big! I had potentially six patients on Phospholine Iodide eye drops, for glaucoma. The Biochemistry Department,

Western Infirmary, measured the level of the cholinesterase in the blood of each patient, initially as a baseline reading.

One or two drops of Phospholine Iodide in each eye was prescribed for each patient, every day, with daily enzyme readings, and I was astonished to see each patient's reading of the enzyme plummet to well below normal, except for one patient.

'Mr Jamieson, are you taking your daily drop to each eye faithfully?'

'Yes, Doctor!'

After a few days, and asking the same question at each visit, the patient looked a bit sheepish. 'Actually, Doctor, I'm really sorry! I haven't been taking the drops as I should.'

The patient was amazed—astonished! He could not understand why this young doctor was so absolutely delighted that he had *not* been taking his required medication!

The paper was published in *The Lancet* (*Lancet* 1965; 2: 272–273), warning of the dangers of scoline apnoea (inability to breathe) during the recovery period just after general anaesthesia when the patient had been using Phospholine Iodide eye drops.

One year later, in New York and also in Israel, there were reports of the severe consequences of scoline apnoea in patients who had used Phospholine Iodide eye drops. The authors of these two separate reports had read the article in *The Lancet* before publishing. There have been many other instances reported in the literature.

A TRADES UNION OFFICIAL

An interesting and amusing episode during a routine outpatients' clinic involved the slit-lamp microscope, which is an instrument designed to examine the patient's eyes at very close quarters. The patient places his or her chin on a rest while pressing the forehead against a firm, fixed strap. This is secure and comfortable. The examiner looks through a binocular microscope and achieves focus on each eye of the patient.

The patient was a Trades Union official. His chin was firmly on the chin rest, and I began the examination. I became aware that his hand was sliding round on the surface of the table which holds the microscope. Underneath his fingers was a paper pound note, which he was clearly offering to me, perhaps thinking I was a poor, overworked young doctor (all true; in that job I was on duty or on call for 132 hours each week).

I thanked him, murmured my protestations, and slid the note back to him. A few moments later, his hand was sliding around the table again. It looked like a diary. All of this was extremely distracting. He had an extraordinarily large mouth. Distracted, instead of asking him to open his eyes wide, I asked him to open his mouth wide!

A flicker of surprise spread over his ample face, but he duly opened this enormous cavern very wide indeed! The beam of the slit-lamp identified his uvula (the wobbly bit that hangs down at the back of the mouth).

What to do? What to say? I said, 'Goo-ood! Now, please close your mouth and open your eyes wide.' All proceeded well thereafter, and it was most interesting to have the memento of a Trades Union diary.

Part Two

OVERLAND TO
AFGHANISTAN: 1968

OVERLAND TO
AFGHANISTAN: 1968

It had been a hard slog, working towards the examination for the Fellowship of the Royal College of Surgeons in Edinburgh (FRCSEd) while in a full-time post in the Professorial Unit, Western Infirmary, Glasgow.

A request came from the south. 'Murray, would you be interested in travelling out to Afghanistan to help with an eye camp? Dr Jock Anderson will be leading the camp in the valley of Bamiyan, over 8,000 feet in the mountains north-west of Kabul.'

Some young people were planning the trip. A doctor and his wife who were to go with the group, travelling overland in a Land Rover, had to drop out because the wife had become pregnant.

All of this was happening in June 1968. The 'crunch' was that my FRCS examination would finish with orals on the Tuesday, results would be announced on the Wednesday, and the group were to leave from London on the Saturday.

Actually, the decision was easy. Pass or fail, I'd had enough of exams, at least for a time, and I decided I was 'out of there', come what may!

THE IMPORTANCE OF TIMING

Looking back, it was very clear that God had planned this trip. Remarkable 'coincidences', extraordinary timing, a place in the Land Rover appearing, the voluntary work in 'eyes', then the leader of the planned eye camp was my senior colleague, mentor, and friend, Dr Jock.

We left London on that Saturday in June 1968—nine of us, in a long-wheel-based Land Rover. In the back of the Land Rover, we lay on top of our kits, each of which should have been not more than one foot square. I was teased by the group because I packed a silk dressing gown!

The team members were Rob and Chris, Pauline, Ann, Chrissie, Neil, Faith, David, and Murray. Five of us were drivers. We travelled through Europe to Greece, Turkey, Iran, reaching Afghanistan in around three weeks.

I was staying with Dr Howard Harper; Monika, his wife; and their three girls. It was my privilege to read stories each evening to their girls.

EYE CAMP IN BAMIYAN

The eye camp was in the valley of Bamiyan, in the Hazarajat region of central Afghanistan. Bamiyan, through the centuries, had thriving communities, being on the ancient Silk Road from China to the Middle East.

There were two massive buddhas carved out of the cliff face, with hundreds of small caves. The biggest buddha was 175 feet tall. This had been a buddhist sanctuary since the 6th century. Later, between the 7th and 10th centuries, with the spread of Islam in the region, the eyes and noses of the two main buddhas were chopped off! In AD 1221, in the extraordinary and disturbing history of this magnificent valley, Genghis Khan and his hordes were said to have killed everything in the valley—'even the rats and the flies'!

In March 2001, during ongoing civil war in the country, these imposing buddhas were blown up!

TRACHOMA IN BAMIYAN

Our camp was in tents in July 1968, at the feet of the 'sightless' buddhas. Dr Jock and I, with our team, went into the schools in Bamiyan to examine the children. Our particular brief was to diagnose and treat the potentially blinding eye infection, trachoma. Certainly, we 'over-diagnosed', but trachoma was epidemic, with more than 50% of children having active trachoma. We had ample supplies of tetracycline eye ointment, which we prescribed for daily application over some weeks.

Of course, the important message to convey to children and their parents, was to improve their general hygiene. If you can encourage children to wash their faces every day, then the prevalence of trachoma in a community can dramatically reduce. Trachoma is spread by flies, fingers, faeces, fomites (e.g., clothing and towels), and 'dirty' faces.

VITAMIN A DEFICIENCY, AND CARROTS

A very significant clinical finding which affected all ages in these communities was vitamin A deficiency. Initially, the evidence of this problem was given by patients complaining that they couldn't see in the dark, described as 'night blindness'.

Vitamin A is required to nourish and sustain the rods of the retina. Of course, in young children there is no complaint of poor vision if it's dark, but you can ask parents if a child seems to bump into objects when it's dusk or dark. We were able to give vitamin A capsules to patients, and in some instances, if the condition seemed very severe, we gave an injection of vitamin A.

One story was of a man who came with severe 'night blindness', and we decided to give him an injection of vitamin A. He came back the next morning absolutely thrilled, saying that he could see in the dark that very same night! The speed of the metabolism involved was startling. He said that it was so fantastic, could we give him another injection in the 'other side'? The first injection had been given intramuscularly in a buttock.

We advised our patients about their lifestyles and what they should eat. So often, vitamin A–rich foods were actually freely available. They should be giving their children dark green leafy vegetables and carrots.

It was good to hear that an entrepreneur in the village bazaar had brought in loads of carrots. He was experiencing a roaring trade because those foreigners up at the eye camp had said it would help people's eyes.

We had set up our tents beneath the main buddha rising around 175 feet in the sheer cliff face. Our clinic was established in tents, one of which was our operating room.

ENTER A WARLORD!

Our second tent housed our operating room. The vivid memory that I have of surgery being interrupted involved a man who was certainly an Afghan leader, and probably a warlord.

I was operating with our surgical team. The flaps of the tent were swept aside, and a man who was clearly used to command and to be obeyed, burst into our sterile area!

He was not tall, but he had a magnificent physique, a kind of square or squat strength. The picture was enhanced by his military garb, with a large and heavy waistband of bullets, and a similar band of bullets angled across his chest and over his shoulder. His automatic weapon was in hand. 'You will see me now!' commanded the impressive interloper.

Through an interpreter, I explained to this commander of men that I was in the middle of a surgical operation and could not possibly see him right away. Perhaps later?

The distinct impression that he was not used to anyone frustrating his wishes and commands hung heavy in the tented operating room. This leader of men, irritated and disgruntled, swept out of the tent!

Would I see him again? I looked out for him later, but he did not reappear. Perhaps that was a relief? I do know that if I were ever involved in a firefight, I would want this guy on my side! Thankfully, that scenario never arose.

CATARACT SURGERY: 'A FEW
YEARS AGO, I WAS 14!'

One of our happy post-operative outcomes involved an old man. 'Old' is a relative term when we consider that life expectancy in Afghanistan was around 45 years. We operated on women in their mid-30s with age-related cataract.

My patient, who was probably about 80 years old, was asked how old he was. He replied, 'Doktar Sahib, a few years ago I was 14'. Afghans in these rural areas probably didn't observe birthdays.

The old man in Bamiyan was recovering after cataract surgery. He had been 'blind' for at least 12 years, with bilateral advanced cataract. The poignant part of his story was his distress, because he hadn't seen his grandchildren clearly for at least 12 years.

After surgery, we placed the temporary post-operative 'aphakic' spectacles onto the old man's face, and I stood back and held up my hand with four fingers extended. 'Chand as?' ('How many?'). He answered in a tremulous and rather squeaky voice. 'Chahr, Doktar Sahib!' ('Four, Doctor Sir!'). He was correct. He could see! Those in the 'ward' who could see all cheered!

GENGHIS KHAN AND THE MONGOLS

A few of us, including our ophthalmic nurse, Frances, went to visit the Red City at the east end of the Bamiyan Valley.

High in the mountains, the Red City had been a thriving community until Genghis Khan and his Mongols appeared. We gazed towards the east and saw the trails curving through the mountains. What a horrendous sight it must have been to see the Mongol horsemen pouring through the entrance to the valley and surrounding the City!

Elsewhere in the valley, having sacked the Red City, the Mongols laid siege to other communities and their fortifications. The story is told that a princess revealed to Genghis Khan the water source to a main community in the valley. The water source was cut off; the community capitulated, but the Mongols slaughtered all the inhabitants, including the princess!

We prayed for Afghanistan and the Afghan peoples high up in the destroyed and derelict Red City.

AN EARTHQUAKE IN IRAN

We drove back to the UK via Meshed in eastern Iran, Tehran, Ankara, Istanbul and into Greece, where we took some days to laze on the beaches. Thence, on through Europe, reaching the UK after four and a half weeks.

The only incident of special note on our trip home was in Meshed, Iran. The local hospital had kindly given us an almost derelict house just outside Meshed, where we could camp. Late that night there was an earthquake! The house shook, but not violently. It lasted for perhaps two or three minutes, and we thought little of it at the time.

The next morning, we proceeded on our way, having already expressed our thanks to the kind folk who had given us hospitality. Our next stop would be the Caspian Sea and then Tehran. Only Ann, from South Africa, was thoughtful enough to contact her parents to let them know that she was safe and the earthquake had not troubled us.

Later the story unfolded. On that Monday morning, my own parents in Bearsden, Glasgow, received a letter from me, written from Kabul, saying we were driving home and would be in Meshed at the weekend.

The *Glasgow Herald* was delivered, as usual, on that same

OVERLAND TO AFGHANISTAN: 1968

Monday morning. My parents glanced at the front page. There was a map with a shaded area and, in the centre of the shaded area, the city of Meshed. The headline read, '20,000 Killed in Terrible Earthquake in Eastern Iran'.

My parents contacted other parents of our group. They contacted the Foreign Office in London, who contacted the British Embassy in Tehran. The British Embassy eventually managed to make contact with us somewhere en route to Tehran ... and were able to report that all was well, at least for our little group.

BACK HOME, AND FISH AND CHIPS

A final memory of that eventful trip is inappropriately light-hearted after the last story. While driving overland, both going and coming, we would occasionally chat about the meal we were going to enjoy on returning home. Of course, it all became more elaborate and ridiculous at times, but when we arrived off the ship at Dover, we parked the vehicle and went straight to the nearest chippy. How we enjoyed our fish and chips out of a paper 'poke'!

Part Three

OUR FIRST YEAR IN KABUL: 1969–70

MEETING RUTH; NEW YEAR'S EVE: 1968 / 1969

A few of us young men, all in our 20s, drove from Glasgow to a conference south of London. This group would meet on a Thursday evening on the south side of Glasgow. Each of us had committed our lives to Jesus Christ. We were discovering more of the person and ministry of the Holy Spirit. One of the group, Alastair Keddie, was to be my best man the following October.

The conference was called 'Prayer and Bible Week', with the purpose of bringing in the New Year with prayer, worship, and Bible study. The leaders and main speakers included Campbell McAlpine, Denis Clark, and Arthur Wallis. An intensive week, we had three sessions each day of over two hours. After a couple of days, you seemed to get a 'second wind'. These were formative days for the many young folk there, who were discovering more about our wonderful God.

It seemed, however, that Campbell and Denis were quietly scheming, with a view to bringing two young people together. God would know what might come of this meeting.

I was asked to meet this lady at the station. It was a simple task, as I had a car. Ruth, who was studying at Theological College (LBC) in London, was coming late to the conference, which had been underway for a couple of days.

A gorgeous-looking girl came off the train, carrying her overnight bag and a guitar. I introduced myself and guided Ruth to the car.

Within minutes I was asking pertinent or impertinent questions! When we came into the College, where the conference was happening, the delegates were all having a meal in the dining room. I went with Ruth to the top table to meet with the leaders, whom she knew. Denis Clark introduced us to each other with a flourish! There was a definite twinkle in his eye!

During the following days of the conference, I was asking the Lord for guidance. 'Is this the girl for me, Lord?' I certainly knew what I felt. I was actually looking through the book of Ruth, in the Bible, hoping for guidance! In the book of Ruth, Ruth meets Boaz, who is described as the kinsman-redeemer. Notice the description 'kinsman'. Soon after, in the Bible story, Boaz and Ruth are married.

I took my 'present-day' Ruth out for afternoon tea in Worthing, on England's south coast, to a quaint little English teahouse, with bubble windows, overlooking the sea. I asked her the question, 'Do you think we could be related?' Remember, it was a question of guidance.

It did seem very unlikely. Living 400 miles distant from each other has always been a long way in UK terms. Ruth's father, Reverend Henry Brash Bonsall, referred to my burning question in his speech at our wedding a few months later. Notice the name 'Brash' in my future father-in-law's name.

It turned out that one of my mother's cousins, Professor James Couper Brash (Professor of Anatomy at Edinburgh University) was one of the Scottish branch of the Brash family.

Sometime after the year 1572, members of the original 'Brasche' family had escaped from France to England and Scotland, one hiding in a barrel on board a ship. They had fled the riotous killing of Huguenots (French Calvinist Protestants) in Paris and throughout France. Targeted assassinations and widespread carnage, largely instigated by Catherine de Medici, had originally flared up on 24–25 August 1572. This became known as the Massacre of St Bartholomew's Day.

We were and are related! Here, surely, was the further

guidance I was looking for. We may have been miles apart, but Ruth received a letter from Scotland every day. Our special theme tune became 'Romeo and Juliet' by Tchaikovsky.

I invited Ruth to come north at Easter to meet my parents and enjoy runs in the country in my MGB sports car. Later I heard that Ruth had some qualms about travelling north. A close friend, June, sat her down and told her to write two lists, pros and cons. The scores were pros 6 ... and cons 2! I still don't know what the 2 cons were!

The first two days were great! I was to play in a rugby match at Balgray, the Kelvinside Academy sports ground. The game was a fun one for Kelvinside Academicals (old boys of the School), Under-27s against Over-27s ('old crocks'). Ruth and my sister, Margery, were coming to watch.

Unfortunately, the two ladies were late arriving at the game. By the time they arrived, I was injured and off the field. Someone had mistimed his tackle and crashed head first into my lower back. I went down, thinking, 'Is it spine? Is it kidney?' Something significant had happened!

My cousin Lorna's husband, Roy Sutherland, an eminent Consultant Radiologist, took me into hospital and X-rayed my back. A transverse process on the right side of my lower spine had fractured and was sitting separated from the bony spinal column. Little needed to be done apart from general support, some analgesia (painkillers) and occasional hot compresses to ease the considerable discomfort.

Our romantic few days together were enormously curtailed. I sat in a chair, waiting for the next painful spasm, with Ruth applying heat as needed. One way of getting to know each other!

A PROPHETIC WORD

A group of us from Theological College visited our good friends Jack and Eileen Kelly in their new home, some miles south of Glasgow.

AN ITINERANT PREACHER

The purpose of the visit was to meet with an Irishman called Denis, who seemed to have an almost unique itinerant ministry. Denis had once been a Jesuit in the Catholic Church.

We were all together as a group in one of the sitting rooms in the stately home when Denis walked in. He spoke very clearly and directly.

'There is a spirit here that is lukewarm!'

The impact on each one of us was startling! We knew enough of the Scriptures to understand that the source of these words was from the book of Revelation, the last book of the Bible. The Apostle John was inspired by God to write Revelation while on the island of Patmos. He was recording the words of Jesus who is addressing the seven churches in Asia Minor (which included most of present-day Turkey). The Laodicean church was described as 'lukewarm' in their faith and practice.

But that wasn't all. The Laodiceans were roundly rebuked for being 'neither cold nor hot!' (Revelation 3:16).

This is God speaking! I remember thinking, 'Lord, I hope it's not me?'

Well, our attention was certainly fixed. During the hour or so that followed, Denis spoke and also prayed specifically and individually for most of us. He prayed for me.

In my mid-20s, an unexpected personal hurt, which happened soon after my undergraduate training, led to a period of very real trauma and struggle.

Looking back, it was clear that God had intervened in that relationship, as the plans I had been considering for the future were not in His purposes.

A WORD FROM GOD

As Denis was praying for me, suddenly his prayer was prophetic. I have it verbatim as it was recorded on an old-style tape: 'God is preparing a place for you which your heart has not yet desired, but God knows what will eventually be the correct desire of your heart. And because you have praised Him, even in the darkness, God is now giving you a complete release!'

Within an hour, I knew that I was different. I was so free, released, and liberated! I look back at that experience so many years ago as one of the pivotal experiences of my life. This was and is reality ... in Christ!

One part of the prophecy puzzled me. Had I praised God, 'even in the darkness'? When had I praised God consistently? Then it dawned on me. At the beginning of my 'quiet time' with God each morning, I had prayed, usually on my knees, and worshipped God, perhaps for ten minutes or so, and often in 'tongues'. Then I read my Bible, meditating on Scripture verses.

That meeting and the word of prophecy was on a Saturday evening in May 1969. The following Saturday, I was in London meeting with Ruth, who was finishing her second and last year at Theological College in London.

A PROPOSAL AND A CALL

I proposed to Ruth that Saturday.

That evening, Ruth's special Aunt Moo (Muriel Ashby) gave us tickets for a wonderful concert, Verdi's *Simon Boccanegra*, in a London theatre.

The following Thursday, I received a telegram from Dr Jock, who was in Kabul. Would I come to Afghanistan for one year, after the summer term at College?

Over the next three days or so, I discussed the telegram with my new fiancée. I was 29, Ruth quite a few years younger. I didn't want to disappear for a year. I planned to get married!

It was decided that I would go to Afghanistan in early July, be a visiting ophthalmologist for about ten weeks, then return for our wedding, planned for 4 October in Birmingham.

I returned in mid-September. We were married in early October, went on honeymoon to Sweden and Norway in my MGB sports car, came back to the UK after two weeks, flew immediately to Kabul, Afghanistan, to begin our work and calling, and complete the year of commitment that had been promised.

But what of the prophecy? When at College, I had sometimes gone to the prayer meeting for China, wondering if God might call me to go there at some time. After all, I was born there; my parents had served there, my father for 30 years; and my grandparents on my mother's side had also been in China.

The prophetic word spoke of 'preparing a place for me which my heart had not yet desired.'

The year before, out of the blue, I had found myself in Afghanistan, involved in an eye camp in the mountains. A gap of an academic year, then a request to go to Afghanistan for a year ...

A PROPHECY AND A PROMISE CONFIRMED

How do you come to love a country or a people? God puts them on your heart! I would find that I was so stirred and moved by writings and photographs of this amazing and yet deeply troubled country and people. Ruth would say to me, 'Murray, please don't buy any more books about Afghanistan until you've read the ones you already have!'

This love for the country and people was to carry me through many sometimes traumatic experiences in the years that followed, and has stayed with me ever since.

'God is preparing a place for you which your heart has not yet desired, but God knows what will eventually be the correct desire of your heart.'

A prophecy wonderfully fulfilled!

'THIS IS THE ONE.'

Here is Ruth's story:

More than fifty years ago, I met Murray at a certain railway station in Sussex. We later discovered that this was actually a set-up, on the admission of two much respected and well-known Christian leaders. This was Prayer and Bible Week over New Year 1968–1969.

I was studying at College (LBC) in London. Murray was at College (BTI) in Glasgow. Within ten months, we were married and in Afghanistan, even though Murray had been out of my orbit and working in Afghanistan for the summer. In fact, we realized that we had only been in each other's company for just over three weeks, between meeting at the very beginning of 1969 and our wedding on 4 October 1969.

How did I know that he was the one for me? After the conference, he went back to Scotland, and I to London. When Murray asked me out during the conference and we visited a little teahouse on the south coast, I knew then, at 24, that I had to have a very clear word from God before venturing out on such an important relationship. At first, God's word to me was 'Trust', 'Rest', and 'Wait', from Psalm 37.

I knew that Murray had had a call from God when he was only 12, to be a doctor overseas. I just wanted to be quite sure I didn't make a mistake!

I come from a family of tall men. My father; both brothers, Charlie and Tom; and sister, Rachel, are tall, and my boy cousins 6' 6" and 6' 7". In contrast, I am the smallest member of my family. An important point for me, apparently.

As I prayed for many days about this young doctor from Scotland, I asked God for a verse to completely remove any doubts.

In my search, I suddenly came upon a verse I had never met before in all my years of studying the Bible. It related to God's choice of a young man to be king of Israel. Samuel, the prophet, was sent with his anointing oil to the house of Jesse—a man with eight upstanding sons (who just happened to be the grandsons of Ruth and Boaz).

Seven of these young men were paraded before Samuel. They were all tall and handsome, and Samuel was sure that any one of them might be a likely candidate. Not so! God clearly had not chosen any of them.

'Are there any more sons?' he asked. 'Oh, yes!' said Jesse, 'Just a young boy, David, who tends his sheep on the mountainside.' 'Bring him here to me,' said Samuel.

As soon as David arrived, Samuel knew for sure that here was God's man! He was young, ruddy, and handsome, with beautiful eyes. God clearly spoke to Samuel. 'Arise, anoint him; for this is the one!' (1 Samuel 16:12).

God's word to me: 'The Lord looks at the heart'!

The verse that completely knocked me for six was 1 Samuel 16:7, when God told Samuel quite clearly that he wasn't interested in looks or height: 'Do not look at his appearance or at his physical stature ... for the Lord does not see as man sees; for man looks at the outward appearance, but the Lord looks at the heart.'

Wow! What amazing confirmation!

The striking thing was that Murray had auburn ('ruddy') hair and his first name is David. Not only this; we discovered that although we lived at different ends of the country, we were actually related through a cousin on Murray's mother's side and my father's family. How extraordinary!

How could I mistake such a clear answer to prayer? I knew that Murray was the man for me!

Now, 54 years on, he still is!

THE MAN IN THE MOUNTAINS

It was the summer of 1969. I was in Afghanistan before travelling home to marry Ruth. Our team was conducting an eye camp in Faizabad, near the base of the Wakhan corridor, the finger of land to the north east of the country that stretches out to its border with China.

For some reason, I was delayed in Kabul and was to travel north, somehow, to join up with the team. A providential meeting with two young American men provided a marvellous opportunity to join our special team in style! These two men had wealthy fathers who were treating their sons to an expedition in Afghanistan. They were flying to Faizabad, and would I like to travel with them in their hired jet?

Our camp was in a District Hospital where we had a few upstairs rooms, one of which we were using for surgery. It was inspiring, between operations, to look out over the soaring mountains all around us!

FIRST PATIENT FOR SURGERY
IN A LIST OF 21

We were reaching the end of our eye camp and had decided not to carry out any more intraocular operations (opening the eye), as we were leaving in two days, returning to our main hospital base in Kabul.

But an older man appeared at our clinic, having travelled some distance down the Wakhan corridor. One eye was completely blind, with hypermature cataract and secondary glaucoma. The vision in this eye was 'no light perception'. The other eye was hardly any better—hypermature cataract, secondary glaucoma and vision of only 'hand movements'.

What to do? Within a few weeks, he would probably be totally blind. I decided to operate, of course, on the eye which had some residual vision.

We tried to reduce the intraocular pressure in the eye preoperatively, to make the eye more suitable for surgery, which was under local anaesthetic. Our patient was first on our surgical list. I made the routine incision into the eye to perform an intracapsular cataract extraction (the technique and method used in those far-off days).

The eye contents began to ooze out of the eye! Even the cataractous lens came out of the eye. I had never experienced this complication before or since. I can still remember the sick feeling in my stomach ... 'He's really blind now!' All I could do was to close the eye as best I could, cleaning the wound. It's still hard to write this.

I put on a pad and bandage. As Rosemary, our nurse, said, 'How we managed to continue our operating list of 21 patients for surgery, we'll never know!'

At the end of the list, I said to Rosemary that we should tell our patient and his family that the operation had not been successful. For most of our Afghan patients, an eye operation is simply an eye operation, and you get your sight back.

Our team at the eye camp were all from Kabul and our NOOR Eye Institute, except for a nonmedical American couple, Gordon and Grace, who were students in Kabul. Rosemary, our British nurse, had vast experience and commitment to our work. There was a junior Afghan doctor who was still in training as an ophthalmologist.

Our patient was lying on a mattress on the floor, near the operating room. I spoke to the patient and the family through our best Farsi speaker, Rosemary. 'I'm so sorry to have to tell you that the operation has not been a success.'

The patient and his family were amazing, full of understanding and even sympathy. 'Would you like us to pray?' I said. Yes, that would be appreciated.

Rosemary, Gordon, Grace, and I knelt beside our patient and prayed, with our hands resting on his head and shoulders. 'They will lay hands on the sick and they will recover'—Jesus's words recorded in Mark 16:18. We prayed in His Name. The Lord's presence was powerfully with us.

The next morning, we took off the bandage and pad. His eye was better than other routine cataract operations we had carried out previously!

That afternoon, Rosemary was packing our equipment and instruments in the operating room. Afghan patients and relatives kept coming to ask her questions. 'You said the eye was 'kharob' ('bad'), but now you say it is 'khub' ('good'). What happened?'

Rosemary told these wonderful people about Jesus and His healing power!

We travelled back to Kabul, a full day's journey in our Land Rover, leaving our Afghan doctor to provide follow-up care for one week.

A week later, I was in the clinic at the NOOR Hospital, in Kabul, when the junior doctor came in, full of news. First, and courteously, he said to me, 'Salaam alekum! How are you, Doktar Sahib? How is your family?' The words then tumbled out!

'That man's eye—he can see perfectly!'

THE STORY OF THE MAN IN THE MOUNTAINS, 30 YEARS LATER!

Fast forward 30 years to my 60th birthday party, where a very special friend of many years asked if she could tell a story. Roseanne and her husband, Henry, and their house church had prayed for us throughout our married life. They had received our account of what happened in the mountains many years before.

She began: 'All those years ago, Murray sent us and our church this amazing prayer letter, with the story of the "Man in the Mountains" and how God healed his eye. Sitting right next to me at that meeting was a young woman, called Elizabeth, who was deaf, particularly in one ear. She was a talented musician who had been born with abnormalities of the tiny bones (ossicles) in her ear. Her increasing deafness meant that she was unable to join a choir or follow her career in music.'

As Rosanne read out our prayer letter, this girl became very excited. She just happened to have her Bible open at the exact place (Luke 22:51) where Jesus dramatically healed a man of deafness. She read the words, 'He (Jesus) touched his ear and healed him!'

Rosanne continued: 'In a sense, Elizabeth put a direct question to God! "Lord, You healed this man in Afghanistan ... what about me?"'

As Rosanne went out into the kitchen to make tea and coffee for everyone, Elizabeth rushed out after her and said, 'Please pray for me now! That amazing story has given me faith, and I strongly believe that God is going to heal my deaf ear!'

Rosanne thought she might choose six of the 40 young people who were together in the living room and go into their dining room to pray. But God spoke to Rosanne. 'What I am going to do now I'm not going to do in secret!'

Rosanne went back into the living room. She explained that Elizabeth had had a word from God and they were going to pray for her.

One lady in the room, a nurse from Australia, said 'The Lord has just told me that He has already healed Elizabeth's ear!' These were the first words that Elizabeth heard really clearly.

That night, Elizabeth found it hard to sleep because of the noise of rain on her bedroom windows. Next morning, she even heard the crunch of someone walking on the gravel of the driveway.

Of course, Elizabeth had regular and appropriate consultations for her hearing, particularly as her musical career had been so disrupted. She went to her consultant, who said that it couldn't be so—it could not be that ear. Impossible! But on checking her records, it was so!

With a lovely singing voice, Elizabeth was able to join a leading choir and pursue her career in music.

How amazing, and how very special, that we were to learn, 30 years after a miracle in the mountains of Afghanistan, what had happened in Kilmacolm, Scotland!

KABUL–TASHKENT–
MOSCOW–LONDON

After ten weeks as a visiting ophthalmologist to the NOOR Project in Afghanistan, I travelled home to the UK for our wedding, which would be celebrated on 4 October 1969.

In Kabul, I made arrangements in good time, to fly Aeroflot to Tashkent, thence to Moscow, followed by a two-day train journey from Moscow to London (including the ship across the English Channel).

THE WRONG DOOR

A transit visa through the USSR required a visit to the USSR Embassy in Kabul, which was on Darulaman Road. This complex of large buildings had the offices of the Intourist Travel Agency, but I found them difficult to locate.

I went through an impressive door which I thought gave access to Intourist. It was a big mistake. A large, open reception area did not provide any welcoming directions. My enquiry of a Russian official was met with an angry response from more than one official.

It is the only occasion in my life when I experienced the well-known 'bum-run'! A burly official grabbed my neck collar at the back of my neck, while his other fist grabbed the top of my trousers at my backside. I was propelled out of the Embassy—or, at least, the wrong offices of the Embassy!

The flights by Aeroflot, with an overnight stay in Tashkent, were largely uneventful. I was placed in a large hotel in central Moscow. The hotel was one designated for visitors to Moscow, and Intourist desks were in the large foyer and entrance hall.

I had two requests of the Intourist officials, all of whom were women. The first was an enquiry as to whether they had churches nearby, explaining that I was to be married in a church in the UK in two weeks' time. The second was about the Bolshoi Theatre and Ballet, which I understood was not far from the hotel.

I was directed to a church only a few hundred yards away, and appreciated going in there amongst a gathering of mostly older Russians.

It was so good to get a ticket for the Bolshoi Theatre that evening. However, it was not the Bolshoi Ballet but Berlin Opera singing *The Mastersingers of Nuremberg* by Richard Wagner. Absolutely magnificent!

RUSSIAN EXPRESS

The two-day, two-night train journey from Moscow eventually reached London, with one change of train en route at the Russian border, the ship from Holland to Harwich, and on by train to London.

Out of Moscow, I was sharing with two fellow travellers in a cabin for three. One was an older Latvian gentleman who was travelling to visit his sister in Latvia. The other was a relatively young Russian, probably in his 30s, who was on a trade mission to The Hague, in Holland. There was virtually no conversation with the Latvian, because of the language barrier, but the Russian and I had a number of interesting conversations, as he spoke good English.

'Is that a Bible you are reading?' he enquired. 'It's called a Daily Light,' I responded, 'but it contains only Bible verses and quotations, usually on a particular subject or theme.' I shared my love of the Bible and its message with this Russian friend.

We discussed many things. This was early autumn 1969. The previous year, 1968, had seen the uprising of the Czech people against the iron fist of communism. This became known as the 'Prague Spring'. My Russian friend advised me that Soviet tanks and armoured vehicles had not crossed the border into Czechoslovakia but remained at the border.

I responded, I hope politely, that this is what he had been told.

A DUTCH FRIEND

Some months later, when Ruth and I were in our first home in Kabul, we were visited by a very special Dutchman, a man of God whom we knew as Andrew. I happened to share with him the story of that train journey out of Moscow and the conversation with my fellow Russian passenger.

When I referred to the 'Prague Spring' and the Russian's reference to military vehicles on the border of Czechoslovakia, Andrew surprised us by confirming that Soviet tanks were certainly in the centre of Prague, the capital. He had driven into Prague when the tanks were there! In fact, he said that his car was just about the only car going into Czechoslovakia. Most were driving out of the country, fleeing a very dangerous situation.

HEALING ON HONEYMOON

Here is Ruth's account of healing on honeymoon:

'Murray and I were married in October 1969, and heading for Afghanistan, a land of deserts and high mountain passes. Our beautiful honeymoon was in Sweden and Norway, courtesy of two special Scandinavian friends. Murray's plan was to spend a week in each country, driving through the most magnificent autumn scenery—rich reds, yellows, and golds—en route.

'As long as I could remember, I had experienced debilitating car sickness as a child, as a teenager, and as an adult. On honeymoon, as we raced through to Oslo, I became quite sick and unable to enjoy the journey.

'Murray suddenly became incensed at this sickness and decided to address it in strong spiritual terms! He laid hands on me and claimed the words of Jesus from Mark 16:18, in faith: "They will lay hands on the sick and they will recover."

'I was healed immediately!

'This was amazing, as two weeks later we were in Afghanistan, near to the Khyber Pass and the huge mountains of the Hindu Kush, where we were driving over mountain passes of up to 12,000 feet and on to eye camps around the country.

'Praise the Lord! I never suffered from travel sickness again!'

PRAYING AROUND THE HOUSE

When Ruth and I arrived in Afghanistan, we were welcomed by a very special family. Dr Herb Friesen, my respected ophthalmologist colleague; his wife, Ruth; and their wonderful kids made sure we felt at home from day one.

There was a banner dramatically displayed on arrival at their home. It was a greeting with a distinct southern American accent!

WELCOME Y'ALL!

In fact, 'American Ruth' said that before she and 'British Ruth' were in Kabul, the place had been 'Ruthless'!

After some weeks, Ruth and I were settling in to our first home in Karte Seh, Kabul. I had chosen a very pleasant property before travelling back to the UK for our wedding and honeymoon in Scandinavia.

Each expat home had its own painted sign, usually at the front gate, with the names of the occupants and their organization. Our organization was NOOR, the National Organisation for Ophthalmic Rehabilitation. 'Noor' means 'light' in Farsi and Arabic.

Our painted sign, beautifully crafted by the sign painter, who assured us that he knew what he was doing, unfortunately had one line stroke missing. Thus:

MURRAY AND PUTH NOOR

That really made our day! Inevitably, in the many years since, Ruth has occasionally had a birthday card written to 'PUTH'!

During those early weeks, I had an increasing sense that we should pray around our house. We were in bed, and once again, I said we should be praying around the house.

Ruth said, 'Well, let's do it!' We got up and began to pray in different rooms, beginning upstairs. We asked the Lord to remove anything that was not pleasing to Him, all the time conscious that we were entering into another spiritual dimension of potential conflict. Having prayed in this way, and asking the Holy Spirit to fill each room with His Presence, we moved on to the next room. So we prayed around the house.

As we prayed into the pitch-black attic, the hairs on the back of my neck sprang to life! Frankly, it was really spooky!

We went to sleep. About 4.00 a.m. we were awakened and startled by a dreadful noise of roaring and shouting! This was accompanied by the crashing of a door somewhere nearby. The 'man' was berserk, yelling and screaming; the door crashed again and again!

I went out onto our balcony, because all of this was somehow very near but not inside our house. Nothing was there or to be seen, inside or out of our high-walled garden. We settled back, trying to sleep.

At 5.00 a.m., exactly the same horrendous shouting and banging of a door! I went onto the balcony again, but nothing!

(Later, our language teacher said that I should not have gone out to the balcony because 'they might have shot you!' He also advised me to sleep with a gun under my pillow, which advice I didn't follow.)

At 6.00 a.m., Baz Mohammed, who helped us in our house and garden, appeared with our morning cup of tea. 'Baz Mohammed, did you hear the noise last night at 4.00 a.m. and again at 5.00 a.m.?'

'Yes!' he replied, 'It was my door that was banging, and the light was switched on in my room. I jumped up, but there was no one there. It happened twice!'

All of this explained why the shouting and banging was outside of the main house. Baz Mohammed slept in a room at the back of our property. We might have prayed in the outbuildings, but Baz Mohammed was sleeping. You wouldn't think of interrupting his sleep to say, 'We're going to pray in your room!'

The following evening, a Thursday, Baz Mohammed left for his day off on Friday and would be away for Thursday and Friday nights. Ruth and I were alone in our sitting room on the Thursday evening.

Suddenly, at about 9.00 p.m., the very same shouting and banging started up. Someone or something was utterly out of control! I picked up an old Afghan sword and gave Ruth a dagger. I went out first as we went into the garden. Again, there was nothing to be seen.

We were given advice that we should call in the police. The following evening, Friday, there was a police officer and his junior in our sitting room, waiting to keep watch. Clearly, they found our situation very frightening, discussing their plan of action between themselves in intense Farsi. Then the police officer turned to me and said that they, the police, would be outside on the road and, if anything happened, we should call them!

I responded that I thought Afghans were tough. They usually are!

In the end, two junior policemen stayed overnight in Baz Mohammed's room. We never saw that senior police officer again. Nothing happened that night.

Ruth and I left on the Saturday to provide one week of eye care at a camp arranged by our associated organization, the Medical Assistance Program (MAP) in the Hazarajat, central Afghanistan.

On our return, we shared the story with a number of folk. One American couple, the Glassmans, were preparing a Farsi/English textbook for people like ourselves who needed to learn the language. After describing our experience, they said that strange things could happen in the spiritual world after prayer.

An Afghan family, our next-door neighbours, were of royal lineage. The father was a retired general in the Afghan military, very gracious and dignified. After an excellent Afghan meal, I was sitting on a couch with a son of the family, a very fine young man whom I had often suggested might be a future Afghan Foreign Minister.

I shared our story; after all, we were neighbours. When I finished, he looked at me and said, 'I believe that was ... but I'm not sure you would agree with me?'

'Go ahead. Try me; I think I might agree with you,' I replied.

'I think that was a djinn, a spirit.'

'I agree with you!'

A few days later, friends of ours, Gordon and Grace, were visiting. We shared the story. 'Have you prayed outside the house?' asked Gordon. 'No, not yet!' I stood with Gordon outside in our garden. He lifted his hands and prayed, 'Lord, this is Your garden, Your house, Your outbuildings ... please, guard and protect; drive away anything that is not of You.'

This incident in our first home was never repeated. But it certainly revealed, once again, the reality and huge significance of spiritual conflict in the Christian life.

Nothing like that extraordinary experience has ever happened again. Since then, Ruth and I have always prayed around any new property or living accommodation.

THE MISTS OF TIME

Soon after we arrived in Afghanistan, Ruth and I were sent on several medical assignments together. Just married, we had no ties, a team of two visiting different fascinating locations in the country.

For one assignment, we were sent due west, to Lashkargah in Helmand Province, on the edge of the Dasht-e-Margo (Desert of Death). We were to examine the eyes of American schoolchildren whose families were posted there, working on a water project in the region. Our particular aim was to make sure that no child was suffering from trachoma, the eye infection caused by *Chlamydia trachomatis*.

Let Ruth describe, in her own words, a uniquely Afghan and historic experience:

'We were given a beautiful room in an American home, with a huge picture window overlooking a vast desert landscape.

'Early the following morning, we were woken by the distant tinkling of bells. There was a little oasis of water right outside our window and a morning mist hanging over the desert. We were spellbound! As we quietly watched, an amazing sight unfolded before our eyes. A large group of Kuchi nomads, with goats and sheep and camels, their little bells all tinkling, were coming down to the water's edge to drink.

'It was not only the animals that caught our attention, but the unveiled Kuchi women, with their fine, sometimes wrinkled, sun-tanned faces, brilliantly coloured dresses, and row upon row of tinkling jewellery around their necks and ankles, leading their flocks to drink. They silently emerged from the mists with their incredibly graceful, swinging gait.

'We watched, mesmerized. Their men were probably nearby,

but it was the women who stole the show! They quietly stayed by our window until all was done, then disappeared back into the desert mists.

'What an honour to be allowed a brief glimpse of an unforgettable scene, a moment centuries old in time.'

MARY AND JOSEPH, IN KABUL

The Kabul Community Christian Church met in a house off Darulaman Road on the south side of the city. The Pastor of KCCC was Dr Christy, a Christian gentleman greatly respected by Afghans and foreigners alike. Christy would pray over circumstances and situations openly, whether with Afghan Muslims or foreign Christians.

Christy phoned us in our new home. Ruth took the call, as I hadn't returned from work. 'Ruth, would you and Murray be willing to act the parts of Mary and Joseph in the KCCC Christmas Pageant? Just married, you're the obvious choice.' Ruth agreed on behalf of both of us.

Each year the KCCC constructed a set, which included a wooden double-storey inn where Joseph would plead for a place for his wife, who was about to give birth to the baby who would be named 'Jesus'.

The set was in the grounds of the large church house. A few rows of terraced seating were then put in place for a gathering of about a hundred, who would come and see what these foreigners were doing and the story they were telling.

There was a live donkey; a flock of sheep with their shepherds; and even, would you believe, real camels!

The evening of the Pageant arrived. Ruth and I were dressed in flowing garments of the time of Jesus' birth. Joseph had a handsome bushy beard. We were waiting at the side of the house for the fine white donkey to appear.

We heard that the shepherds were confused about proceedings. There had been a dress rehearsal, but the shepherds thought this was the real thing and had begun to wander off. The shepherds and their sheep were retrieved, but a sheep fell down a well! The loss of a sheep would have been an absolute disaster. The sheep was saved!

The background music had begun. Our blind brother, Zia, had begun the running commentary. Where was the donkey?

Then a 'clip-clop', and around the back of the house came our magnificent white donkey! I lifted Ruth on to the donkey, as planned, and we began our trek to the inn. All seemed to have come together. But there were a couple of mishaps still to happen, one quite serious, the other amusing.

One of the wise men fell off his camel! Abraham, from India, was an imposing and substantial figure who, incidentally, had a very fine tenor singing voice. Fortunately, he was uninjured.

The more amusing mishap was as Ruth, the donkey, and I traversed the grass towards the inn. About halfway there, the donkey stepped on my foot. It wasn't painful, as the hoof was on the soft leather of my fleece-lined shoe. But the donkey had stopped, and I had to stop!

Later, someone said to me, 'Really good acting, Murray! The way you stopped halfway across and surveyed the scene before moving on was quite impressive.' I was, in fact, trying to get out from under the donkey!

The wonderful story of the birth of our Lord Jesus Christ had been told once again. It was so good to have played the roles of Joseph and Mary, recounting the message of hope for a very troubled world.

CONCERTS IN KABUL

Our first year in Afghanistan was full of surprises. Our first home was an attractive two-storey house with a walled garden. Many American expats had delightful homes with courtyards, while the British Embassy was a truly palatial white-domed building with extensive gardens.

One summer's evening, there was an outstanding performance of Shakespeare's *A Midsummer Night's Dream* in those grounds, with lanterns and 'fairies' adorning the huge historic trees. What a sight!

Our church choir had opportunities to sing in front of various audiences. We sang Stainer's *The Crucifixion*, with our 'wise man' and tenor soloist, Abraham, from India. Abraham and I (baritone) sang the duet from *The Crucifixion*, which I had sung previously, and informally, with my father.

One of the most extraordinary features for Ruth, in 1969 and 1970, was the Kabul School of Music, led by Professor Walter Fleischmann of the Vienna School of Music. Ruth was already teaching music at Ahlman Academy, an outstanding international school, with 100 children of 26 nationalities. But what a blessing, all those years ago in the capital of Afghanistan, to have superb piano lessons from Professor Fleischmann, himself a concert pianist.

Soirees were often held in different expat homes while the British Ambassador's wife happily worked on her embroidery.

International gatherings with many from very different countries shared the joy of wonderful music in Kabul, Afghanistan.

THE VALLEY OF BAMIYAN

One of our favourite places in Afghanistan was the valley of Bamiyan in the Hazarajat. It was there that I had been involved in an eye camp when nine of us drove overland to Afghanistan.

A DELAYED FLIGHT

Ruth and I were in Bamiyan and staying overnight in the small hotel before flying back to Kabul. Both of us needed to get to Kabul.

We were sitting in the dining room, having a meal before our flight back to Kabul in the 20-seater Bakhtar Airlines plane. Conversation in the dining room amongst the guests, who were mostly tourists, seemed to increase in volume, with an anxious buzz. Someone had counted the number of potential and booked passengers who were to fly on the waiting Bakhtar plane. It became apparent that our plane did not have enough seats for the number of booked passengers!

Individuals in the dining room began to stand up! They began to move to the door. Attempts to appear nonchalant, while moving with increasing speed, soon discarded any attempt at pretence.

We arrived beside the much-desired plane. Quite a number of folk had already found their seats and seemed to stare fixedly straight ahead into the middle distance. One German gentleman sat with grim determination etched on his face. An American lady said, 'Well, I gotta go!'

When Ruth and I arrived at the plane, no seat was available.

We trudged back to the hotel and spoke to the young manager.

But there was one more episode in the saga of the overbooked and overfilled plane. The next morning, our manager friend came to us with a mischievous smile on his face!

'The Bakhtar plane that you were not on because you didn't run ahead to get a seat ... on their flight to Kabul (about 100 miles), they encountered a storm, and safety requirements dictated a detour in their flight. They flew around the storm and landed at Jalalabad, a further 100 miles beyond and east of Kabul!'

We couldn't help smiling. At least everyone was safe.

A CHARIOT RACE

Ruth and I were in Bamiyan with special friends of ours, Gerry and Irma. They were valued members of our team in Kabul.

Horses and traps were readily available for hire. Each could seat two people. Very much in holiday mood, Gerry and I hired a horse-and-trap each. Irma and Ruth climbed aboard beside their husbands, and we set off.

Whether or not we thought of the epic movie *Ben Hur*, is in question. But Gerry is a cheerful, warm-blooded Frenchman, and soon we were careering along the dirt track and rutted road at a spanking pace!

The chariot race was dangerously underway. There was not really enough room on the dirt- and stone-strewn road for two chariots, side by side. But our steeds responded with vigour and abandon as we found ourselves racing in true Ben-Hur style!

Utterly foolhardy! Never again! Thank the Lord, no one was hurt, and we made it to the finishing line with whoops and shouts. It was a dead heat!

ACROSS THE GENERATIONS

Ladd and Thea were in Afghanistan when Ruth and I were there. Ladd was minister to the Anglican congregation in Kabul. He was also a well-respected teacher at Ahlman Academy in Kabul, where Ruth was teaching music.

Ladd, a tall, well-built American (Thea, a gracious English lady), was certainly a very fine tennis and table tennis player. Very competitive!

Years later, Ladd was chaplain at a school in Perthshire, Scotland, where the boys wore kilts. Rannoch School had a Sunday evening service, at which I spoke a couple of times. In later years, our son Andrew spoke at the same service.

Danny, a son of Ladd and Thea, was a great friend of our son, David. When we lost David in a car accident in 2020, Danny wrote a very moving poem in memory of his friend and our dear son.

Another son of Ladd and Thea, Jonathan, became a doctor and married a doctor, Gwendolyn, a very fine paediatrician who has cared for one of our grandsons.

The links and interests go on! Jonathan and Gwendolyn have two sons who are professional rugby players. Zander Fagerson, still in his 20s, has been capped over 60 times for Scotland, as a prop forward. He was chosen for the British and Irish Lions on their tour of South Africa in July and August, 2021. Matt Fagerson, in his mid-20s, has been capped over 40 times by Scotland as a back row forward. Matt was 'Man of the Match' in the win against England in 2022!

God called the grandparents, Ladd and Thea, to

Afghanistan. He also called us, Murray and Ruth, to that much-loved country.

Now back in Scotland, we continue to share common interests across the generations, in our Christian faith and also in rugby, particularly Scottish rugby!

SOME PATIENT REPORTS

LEPROSY IN THE MOUNTAINS

Ruth writes:

In the holidays, I joined Murray to assist on eye camps around the country. Our first year of married life was amazing! Sent around the country on special trips and thoroughly spoiled, in general!

An extraordinary experience was a week in the central mountains of Afghanistan, in Yakaolang (the Hazarajat), assisting the team of our sister organization, The Medical Assistance Program (MAP). While there, Murray was busy examining and treating so many patients with eye problems, and I worked alongside him most of that week.

One particular little lady made an indelible impression on me. She was so very, very sad. She had leprosy. I spent quite a lot of time removing the crawling maggots that had eaten away at the flesh of her nose. Very little was left!

Each day, I talked to her, smiling and showing all the healing love and encouragement I could. Gradually, she began to smile back, and by the end of that week, she had changed dramatically! What a blessing to see her face full of smiles!

A NEW EYEBROW

An Afghan man, aged about 30, presented at the Avicenna Hospital in Kabul. 'Doktar Sahib, I'm getting married soon. But I've suffered a severe burn of my face, and I've lost an eyebrow. Can you give me a new one?'

Where his eyebrow should have been, there was only scar tissue. Otherwise his face had minimal post-burn scarring.

At that very time, a British leprologist was visiting Kabul. He had just described for us, three ophthalmologists, a new surgical technique to replace an eyebrow. One distressing problem that patients with leprosy may have is a condition called madarosis. This can involve the loss of both the eyebrows and eyelashes.

I was delighted to mention to the visiting colleague that a patient had just appeared and needed a new eyebrow. Could he demonstrate the technique for us and provide the new eyebrow requested by the patient?

'Actually, I've never done the operation,' said our colleague. 'I was simply describing the procedure, but without any personal or practical experience.'

We arranged for surgery in the Avicenna Hospital. I would carry this out with a local anaesthetic. Not ideal, but these were early days before we had our 100-bed NOOR Eye Institute.

The technique involved resecting a graft of hair-bearing skin from the side of the head and rotating the graft, with a view to placing it into a prepared 'bed' where the eyebrow should be. This meant that the 'bed' must be prepared, but also a tunnel under the skin, over the zygoma bone, between the hair-bearing graft and the 'bed' at the eyebrow site.

An important feature of this procedure was to retain the vascular supply of the superficial temporal artery, feeding the hair-bearing graft.

We proceeded with surgery, preparing all required as

described above. But with all the manipulation and local anaesthetic, the superficial temporal artery went into spasm. How disappointing! Of course, I could simply use a free skin graft, without the artery, but ...

The patient was awake, as this was done under local anaesthetic. I asked him to stick his legs in the air (on the operating table) and 'bicycle', as we've all done, with his hands under his bottom! Within seconds, the tiny artery was pulsating, and we proceeded (legs back on the operating table), reaching a satisfactory conclusion to the operation.

Ruth phoned through while we were operating, just when the patient was working hard to follow my instructions. Frances, our excellent theatre nurse, answered Ruth's question as to whether the operation was going well.

'Fine!' said Frances drily. 'The patient is bicycling on the table!'

Yes, it was a success, even if the hair of the new eyebrow grew upwards and forwards. I trust his bride appreciated the plastic repair, providing two 'balanced' eyebrows.

THE GIRL WITH 'HYSTERICAL BLINDNESS'

It was a Saturday morning, and I was operating in our surgical theatre at the Avicenna Hospital in Kabul. One of our Afghan nurses, Zilayikha, came breathlessly into the operating room. 'That girl with the hysterical blindness, she's tried to strangle herself!'

'How is she now?' I asked, very concerned.

'She's settled. The family is there.'

'We'll finish the surgical list and then go and see her.'

The teenage girl had developed a dramatic type of 'blindness' more correctly described as 'Dissociative Conversion Disorder'.

Her father and brother had fought with each other, and her distress showed itself with this condition. She was utterly depressed, withdrawn, and showed no evidence of any visual capacity. We had invited a psychiatrist to see her, but there was no change in her condition.

I walked into the room where she was in her hospital bed. Rosemary, our British nurse, was with me. Members of the family, including the girl's mother, were standing around her bed, very anxious and distressed.

In later years, in London, I used to give a lecture entitled 'Customs, Cultures, Beliefs and Eye Disease'. I would ask our often senior student colleagues studying for the *Diploma in Community Eye Health* how often they had walked into a ward or a room and the family of the patient looked at you, enquiring 'What are you going to do, doctor?'

This is exactly what happened on that Saturday morning in Kabul, Afghanistan. I found myself saying to the family, especially the mother, 'Would you like us to pray?'

'Yes!' The mother and family would appreciate prayer. Rosemary and I prayed for the girl, according to the Scriptures, with the 'laying on of hands', in the Name of Jesus. The sense of God's presence was very real and special. My faith soared!

We finished praying and looked at the girl. Nothing had changed. Really quite disappointed, I went home for lunch. An hour or so later, the Afghan resident doctor phoned. 'Dr Murray, that girl, she can see perfectly, and I've sent her home. Oh! ... and ... er ... all the other patients want you to come and pray for them!'

Of course, it was 'good psychology', but I believe God intervened. Although her problems at home were not over, the next time I saw this young girl, her utterly depressed expression was transformed!

She was simply radiant!

Years later, when I wrote articles for *Triple Helix* and *Developing Mental Health*, the senior consultant psychiatrists of the DMH Editorial Board advised me that the correct description is 'Dissociative Conversion Disorder' instead of 'Hysterical Blindness'. *Developing Mental Health* had the title 'Dissociative Conversion Disorder; and Prayer'.

ANNE'S VIRAL KERATO-CONJUNCTIVITIS

One of our NOOR nurses, Anne from the UK, developed very unpleasant red and inflamed eyes with some watery discharge.

There were three foreign ophthalmologists working with NOOR at the time: Dr Herb, from the USA; Dr Jock, from the UK; and myself, also from the UK. It is a pleasure to recall the joys of working with these two colleagues, both highly qualified, Herb with the American Board of Ophthalmology qualification, and Jock, the UK Fellowship of the Royal College of Surgeons in Ophthalmology.

However, in the case of Anne, our practice of medicine might have left something to be desired. Over the course of a week to ten days, Anne saw each of us, and different treatments were tried. Certainly, a presumed diagnosis on clinical grounds suggested to each one of us that this was a viral kerato-conjunctivitis affecting one eye more than the other. Anne's eyes did not show any improvement with our treatment.

It was a Sunday evening, after a full working day. (In Afghanistan, our weekend was Thursday and Friday, with Friday the holy-day, when Afghans attended the mosque and we went to our church). Unusually, on the Sunday evening I drove round to discuss some NOOR matters with our nurses, Anne and Rosemary, who shared the same home.

I recall very vividly that I was sharing some thoughts and plans relating to our work. Undoubtedly, I was really preoccupied with these concerns.

After an hour or so, I left. As I drove away, I had such a strong sense that I should have taken time to pray for Anne and her eyes. It was so real that I was disappointed with myself. I felt I had missed it!

The next morning, I left for work in good time so that I could visit Anne and Rosemary with a view to praying for Anne. But as I drew up outside the house, Rosemary was disappearing in a taxi, heading for the hospital.

'Lord, I can't go in and pray for Anne without Rosemary being there!'

Rosemary, in the back of her taxi, turned right round, saw me through the back window, stopped her taxi, got out, and walked back to my car. 'What are you doing, Murray?' she asked.

'I believe we should pray for Anne and her eyes. We should have done this last night.'

Rosemary and I went back into the house. Anne had not been going to work because of her eye inflammation and infection. We prayed for Anne, 'coming against' the infection and praying for healing in the name of Jesus Christ.

My colleague, Dr Herb, had told Anne that a viral kerato-conjunctivitis would run its own course, perhaps lasting a further ten days or so, but then would probably resolve, with or without corneal scarring.

We prayed that Monday morning around 8.00 a.m. During the morning, the discomfort and pain gradually eased. By lunchtime, the redness had largely disappeared. By the evening, the eyes had become 'quiet' and inflammation had completely gone!

Two days later, Herb, my totally convinced and appreciative

colleague, said, 'Murray, I sure did like your treatment!' He and I knew the Source of that healing intervention, just as described in the Bible records!

'Jesus Christ is the same, yesterday, today and forever!' (Hebrews 13:8)

EYE CAMP IN THE PANJSHIR VALLEY: 1970

The Panjshir Valley, a few hours north of Kabul by car or truck, is a magnificent natural linear fortress, extending for many miles due north from its entrance, beyond the plain of Gulghandi, famous for its beautiful flowers in season.

Away back in 1970, we were to plan and carry out a small eye camp, some distance into the valley. Our small team was Rosemary, Ruth, and myself.

In later years, from 1979 onwards, Panjshir would see extraordinary resistance to the Soviet invasion and occupation of Afghanistan. Indeed, it might be argued that the Soviet presence partly foundered on this particular rock of stubborn Afghan grit and determination!

The leader of this dreaded and respected Afghan militia was Ahmad Shah Massoud, the Lion of Panjshir. An engineer by training, Massoud gathered around him a naturally warlike Afghan fighting force, and Soviet soldiers must have been enormously apprehensive about any sortie into the Valley.

The years passed, and, in 1989, Soviet troops were withdrawn from Afghanistan.

In 2001, two men visited the Panjshir, posing as photographers. Their 'camera' was effectively an explosive device, and they blew themselves up while 'interviewing' Ahmad Shah Massoud.

Two days later, on 9/11, the date etched hideously in our world's history, the destruction of the twin towers took place in New York.

In the Spring of 1970, Ruth and I, with our nurse, Rosemary, travelled to set up the eye camp some miles into the Panjshir Valley. The camp was to run for ten days.

Preparations for a camp always involved careful planning, with information being provided for all the Afghan settlements near to the camp—including, as appropriate, radio announcements.

Hospitality was provided by the Governor of Panjshir. But this was a basic camp with basic facilities. The clinic was set up in unused outbuildings. Surgery would be carried out in a substantial mud building, where it became necessary to fix a carpet to the ceiling to keep dust from falling on the patients.

Our host, the Governor, provided accommodation for us and supplemented our provisions for meals, even providing an Afghan waiter, who apparently had a conviction for murder!

In this small camp, I examined about 60 patients each morning and then, in the afternoon, operated on 10 or 12 patients. It was such a 'gentle' camp that, after surgery, Ruth, Rosemary, and I would walk a mile or so upriver, sit down on the bank, and enjoy the wonderful scenery, with all the beautiful spring blossoms. I was reading *Tom Sawyer* by Mark Twain.

As we were walking upriver one day, a little girl in colourful dress ran away from us screaming, 'They'll take my heart out!' Oh dear! Had her mother warned her about these foreigners? How were we described to her daughter?

These were tribal people, very conservative and reserved, but with their own dignity and self-assurance in their own land. Some of them might never have seen a foreigner.

One woman came with her husband to the morning clinic. To her husband's consternation, his wife would not unveil in front of me. Later, I understood from an Afghan friend that for a woman to unveil in front of a stranger in this way was a 'great sin'—his words! Of course, it's extremely difficult to examine someone's eyes if there is a cloth grill barrier in front of them!

The husband, by this time, was in a real stew. 'He's a doctor! He's a doctor! He's not a man at all!'

I wasn't too sure about this description!

The reluctant patient maintained her dignity, tore a small hole in the cloth grill, and held the hole over one eye, which I then examined. This accomplished, she shifted the hole to the other eye, for a final viewing!

It was astonishing, as a western-trained ophthalmologist, to observe the versatility of these Afghan patients. They would walk into the operating room, having been 'prepped' by Rosemary; swing a leg onto the operating table; settle back with their head on the headrest; and await developments.

Ruth and I were scrubbed and gowned, waiting for each patient. The patient was draped appropriately with sterile gowns, local anaesthetic was given, and a cataract operation (or other procedure) was carried out.

We received a visit from an important group of women from different countries who called themselves 'The Diplomatic Wives'. Most of these influential ladies had husbands who were ambassadors or other senior diplomats, appointed by their countries to postings in Kabul, Afghanistan.

A small group of these visitors watched Ruth, Rosemary, and myself operate on a patient with cataract in our somewhat makeshift operating room.

These supportive ladies had donated a large tent for our camp and work. The tent was erected not far from the operating room. Post-operative patients had wicker or camp beds inside the tent. Very quickly, the tent was full and overflowing with patients.

Surgery had to continue. The patients kept coming and were listed for surgery. Many of these patients had bilateral, blinding cataract. I decided that we must continue to operate. These trusting patients had no alternative prospect of surgery.

As usual, the patient was guided into the operating room, swung a leg onto the operating table, lay back, and surgery commenced. After 15 to 20 minutes, with a pad and bandage in place, the patient climbed down and disappeared to … we know not where!

The next morning, patients who had been operated on the previous day came back from wherever they had slept, for dressings.

All of these patients did very well. We had no post-operative intraocular infection. Sight was restored, particularly when each patient received their aphakic spectacles (often + 10 dioptre sphere lenses).

There was some personal enjoyment in later years when colleagues talked about day-release cataract surgery. I was able to say, with a wee smile, 'We were doing that a long time ago, away back in 1970!'

A TRACHEOSTOMY—ON MYSELF?

A grateful patient appeared at our accommodation rooms. Expressing his thanks, he handed me a few small fish. Generally, we couldn't eat fish safely in landlocked Afghanistan. However, they seemed fresh, and the Panjshir river was flowing freely with the melting of the winter snows.

There were insufficient fish for all three of us, and so it was decided that I should eat them. After eating them, and they were tasty, I settled down to some other diversion.

To my consternation and alarm, I became aware that my larynx and upper oesophagus were 'closing', and swallowing and breathing became disturbingly difficult! I was the surgeon. But how successfully could I carry out a surgical opening into my own windpipe (tracheostomy)?

Thankfully, with prayer, the swelling subsided, and I made a full recovery.

AN INVITATION TO DINNER

Ruth and Rosemary returned south to Kabul, leaving me alone to look after the follow-up of patient care for a few days.

The relative of one of our patients invited me to his home for an evening meal, the traditional time to entertain in most cultures. The night was very dark when my host came to collect me. We walked for possibly a mile, winding up the hillside following a single track, with my host ahead of me. In one hand he had a torch; in the other hand he had a gun, at the ready! I tried to ask him if the gun was for wild animals or for human beings. His response was rather noncommittal!

We arrived safely at his home, high on the mountainside. His wife would have been cooking for hours. The food was good! The only problem was that his wife had not been able to pick out many of the tiny stones that were widely dispersed in the rice. As I ate my food with relish, quite often my teeth would crunch on a stone, which was impossible to cover up or accomplish silently. Each time, my host winced visibly! I do hope he was kind to his wife later, and I was profuse in my appreciation and expressions of enjoyment of the meal afterwards.

My host guided me safely back to the Governor's compound without any mishap.

EARLY-MORNING COMPANIONS

On a couple of occasions, in the early morning, I wandered some way up the hillside, sat on a grass-covered mound, and enjoyed a time of quiet and prayer. My study Bible was fairly large, with a wide blank margin for notes.

It was an oasis of peacefulness in a place with superb vistas, both nearby and up and down the Panjshir Valley.

But then a young man appeared. Then another! And another! Each boy or young man settled comfortably and respectfully a few yards from me. Within a short time, perhaps 30 minutes, there were around 30 boys and young men sitting beside me, looking enquiringly at me.

A spokesman courteously asked, 'Doktar Sahib, what are you doing?'

I replied, 'Dua makenam' ('I am praying').

'What is the book?'

'This is the Injil (Gospel / Holy Bible).'

'What does it say?'

'It tells me about Isa (Jesus),' I explained a little with my limited Farsi.

These young men and boys had been taught to respect a Holy Book, although they would know nothing of its content.

I prayed briefly, openly and out loud, that God would reach out and bless these fine young Afghans.

MY BIBLE

My Bible was a study Bible. It was not small and was quite heavy, with a hardback cover. Later in Kabul, Helen Perry, one of our optometrists, told me that I could get a very good and lighter leather cover in a particular shop. I went to the shop, explained my request to the owner, who nodded his understanding.

As he took the Bible from me, he commented, 'This is your Holy Book, I think.' The shopkeeper took my Bible in both hands with great reverence, carrying it high in front of him and placing it on an upper shelf, with nothing on top of it.

There was a lesson here for me. While we rightly emphasize

the content and wonderful message of the Bible, there should be suitable reverence in how we treat this God-inspired and great book. Further, if treated with perceived disrespect, it can be a real stumbling block to those of other faiths in many countries.

I was travelling in a train in Pakistan. It was a fairly long journey, and I settled back with my feet on my small suitcase in front of me. I thought I might read my Bible at some point and so took it from my case and placed it on the suitcase.

A short time later, the man across the aisle from me leant over and asked, 'Is that a Bible you have there?'

I replied, 'Yes, it is a Bible.'

In a tone of clear rebuke, the man said, 'We would never put our feet beside a Holy Book'. Because of that experience, and others, I never like to see a Bible placed 'casually'—for example, on a floor. The point and significance is surely 'to be all things to all men', and to be sensitive to the culture and people with whom we have to do.

Part Four

SCOTLAND: 1970–1975

SAILING HOME: SOUTH AFRICA AND RHODESIA

It was early autumn in 1970. We took an unusual route to travel from Afghanistan to our home in the United Kingdom.

An Afghan bus took us from Kabul to Torkham on the Pakistan border. Then a taxi from the border drove us on to Peshawar. From Peshawar, it was the train overnight through the length of Pakistan to Karachi.

The Italian Lloyd Triestino ship sailed Karachi to Bombay (Mumbai, India), then to Mombasa (Kenya) and on to Durban (South Africa). We disembarked at Durban and spent five wonderful weeks visiting friends and touring in South Africa and Rhodesia (now Zimbabwe), reaching the border with Zambia.

Following the Garden Route south to Capetown, we boarded the next ship of the same Lloyd Triestino line and sailed northwards from the Cape of Good Hope, eventually reaching the Mediterranean and Venice, our final port of call.

The bus journey in eastern Afghanistan had only one memory. I had bought a Japanese Akai tape recorder in Kabul and declared this to the Afghan customs official on the bus. He was difficult and officious! I felt a little uncomfortable murmuring to the official that I was an eye doctor and had been working in Afghanistan for a year. The official was transformed, embarrassingly so! It seemed that he then recognized me. Had his mother been a patient? He made a speech of personal approval to the whole bus, after which I was allowed to take my Akai recorder without let or hindrance.

On board ship after Karachi, we met a delightful Indian family who were to disembark at Bombay (now Mumbai). As we had an overnight stay in Bombay, they kindly invited us to their home, where we enjoyed great Indian hospitality, including a guided tour of the All India Cricket Club.

Thence to Mombasa (Kenya), and on to Durban (South Africa), where we disembarked to begin our southern African adventure. Colourful tribal dancers leapt high into the air as our ship docked at the quayside. As we began our travels, we were so taken with the colours and magnificent blossoms of the jacaranda trees. We had friends and contacts on all our travels during five amazing weeks, driving 6,000 miles in South Africa and Rhodesia (Zimbabwe), reaching the Zambesi River and looking over into Zambia.

A very African picture has remained with us over the years: a huge herd of buffalo, standing motionless, having stirred the dusty ground, with a glorious sunset behind them!

ADVENTURE BY THE ZAMBESI

We drove on to Rhodesia's largest Game Reserve, the Hwange National Park, which has the Zambesi River at its northern border.

Our plan was to spend two or three days in the Game Reserve but come out of the Reserve each evening. Of course, instructions are very clear. You do not get out of your car at any time. The wildlife was magnificent! To be a few feet from a stately family of cheetahs, still and watchful, was very special. Hippos in the river, evidence of crocodiles, deer coming with furtive glances for a fleeting drink of water!

On our last day, we drove very close to the Zambesi River— too close! To my horror, the car stuck fast in the sand! There were crocodiles and large beasts nearby, and around us there was evidence of dusk falling.

'Ruth, I'm going to get out of the car and walk a couple

of hundred yards up to the main dirt track road, looking for someone in a vehicle.' It was a concern that there seemed to be very little evidence of any other vehicle or person in the vicinity. The Reserve was about to close.

'If you are getting out of the car, I'm coming with you!' said Ruth. Quickly, and as silently as possible, we got out of the car, made it off the sand and up the bank to slightly higher ground. Frankly, with hearts pounding, we made our way towards the main road, still a long way off, and praying fervently!

To our sheer joy and relief, a game warden appeared driving his Land Rover!

'What are you doing?' he almost yelled. 'I never come this way at this time! You could have been stuck here over the weekend!'

'If you survived' was the grisly inference.

We told our saviour, with enormous gratitude, that he was an answer to prayer. Our vehicle was extricated without mishap using the warden's tow rope.

Our next exciting venture was to view the Zambesi's magnificent, cascading waters of the Victoria Falls. What a mighty spectacle! The Victoria Falls were first named by the Scottish medical doctor and explorer David Livingstone, in 1855. The indigenous Lozi language has such an apt description: 'The Smoke That Thunders'.

Walking along a mud-packed path opposite the Falls, three of us had a fright! Two of us, namely Murray and Ruth, surprised a warthog trotting along the path in the opposite direction. Probably, we were not particularly attractive to the warthog either, and it is certainly a question who had the biggest fright. It was almost endearing to observe the robust little pig disappearing into the bush with its tail vertical and its trot almost becoming a gallop.

Our journey into Rhodesia was at a very sensitive time politically. The Unilateral Declaration of Independence, declared in late 1965, had resulted in highly strained relations between Rhodesia and the United Kingdom. Certainly, the border officials, both of whom were 'white' Rhodesians, were not at all friendly when we left, suggesting that we shouldn't think of returning. One said that he didn't believe I was a doctor at all.

Then, back south into South Africa, we headed for Johannesburg. As I drove, we would stop to buy fruit from vendors at the side of the road, especially oranges in large net bags. There would be about 40 oranges in each bag. How refreshing it was to be fed oranges by Ruth while I drove. My vitamin C level was in very good order.

An extraordinary South African experience in the environs of Johannesburg was visiting a gold mine, way down below ground. It was fascinating to see rows of ingots within touching distance!

Another attempt to experience a thrilling South African occasion sadly met with failure. South Africa (Springboks) were to play New Zealand (All Blacks)! The rugby match was to be played at the famous Ellis Park stadium in Johannesburg. I tried to get tickets. Not even a mention that I had played rugby against the Springboks in Scotland brought any response.

I recalled the dinner after the match versus South Africa away back in 1961. Our South African counterparts told us that they would not dare go outside on their own wearing the Springbok blazer, because supporters would want pieces of the blazer as souvenirs. In short, those tickets were gold dust!

RIDING AN OSTRICH

We journeyed along the Garden Route, heading for Capetown.

Our next dramatic memory was to visit an ostrich farm. It was extraordinary to stand on a huge ostrich egg. Our guide advised us that the egg could provide us with at least 15 omelettes!

The real climax was riding on the back of an ostrich. At least, Ruth managed it fairly well, hooking her knees over the upper joints on each side. Only two or three of our visiting group dared to ride an ostrich. My turn followed Ruth's. I climbed on, hooked my legs over the ostrich legs, as instructed, and encouraged the flightless bird forward. Without warning, the ostrich stopped abruptly! Murray went flying through the air, over the wobbly and sinuous neck and head, landing in a crumpled heap right under the steely gaze and beak of a very large ostrich.

That was all very well. I had just been told that an ostrich can 'split you down the middle' with one vicious swipe of its claws! Our group was indulging in chortles and amusement at my predicament, while I scrabbled clear of my victorious and feathered steed!

THE SCOTTISH
SCENE: 1970–1975

On our arrival in Scotland, we needed a place to stay, and my friend David Lawson, with whom I had studied medicine, offered his home north of Glasgow for a year. David and Alison were to spend a year in the States as part of his career path. The timing for us was perfect.

Meanwhile, Professor Wallace S. Foulds had created a Senior Registrar post for me at the Tennant Institute of Ophthalmology, Western Infirmary, Glasgow. It was a real privilege to be invited to join the Professorial Department, but it was far from an easy experience, at least for the initial months.

It was nearly two years since I had been in an academic set-up, which had reached some kind of fruition in 1968, with the FRCS examination in Edinburgh. In those intense days, in a very active Department of Ophthalmology, we had a heavy workload of clinics, inpatient responsibilities, and surgery. We were aware of current opinion and practice, involved in research and publications in the medical literature, sharing these findings at medical meetings and conferences.

After returning from the overland trip to Afghanistan in the autumn of 1968, I had enrolled for an academic year studying systematic theology, church history, and philosophy of religion. Then, in the summer of 1969, the invitation came to be a visiting ophthalmologist for one year to NOOR in Afghanistan. There was excellent opportunity for practical experience in that year. Surgical skills were certainly enhanced with the high volume of surgery, but academic study, discussions, and lectures were not yet significantly part of the NOOR programme.

At the beginning of 1971, to be thrust into the high-powered environment of a front-line Professorial Unit with so-called grand rounds, seminars, and discussions about the latest research was frankly traumatic! It did mean, however, that I had to get back into the academic stream, and quickly. Also, I was considering which field of research I should explore.

In 1972, with generous parental help, we were able to buy a property near Canniesburn, north-west of Glasgow. No. 2 Speirs Road, Bearsden, was to be our home until we returned to Afghanistan in 1975.

By this time I was pursuing a study into inflammation of the sclera ('white' of the eye) and its association with rheumatoid disease. ·

Ruth was very much into preparing for one shot at an LRAM piano exam. This involved a complicated section on the theory of music (much of it new territory), not to mention one hour of scales each day. In the exam, all went well with the practical, but it was the theory that proved to be the sticking point. Apart from which, it was a race for time before the birth of David!

Three weeks after we moved into Speirs Road, in April 1972, David Charles Murray was born at Rottenrow Maternity Hospital, Glasgow. This famous Hospital, with its unusual name, was first a maternity unit in 1834. In November 1974, Andrew Stuart Brash arrived on the scene, again at Rottenrow.

RESEARCH AND MD THESIS

Any doctor who hopes to become a Consultant in any speciality in medicine must pursue research topics and publish these findings in the medical literature.

There was a significant 'difference' in the United Kingdom, which is important to explain to readers from other countries. The degree of MD (Doctor of Medicine) is a higher qualification, more equivalent to a PhD. Why this is the case is lost in the mists of time or, at least, the history of UK medicine. In the United Kingdom, we qualified as doctors with the degree MBChB or MBBS (Bachelor of Medicine / Bachelor of Surgery). All of this has to be explained to American, Afghan, and other colleagues, who, very logically, have 'MD' as their first and initial qualification.

Although it is not obligatory, each of us had a choice, whether to give time and effort to a Research Doctorate, such as an MD (Doctor of Medicine) or ChM (Master of Surgery), or a PhD (Doctor of Philosophy). The MD and the ChM usually involve clinical research. All research must be original, building on studies formerly published in the medical literature. Most often, these studies were made while holding down a full-time post in the chosen speciality. Because of this, Ruth said to me that she was extremely glad that I had completed other qualifications before we were married!

Knowing that I was interested in a project of clinical research, my excellent supervising consultant, Dr John Williamson, suggested that I might study patients with inflammation of the sclera ('white' of the eye)—that is, scleritis—and its association with rheumatoid disease.

John was studying dry eyes and a triad of signs called Sjogren's Syndrome. He received an excellent award for his own study.

I was delighted and followed a study over four years, returning to visit John's patients and adding my own, which made the whole study one of some length and, I believe, significance.

Professor Foulds created a Scleritis Clinic at the Western Infirmary, and I visited and examined patients with rheumatoid disease in the Centre for Rheumatic Diseases, Glasgow, under the expert and enthusiastic eye of the eminent Professor Watson W. Buchanan.

The research was published in two volumes:

Episcleritis and Scleritis: A Detailed Study of their Manifestations and Association with Rheumatoid Arthritis.

Now, dear reader, that is enough writing on medical research, except for a reference to the final paragraph of the text. Two leading American ophthalmologists, P. Henkind and D. H. Gold, had written in the medical literature words that gave me a marvellous opportunity to state the relevance of the study.

The text in my final paragraph reads, 'In a recent publication reviewing ocular manifestations of rheumatic disorders, Henkind and Gold (1973) make the plea for including detailed ocular examination by an ophthalmologist in the protocol for any prospective study of rheumatic disease. During the preparation of their paper they said that they "could only look with envy and frustration at the enormous series of patients reported in the literature, recording every conceivable clinical and laboratory finding in these diseases and yet including little, if any, data on their ocular status."'

Their plea for cooperation in the correlation of clinical findings concludes, 'We hope to have stimulated some of our readers to do just that.'

My final paragraph continues, 'This study has anticipated their (Henkind and Gold) request by some years and attempts to collate the ocular manifestations of episcleritis and scleritis with rheumatic disorders, in particular, rheumatoid arthritis.'

When I heard, over the phone, that a good level of award was likely from the assessors of my work, Ruth really enjoyed my reaction. 'Murray, I've seen that expression on your face when Scotland are scoring a try at rugby!'

GRADUATION AND A CONVERSATION STOPPER!

The graduation was a grand occasion. There was a pack-out in the Bute Hall of Glasgow University. The academic gown for the MD was vividly scarlet, and our son David informed my sister, Margery, that 'Daddy was at a decoration party and got a new dressing gown!'

After the ceremony, Ruth and I went out of the Bute Hall and strolled on the terrace of the magnificent buildings of the University, gazing towards the historic buildings of the Kelvingrove Museum and Art Gallery. Surprisingly, standing entirely on his own was the Post-Graduate Dean of Medicine, still in his academic gown. He very kindly expressed his congratulations. Searching for the right words, I told the Dean that I had dedicated my research thesis to Ruth, my wife, using the words of Proverbs 31:10: 'Who can find a virtuous woman? Her worth is far above rubies.'

The Dean informed me that he had completed his MD thesis 'despite his wife!' That really was a conversation-stopper, but it didn't detract from a joyful day! Now we could move on to the next stage of our story.

MEANWHILE IN AFGHANISTAN: COUP D'ETAT 1973

UNREST IN KABUL

In the early 1970s, ideological differences between followers of Islam and Communist supporters boiled over with the publication of a 'Parcham' poem praising Lenin but using terminology more often used in Islamic texts. This poem was condemned by leading clerics, including Professor Sibghatullah Mojaddedi, whom we were to meet later.

Tensions increased; unrest and demonstrations followed. While these political and religious tensions were rife in Kabul, the nation was experiencing a major economic crisis, compounded by the failure of winter snows over some years, with much reduced rivers for irrigation. Crops failed, livestock died, and the people were in dire straits.

When Ruth and I left Afghanistan in 1970, our very special dog, Sam, a golden Alsatian / Afghan hound mix, was given to a group of our foreign nurses. We heard later that Sam had constantly tried to escape and eventually disappeared. Very sadly, there was speculation that he might have been taken because of the famine!

A further strain on the national economy and food supplies was the number of travellers—hippies who were pouring through Afghanistan from Europe and elsewhere on their way to India. Many were smoking hashish and raw opium. Occasionally, I had been asked if I would see a hippie who might have hepatitis or some other ailment.

Opening of the NOOR Eye Institute

So much was happening in the early months of 1973. One very positive event was the opening of the NOOR Eye Institute in Kabul, with a service of dedication on 4 March 1973.

Dr Jock gave a speech which so sensitively set the tone and vision for a great work:

> However much we value this building, it is the people who come here that we must value even more. The best doctors in the world, and the best nurses in the world are those whose first concern is not for the money that they earn, but for the patients they treat.
>
> God cares for the poor, the blind, and the lonely. It is He who wants to fill our hearts with love for people. We can be His fingers to touch them, His hands to heal them, and His heart to love them. Do we care for people as He does? If we do not, then let us ask Him to forgive us, and to fill us with that kind of love. This building is important, but people matter more than things.

King Zahir Shah Is Deposed

In June 1973, King Zahir Shah travelled to Italy, apparently for treatment of an eye injury. The King's eye problems were well known, and Dr Herb had previously referred him to a retina specialist in London. The diagnosis was retinoschisis ('splitting' of the layers of the retina).

On 17 July 1973, Mohammed Daud, the King's cousin, ordered his army units to attack the palace. Queen Homaira, with some kind of pre-knowledge of events, ordered the royal guard to surrender. None of the royal family had any injury.

ALSO IN AFGHANISTAN: DEMOLITION OF KCCC

The Kabul Community Christian Church (KCCC) had previously had services every Friday morning in a large house just off Darulaman Road on Kabul's south side.

The Pastor from the States, Dr Christy, had contacted senior Afghan authorities. It was a sensitive issue. Would permission be given to construct a Christian church in Kabul? The request even reached the King, Zahir Shah.

Permission was granted. The site of the new KCCC was on a piece of prime land beside the church house, just off Darulaman Road. It was a very impressive building, with a shining turquoise roof and very fine Afghan marble flooring. Perhaps it was even too dramatic and conspicuous?

The year was 1970. The day of the dedication of the Kabul Community Christian Church arrived. My mother and father were visiting us in Afghanistan. My father led the congregation in prayer. It was my privilege to sing the beautiful song from Psalm 84:

> How lovely are Your dwellings, O Lord of Hosts!
> My soul longs, yes, even faints
> for the courts of the Lord;
> My heart and my flesh cry out
> for the living God!
> Even the sparrow has found a home
> And the swallow a nest for herself
> Where she may lay her young--
> Even Your altars, O Lord of hosts,
> My King and my God!

ELLEN RASMUSSEN AND THE LITTLE PRINCESS

A marble plaque of dedication was unveiled by a fine Danish nurse, Ellen Rasmussen. Ellen had taken on the heavy responsibility of nursing and caring for a princess. Mawari was a daughter of the King, premature at birth, weighing only about two pounds. It was too frightening a commitment for any Afghan nurse to care for such a tiny princess, but Ellen said she would take on the responsibility.

Princess Mawari thrived in Ellen's care! We have a happy picture of Ellen and Mawari visiting our home in Karte Seh, Kabul.

RAZED TO THE GROUND

In February 1973, Ruth and I were back in the UK. We heard the disturbing news that the beautifully constructed church was under threat. The word was that KCCC was to be demolished! Many around the world were praying, but rumours were rife. Some expressed great concern and even warnings about this prospective demolition of the church. Destruction of this House of God would have consequences!

Subsequently, reports reached us that the church had been demolished. Every stone and piece of the building was removed. The church had indeed been razed to the ground! Very soon after this distressing event, Afghan rulers and government fell! There was an almost bloodless coup d'etat. The King was deposed by his cousin and brother-in-law, Mohammed Daud.

Thus, the Republic of Afghanistan was declared and established in July 1973. How far the church demolition influenced the downfall of King and government is an open question. The timing was certainly dramatic! God knows, and we can rest with that.

Part Five

RETURN TO AFGHANISTAN; 1975 NOOR PROJECT SAUR REVOLUTION

RETURN TO
AFGHANISTAN: 1975

Sometimes there are long periods of waiting. If we are longing for God's word to guide us in a present and pressing situation, waiting can be very difficult.

Ruth and I were waiting for our visas to return to Afghanistan. The year was 1973. I was completing my doctorate and was to hand this in to Glasgow University's medical office by 31 August of the same year. The two bound volumes were handed in to the University on that final afternoon.

Our visa applications for Afghanistan had been made months before. My colleague, Dr Herb, working as the one foreign ophthalmologist, was desperate for my support at the NOOR Eye Institute in Kabul.

There was another very significant deadline relating to the same date, 31 August. Ruth was expecting our second child (Andrew) and would be too far on in the pregnancy after that date to fly to Afghanistan. In fact, when the visas were not granted by midnight on 31 August, Herb, in Kabul, sent a telegram of enormous regret that they would not see us, at least for some months.

During the months while we waited, a further apparent setback was the news that the Afghan authorities only wanted 'professors' to come to Afghanistan. Elsewhere, I've referred to the seniority of medical professionals and their titles. In the States, there were 'full' professors, 'associate' professors and 'assistant' professors. But in Great Britain we only had 'full' professors. Anyway, Professor Wallace S. Foulds, onetime President of the Royal College of Ophthalmologists, kindly provided a rather glowing account and document regarding my qualifications and seniority, which seemed to satisfy the Afghan authorities.

During these many months of waiting, while maintaining the conviction that God wanted us to return to Afghanistan, a request came from a respected colleague to go to Meshed, eastern Iran. Dr Howard was now in Meshed, setting up an ophthalmic programme there. Would I come to Meshed, with Ruth and our two boys, as Associate Professor?

This was a serious offer from a known colleague. Was God saying something to us? Ruth and I decided to bring the offer and request to God in prayer.

'Lord, what do you want us to do? What is your plan for us?'

We decided to 'take a position' before God, individually and separately. We took the position that we should be going to Meshed, Iran, responding positively to the invitation. For a full day, we separately offered this position and plan to God, asking Him to confirm this appointment—or otherwise.

At the end of the day, we compared our sense of what He was saying to us.

Quite clearly, we both felt that God was saying, 'No! Not Meshed at this time. You wait for the visas to come for Afghanistan.'

Subjectively, neither of us felt peace about changing course. We had to wait.

Waiting is long! But we had an absolute conviction that God's timing would be made very clear. It was a further five to six months before the visas came for the beloved country—in total, fourteen months of waiting.

THE NOOR PROJECT AND NOOR EYE INSTITUTE

The letters 'NOOR' stand for 'National Organisation for Ophthalmic Rehabilitation'.

The vision and inspiration for NOOR owes so much to Dr Howard, an ophthalmologist from New Zealand. Howard, with his wife, Monika, and family, came to Kabul and were involved in the setting up of the NOOR Project in 1966. This included visiting the Afghan Ministry of Health multiple times.

Dr Jock, with his wife, Gwendy, and family, came to Afghanistan in 1967. Both Howard and Jock had lived and worked in Pakistan before moving across the border into Afghanistan.

Dr Herb from the USA arrived in Afghanistan with Ruth, his wife, and family in 1969.

These very well qualified ophthalmologists were so important and critical to the early vision and ongoing development of the NOOR Project in Afghanistan.

INTRODUCTION TO AFGHANISTAN AND NOOR

My own introduction to Afghanistan had been over a few weeks, in the summer of 1968, when nine of us drove out from the UK.

Those early years of the NOOR Project found facilities for eye care in two of the main hospitals in Kabul. The Avicenna Hospital and the Wazir Akbar Khan Hospital also provided operating room facilities and some staff support.

However, specialist and support personnel were few. I had one occasion when I was operating in Wazir Akbar Khan without any assistance. Our two British NOOR nurses were away with Dr Jock on an eye camp.

I've always known that the expertise of our nurses in surgery is absolutely vital. This recognition became a total conviction after my experience operating in Wazir Akbar Khan Hospital all by myself. As I was alone, I had to sterilize all my surgical instruments, lay them out, scrub up, and begin surgery on the first of two cataract operations. In the middle of surgery, I needed a particular instrument, but it wasn't there. There was nothing else for it; I had to break away, locate the instrument, sterilize it, place it on the surgical instrument tray, and scrub up again!

These Afghans are so trusting and stoical. My patient quietly waited, no doubt believing that all was proceeding as it should. Practically all of our surgical procedures in those days were carried out under local anaesthetic. All seemed to go well after this, with the only disturbance being the appearance of a cleaning lady, who wanted to mop the operating room floor while I was operating. She readily agreed to come back another time!

Any surgery should ideally have a focused and dedicated team.

We conducted a clinic in the Chaman district of Kabul, by the Jashn grounds. The Jashn (celebration) grounds were originally named to celebrate Afghan independence from the British in 1919. An Independence celebration was observed there each year, which was most interesting to attend. It included a march past, military vehicles, and even a fly past. Sadly, one year the crowd saw a fighter jet crash into a hillside while the occasion was well underway.

This clinic was extraordinarily busy! It became very much a screening clinic, providing immediate treatment where appropriate, referring patients to other clinics, listing patients for surgery, and the like.

On one occasion, I examined 130 patients in three hours, very much supported by our nurses, Frances and Pauline. We were being formally observed by nursing colleagues who were visiting Afghanistan and who complimented us that, in the middle of the clinic, despite the numbers of patients, we still paused for a quick cup of tea. You will understand, dear reader, why this had to be a quick screening and referral clinic.

In 1970, a small building was constructed on open ground, off Darulaman Road on Kabul's south side. This open area was later to accommodate the 100-bed NOOR Eye Institute, for which funds were being solicited around the world.

The smaller building became our eye clinic and operating facility, all of which was temporary. But at least we were beginning to have a focus and a hospital site, so important for public awareness that an eye care facility was now in place. Patients might travel for days to reach good eye care.

THE BLIND INSTITUTE

Later, this building became the Institute for the Blind. So many Afghans suffer blindness, often from a very young age. The work of Betty, wife of our church pastor, brought so many out of despondency and hopelessness, teaching Braille and providing reading materials and the potential for further studies.

DR HERB

During the years 1971 to 1975, back in the UK, I was preparing and completing my research doctorate. In Kabul, the building which was to become the NOOR Eye Institute was under construction. It was opened in March 1973.

A heartfelt tribute to Herb, from the USA, is so appropriate here. The workload that Herb sustained for years was quite phenomenal, running a programme of clinics and surgery, developing a training schedule which became increasingly demanding, and supervising the building of a large hospital, where his medical advice and understanding was so important.

Nevertheless, when I rejoined the team in Afghanistan in 1975, Herb told me that he had been advised to go home to the States for two years of rest.

TIME OF MY LIFE!

So it was that in May 1976, I was appointed Project and Medical Director of the NOOR Eye Institute. That appointment and those five years up to and including 1980 were undoubtedly the most challenging, fulfilling, and extraordinary years of my life!

There was such a wealth of experience, with pressure—professionally, personally, and also spiritually—compounded by a military coup d'etat on 27 April 1978, followed by the subsequent invasion of Soviet troops from the north at the end of 1979.

But what of the calling to which we had sought to respond? How did all of that work out in practice? How did it impact our personal and family lives?

Ruth and I had arrived in Kabul in 1975, with two brand-new boys, David and Andrew, both born in Glasgow. Our daughter, Caroline, was born a year later, in Kabul.

After the Saur revolution (coup d'etat) on 27 April 1978, our NOOR foreign staff and members of our international team met together for a conference to discuss our way forward. There was a firm conviction that God would guide us in our decision-making. It was wonderfully reassuring that so many around the world were praying with us and for us.

Many other organizations were leaving, particularly those

with families and children. We decided to stay on, and for 20 months we lived and worked on in Kabul (and in Herat), each of us with a suitcase packed, ready for evacuation, if required.

Into the mix came the request from the United States Embassy to be a Warden for the potential evacuation programme. We reached Phase 2 of the evacuation schedule a number of times because fighting had erupted, which meant 'Stay where you are, confirm where your family is, and any others you are responsible for, and be ready to move.'

It was a season in our lives when we were providing a high standard of eye care in the country and training our Afghan colleagues for future leadership.

NOOR KABUL AND NOOR HERAT: ANNUAL REPORT 1979

Each 'Western' calendar year, an Annual Report was submitted to the Minister of Public Health. It was my task to compile these Reports for the years 1976, 1977, 1978, 1979, and 1980.

The following is an abbreviated 1979 Annual Report to the Minister of Public Health. Despite the political instability and insecurity after the coup, the work continued. Please feel free to skim over these lists and numbers.

DEMOCRATIC REPUBLIC of AFGHANISTAN
THE NOOR PROJECT
ANNUAL REPORT 1979
Submitted to: THE MINISTER OF PUBLIC HEALTH
'Serving the People of Afghanistan ...'

Significant advances in ophthalmic care services to the people of Afghanistan.

1. 1 July, 1979, the NOOR-Herat Ophthalmic Centre (36 beds) was opened officially.
2. In August, 1979, the staff of the University Department of Ophthalmology joined us at the NOOR Eye Institute.
3. The first full eighteen months' course in Auxiliary Ophthalmic Nursing commenced on 1 June, 1979.
4. The NOOR Project welcomed requests ... the development and supervision of provincial eye departments in Kandahar, Nangarhar, Mazar-i-Sharif and Kunduz.

5. Dr S M A Raheen, trained in our post-graduate course, appointed Ophthalmologist in Charge of the Department of Ophthalmology, Kandahar General Hospital.

Statistics of Patient Care: 1979
NOOR Eye Institute, Kabul:
40,707 outpatients were examined
1,413 inpatients were admitted to our wards
2,590 surgical procedures were performed
3,870 refractions were carried out

NOOR – Herat Ophthalmic Centre: July – December 1979
6,018 outpatients were examined
212 inpatients were admitted
531 surgical procedures were performed
500 refractions were carried out

University Department of Ophthalmology
We welcome our colleagues, Professor Yunossada, Dr Seddiq, Dr Wahedi, Dr Gran and Dr Rahima from the University Department, who have joined us at NOOR. There is the opportunity to cooperate in the teaching of undergraduates, together with our post-graduate teaching programme.

Visiting Professors
Dr H Kennedy FRCS (UK) (February) and Dr T Barrie FRCS (UK) (July) taught our post-graduates. Their lecture topics – Diseases of the Retina, Toxicology and the Eye, Clinical Evaluation of Proptosis and Ophthalmic Pathology.

Diploma in Ophthalmology (Afghanistan)
Six candidates will be eligible to sit this examination in
1980.

Nursing Procedures Manual Training Course
In April, May and June, 1979, a course based on our
Nursing Procedures Manual was conducted by our
Nursing Ward Supervisor, Mr Mahmood, supported by
Mrs Marita (Sweden) and Miss Elizabeth (Germany). We
found that our foreign nurses, who came from the United
Kingdom, Sweden, Canada, Finland and Germany, might
have some differences in their approach to nursing, for
example, how to give a sub-conjunctival injection. I
asked the highly competent Mrs Marita, from Sweden,
to chair a nursing committee and devise a document,
The Nursing Standard Procedures Manual, with agreed
standards and protocol for most nursing care procedures.

Department of Ophthalmic Optics: Courses for
Ophthalmologists in Training
1. Helen Perry conducted a comprehensive Course in
    Ophthalmic Optics and Refraction for two of our
    doctors. A further Course is planned.
2. Helen Perry gives separate weekly tutorials to our
    junior doctors, to staff members of the Optical and
    Artificial Eye Departments, and to medical students.
    Occasional lectures are given to our nurses.
3. Helen Perry and Hans Ek have been planning a
    Course for Dispensing Opticians.
4. We are able to provide most lens corrections and
    complete the spectacles for our patients on the day
    of their refraction examination.

New Equipment

1. Zeiss Opmi-1 operating microscope. (The smaller wall-fitted Zeiss operating microscope has been transferred to the NOOR- Herat Ophthalmic Centre).
2. Sony Video System for teaching.
3. Goldmann Static and Kinetic Perimeter.
4. Two Haag-Streit slit-lamp microscopes added to clinic facilities.

NOOR-Herat Ophthalmic Centre

The opening of the NOOR-Herat Ophthalmic Centre on 1 July, 1979, was the culmination of years of planning. This new development provides the first example of the potential for ophthalmic care in a Centre situated in the provinces. We pay tribute to the staff who shared in the planning and preparation of the hospital and to those who now form its staff. We look forward to the establishment of other provincial Centres so that the treatment of eye disease will become readily available to people in all parts of Afghanistan.

Other Provincial Centres (Kandahar, Nangarhar, Mazar-i-Sharif, Kunduz)

We have responded positively to the request of the Ministry of Public Health in regard to the supervision and equipping of Eye Departments in Kandahar (a NOOR Afghan ophthalmologist is already appointed there), Nangarhar, Mazar-i-Sharif and Kunduz.

Projected Plans for 1980

1. Review of equipment and general facilities of the Department of Ophthalmology, Kandahar General Hospital.
2. Development of the Eye Department in Nangarhar.
3. Establishment of an Audio-visual Department at the NOOR Eye Institute, with particular emphasis on public health education for prevention of eye disease.
4. Continuing development of programmes for under-graduate and post-graduate teaching of medical personnel.
5. Completion of the first eighteen month's course for auxiliary ophthalmic nurses.
6. Course for dispensing opticians in Kabul.
7. Examination of candidates for the Diploma in Ophthalmology (Afghanistan).

VISITING PROFESSOR PROGRAMME

One programme we valued so much was the Visiting Professor Programme. Ophthalmic specialists were invited to join us at NOOR for a minimum of one month, when they would teach on the wards, in clinics, and in surgery, complemented by lectures (each morning at 8.15 a.m.) in their own area of particular interest.

The information about these welcome visitors was always included in the Annual Reports to the Minister of Public Health, but, for the purposes of this record, it seemed better to describe their contributions in a separate section. I have chosen the years 1976, 1977, and 1978.

It should be kept in mind that 1978 was the year of the coup d'etat (27 April), and so the number of visitors was subsequently much reduced.

Visiting Professor	Specialist Interest
1976:	
Dr T. Gettelfinger (USA)	Paediatric Ophthalmology; Strabismus
Dr W. J. Holmes (USA)	Tropical Eye Disease; Xerophthalmia
Mr R. Stevenson (UK)	Refraction Course
Dr H. Kennedy (UK)	Neuro-ophthalmology
Dr G. R. Sutherland (UK)	Radiology
Dr J. W. Reed (USA)	External Eye Disease; Keratoplasty
Prof. R. Tornquist (Sweden)	Retinal Detachment

Prof. A. J. Elliot (Canada)	Eales' Disease; Retinal Physiology
Dr G. Jeffery (USA)	Blow-out Fractures; Pharmacology

1977:

Dr John Gourgott (USA)	Vitreous Haemorrhage; Farah eye camp
Dr C. Candray (C. America)	Extraocular Muscles
Dr J. Hetherington (USA)	Glaucomas
Dr Helena Frank (UK)	Congenital; Phakomatoses
Dr Hans Kolder (USA)	Neuro-ophth.; Red Eye; Trauma
Dr James Reed (USA)	Cornea

1978:

Dr Peter Graham (Australia)	General; attended Kunar eye camp
Prof. Ron Fisher (UK)	General Ophthalmology
Dr Jon Bayers (USA)	General Ophthalmology

PATIENT CARE AT THE NOOR EYE INSTITUTE

Statistics can be so dry and boring. But let me relate some human stories behind the facts and figures, looking particularly at our records for the year 1979. Again, please feel free to go forward to further stories in Afghanistan and other countries.

CATARACT

Cataract is opacity in the lens of the eye, and the most common associated factor is the age of the patient. When one considers that life expectancy in Afghanistan was around 45 years in those days, it was not surprising that cataract presented early. Still, it was a real surprise for a Western-trained ophthalmic surgeon to be operating on women of 35 years with age-related cataract.

Considering the causes of cataract, the Afghan environment contributed enormously to the early onset and 'maturing' of the cataractous lens. Poor nutrition, excessive ultraviolet light (Kabul itself is at 6000 feet), acute dehydration earlier in the life of the patient (most Afghans had bowel infections), and, for women, multiple pregnancies (a girl might marry aged 13 years old) all may have been factors in the onset of cataract at much younger ages than those in the West.

A relevant note here relates to the onset of *Presbyopia*—the need of plus lenses in a patient who has not required a correction (glasses, spectacles) for reading or close work, but who has this need usually by mid-life. In Western countries this might be in the mid-40s, but in Afghanistan it could be in the mid-30s. Clearly, this relates to the ageing process.

In 1979, there were 509 patients, male and female, with immature cataracts; 807 patients with mature cataracts, of which 113 were mature 'blinding' cataracts in both eyes. 967 cataract operations were performed.

THE GLAUCOMAS

Glaucoma often presented late in the disease process. One factor was the distance patients might have to travel to find good eye care. It might involve days with different modes of transport. The statistics are disturbing.

In 1979, in patients where the diagnosis proved to be one of the glaucomas, open-angle glaucoma was found in 135, narrow / closed-angle glaucoma in 67, and 177 patients were categorized as 'absolute' glaucoma.

Absolute, blinding glaucoma with 'no light perception' in the affected eye is a consequence of irreversible damage to the optic nerve at the back of the eye. Absolute glaucoma was most often caused by an enlarged, cataractous lens which had blocked the drainage channels out of the eye, together with abnormal proteins in the aqueous fluid, also causing blockage of the drainage channels.

The figures for 1979 provide a sobering finding. In new patients where the diagnosis proved to be one of the glaucomas, approximately 46% had absolute blinding glaucoma in one eye.

The treatment for an eye which still has good 'light perception' or 'hand movements', or better, is to remove the swollen, cataractous lens surgically.

The importance of increasing public awareness of health issues was so very evident. Courses and information-sharing were also needed for doctors, nurses, pharmacists, and all health professionals. These we sought to set up in our own field of medical care, for example, by programmes on Radio Afghanistan. Our NOOR President, Dr M. H. Sherzai, would read the news in Pashto on TV.

STEROID-INDUCED GLAUCOMA

A very sad illustration of the need to inform doctors, nurses, pharmacists, and the general public relates to a young man aged about 18 years and just beginning adult life.

This boy presented with one of the secondary glaucomas, specifically steroid-induced glaucoma.

Indiscriminate use of topical steroids in the eyes of susceptible individuals can cause the intraocular pressure to rise.

This young man had developed sensitivity to pollens and other allergens resulting in an allergic conjunctivitis, known as spring (or vernal) catarrh. I speculated, in sharing the story, that this boy, perhaps when he was about 11 years old, had developed irritable and red eyes after working in the fields with his father. In the spring and summer, when his red and inflamed conjunctivae were 'active', the itch was awful!

His parents took him to a Basic Health Centre somewhere in rural Afghanistan. The doctor at the Health Centre, looking for a quick and effective response, prescribed topical steroid eye drops, possibly with steroid eye ointment at night.

The results were dramatic! Within days, the eyes were quietening, the conjunctivae no longer swollen and red, and the itch was disappearing.

Perhaps it became winter, even with snows in higher places. Our lad could leave off using the drops and ointment. Spring returned and moved into summer. Work was needed in the fields after school was finished each day.

Then it happened again! Red, irritable eyes, swollen conjunctivae, and such an itch. Those drops and that ointment ... where were the empty bottles and tubes? The parents found them and went straight to the Basic Health Centre. But the doctor was no longer there! Never mind, there is a pharmacist in the nearby town.

The pharmacist sold steroid eye drops and ointment to the parents. Again there was a marvellous response. A pattern began to emerge: red, irritable, and so itchy eyes developing in the spring and summer, but with a ready answer found in the topical steroid treatment.

But our patient began to have difficulty with his vision. First, his schoolwork was affected. Then even his work in the fields.

He came to the NOOR Eye Institute, aged 18, a strapping lad, now an adult, but he was blind!

Examination showed bilateral cupped optic nerve heads. Both eyes had optic nerve atrophy, where steroid-induced raised intraocular pressures had severely damaged the optic nerves where they enter the back of each eye.

It is important to emphasize that topical steroids, used

with supervision in the 'right' situation, can often be a sight-saver. They may dramatically and effectively reduce intraocular inflammation, so saving sight. But their use must be carefully monitored by a health professional who is trained and competent. It will require regular checks of the intraocular pressures as part of the treatment process.

The original condition affecting this young man was *Spring* or *Vernal Catarrh*. The importance in Afghanistan of wise and informed treatment of this inflammation is emphasized by how common it was and is in the country.

In 1979, *Classical Vernal Catarrh* was diagnosed in 1700 patients, 575 of whom were children.

TRACHOMA

Trachoma is widespread in Afghanistan. Infection with *Chlamydia trachomatis* is easily spread.

Advanced trachoma results in conjunctival scarring and, potentially, corneal scarring. We graded trachoma in four grades, grade IV being the most severe, with manifest scarring complications.

2412 patients were diagnosed with grade I or grade II *Trachoma*.

440 patients were diagnosed with grade III or grade IV *Trachoma*.

Trichiasis is the condition where the eyelashes are turned in and rub against the eye itself—usually, in Afghanistan, as a consequence of the scarring of trachoma.

Trichiasis: This highly irritable eye disease was found in 207 patients in 1979.

Another possible consequence of trachomatous scarring is inflammation of the tear sac and canaliculi (dacryocystitis), associated with dry eyes and a propensity to bacterial infections.

Acute Dacryocystitis was found in 867 patients. *Chronic Dacryocystitis* in 108.

VITAMIN A DEFICIENCY

The results of *Vitamin A Deficiency* can be devastating, not only affecting the eyes, but even be a danger to life. A vitamin A–deficient child may die within months of reaching the vitamin A–deficient state. Yet one capsule of vitamin A popped in the mouth of a child every 3–4 months can save the child from awful consequences. Further, vitamin A–rich foods are often freely available in the bazaar.

Breast milk contains vitamin A. This means that the danger of deficiency is there for the child who is weaned off the breast, often after a new baby is born into the family.

In children, the eye problems can be sadly dramatic! Changes to the conjunctiva in the child can result in 'foamy' patches, called Bitot spots. But the most serious, sight-threatening damage is to the cornea, often of both eyes, although invariably one eye is affected more than the other.

The cornea 'melts'! This is called keratomalacia. Of course, vision is profoundly affected.

In practice, when treating vitamin A deficiency, it is effectively a matter of saving the second eye. Many times I've thanked God that we have been given two eyes!

In children who survive the acute vitamin A–deficient state, the scarring of the anterior eye is obvious and unsightly.

Anterior Staphyloma (scarred cornea bulging forward with iris adherent behind) was recorded in 57 patients, and *Phthisis* (scarred and shrunken eyeball) in 83.

RETINAL DISEASES

Retinal Detachment was diagnosed regularly in our clinics.

Retinal Detachment surgery was performed on 36 patients in 1979.

Eales' Disease (Periphlebitis Retinae / Primary Retinal Vasculitis) was a regular, if occasional retinal finding, although only recorded in 8 patients in 1979. *Tuberculosis* was found in the country in both human beings and cattle. The potential association between tuberculosis and Eales' Disease affecting the retina has long been recognized.

It was certainly a challenge to attempt surgical correction of a detached retina in an eye which had the (minor) inflammatory changes of periphlebitis retinae!

Retinitis Pigmentosa (Primary Pigmentary Degeneration) is an inherited condition which is relatively common in Afghanistan. The very common marriage of first cousins will have significance and contribute to the relatively high prevalence of this eye disease.

Usually this eye disease will develop slowly in the early years, in due course with the appearance in the peripheral retinae of pigment clumps or clusters and the gradual onset of reduced visual fields, associated with bilateral optic nerve atrophy. All of these changes may progress in the 20s, 30s, and 40s, with variable but sometimes profound visual loss.

In 1979, there were 48 patients diagnosed with *Retinitis Pigmentosa*: 34 males, 8 females, and 6 children.

BASAL CELL CARCINOMA

Another condition that should be mentioned is a skin cancer, relatively common in Afghanistan, which regularly presented at NOOR. *Basal Cell Carcinoma*, or *Rodent Ulcer*, is a locally growing and typically ulcerating skin tumour that may appear around the eye, eyelids, and face.

In 1979, 16 patients presented with *Basal Cell Carcinoma*.

Constant exposure to the elements, ultraviolet light (particularly in the mountains, with deflected sunlight during the winter snows), dust, and sand must be such an assault, even on tough and leathery exposed skin.

I recall resecting a rodent ulcer of the lower eyelid (cutting clearly away from the diseased tissue), grafting in a pedicle graft in a two-stage procedure, and seeing the graft 'take' well.

Follow-up was often very difficult, as most Afghans travelled long distances for care, probably after waiting many months to see if the problem would go away.

The most dramatic and distressing rodent ulcer, the worst by far that I have ever seen, involved virtually the whole side of this middle-aged man's face! Afghans wear their turbans with a tail, usually lying down over one shoulder. This man had the tail over the side of his face, obscuring a grossly damaged and unsightly cancer. When he shifted the tail to the side, a huge basal cell carcinoma had 'eaten' the whole side of his face, down to bone, teeth, and sinuses.

SOME OTHER SURGICAL PROCEDURES

Reflecting on the differences in surgical requirements in Western countries, compared with Afghanistan, the following may be of interest.

In 1979, there were 173 operations for *Trichiasis* (turning in of the eyelashes).

Tarsorrhaphy, which is the partial stitching together of the upper and lower eyelids, was performed on 91 patients.

Often temporary, it may be used to protect an exposed cornea.

Dacryocystorhinostomy, an operation to rectify blockage of the tear ducts, was carried out in 153 patients.

Pterygium, a 'wing' of tissue growing across the cornea, required surgery in 107 patients.

A *Corneal Graft* was carried out on 4 patients in 1979.

It was always difficult to obtain suitable donor corneae for corneal grafting. Eyes were generously sent to us occasionally from the Eye Bank in Sri Lanka. But the logistics of at least two flights—Colombo to New Delhi, New Delhi to Kabul—were sometimes too complicated and disappointing, with the preservative fluid leaking from the donor package, perhaps if the package had been passed on upside down.

It was even suggested to me (by an Afghan Health Official) that the military hospital in Kabul would have 'donor eyes available', since so much fighting was going on in the country, and that many young men were dying! I promptly declined the suggestion of a 'quiet visit', pointing out that such a visit could have disastrous consequences, both personally and for our work, in this deeply religious country!

One American professor, visiting for one month, had a particular interest in corneal grafting and brought some donor corneae from the States. He demonstrated his techniques of corneal grafting on suitable and needy Afghan patients.

An *Orbitotomy* procedure—that is, exploring the bony orbit behind the eyeball itself—was performed in 8 patients.

This operation is usually to explore the nature and potential removal of a tumour (swelling) behind the eye which causes proptosis (forward protrusion of the eye).

An unusual finding for a Western-trained ophthalmologist was a tumour which was, in fact, a cyst. Sometimes this hydatid cyst located itself within the bony orbit so that the patient presented at the eye hospital with proptosis.

The patient with these cysts has infection with *Taenia echinococcus*. This may become a chronic disease, and cysts may form throughout the body, including the liver, lungs, and brain.

One visiting professor, with us for one month, was operating on an Afghan patient, an orbitotomy. He had opened the orbit from the temporal side and was exploring this extremely solid tumour behind the eye. In my limited experience, I had seen and operated on intraorbital tumours and had found that even very solid tumours could be a hydatid cyst, but they did not seem cyst-like at all.

I murmured to our visiting professor that this could be a hydatid cyst he was dissecting out. Clearly, he did not agree. Body language speaks loudly. But remember this was a fine ophthalmologist. He proceeded with surgery ... and the cyst burst!

A VISIT FROM THE PRESIDENT

Protocol required a formal arrangement and appointment for a very senior and important Afghan leader. The President of Afghanistan, Mohammed Daud, was to come to the NOOR Eye Institute for an eye examination.

The President's administrative staff arranged the date and the time. All was subservient to the President's calendar and preferences, and because of security concerns, NOOR staff and patients were kept away from the parts of the Hospital where the President would arrive and be examined in the private clinic.

President Daud would be examined by the foreign ophthalmologist.

The day in April 1978 arrived. President Daud's limousine swept in through the hospital gates, with an entourage of security vehicles. Before the President alighted from his car, security men poured out of their vehicles, all of them wearing white coats, trying to look like medical staff. That impression did not work! But security was the main issue.

Ruth was in my spacious office, one floor up, taking photos. Rather unwise, in retrospect. A camera behind a curtain might have looked suspicious!

Dr M. H. Sherzai, our NOOR President, and the NOOR Project and Medical Director, formally welcomed President Daud. Senior Afghan NOOR doctors were respectfully at a distance in the reception hall of the Hospital.

I examined President Daud in the private clinic. It was a straightforward history and examination, with no significant problems found. All that was necessary was a prescription for reading glasses.

It was interesting and a privilege to meet the President

of Afghanistan. Little did we know that further great and catastrophic events were about to take place.

Three weeks later, on the night of the coup d'etat of 27 April 1978, President Daud and many members of his family were killed. Reports describe President Daud and his brother, Mohammed Naim (also a former patient at NOOR) coming out of the palace firing pistols—their final actions.

THE SAUR REVOLUTION: 27 APRIL 1978

EYE CAMP IN KUNAR PROVINCE

The particular significance of the eye camp in Kunar was that it was set up and took place just a few days before the coup d'etat of 27 April 1978.

Kunar Province, with its capital, Asadabad, is in eastern Afghanistan, north-east of Jalalabad. Kunar, situated at the border of Pakistan and Afghanistan, was to become a Province of much fighting and mayhem in the years that followed.

Our visiting professor who attended that eye camp was Dr Peter Graham from Australia. This fine ophthalmologist had chosen a month towards the end of which momentous events were to take place!

Ruth, Rosemary, and I made up our small foreign team at the camp.

We returned to Kabul. The events of the next few days were about to erupt all around us.

COUP D'ETAT

We had very little warning that there was to be a coup d'etat, deposing the President, Mohammed Daud, and his government. Others were aware, however, and even tried to warn us.

Our 'parents' in Afghanistan, Izatullah Mujaddedi and his wife, Aisha, told us later that they had been sending their children out of the country two by two in the weeks before 27 April. At that time, our son David was given a camel stool by his 'grandparents'. We still have that stool.

On 17 April, Mir Akbar Khyber, head of the Parcham communist party, was shot in Kabul. Who was responsible? As many as 15,000 angry people lined the route of Khyber's cortege when it later wound through the streets of Kabul.

President Daud, fearing a coup, arrested Nur Mohammed Taraki (Khalqi communist) and Babrak Karmal (Parcham communist), and others.

On 27 April (7 Saur in the Afghan calendar) he called a cabinet meeting which was interrupted by shell fire and jets flying low over Kabul.

We were having our biannual conference in a large house in Karte Seh. The children of our families were in a house nearby.

At one point in the day, I left the conference to check information about one of our team's arrival at Kabul Airport. When I drove up Darulman Road, returning to the conference, I found myself driving behind tanks going in the same direction, south, along Darulaman Road.

Back at the conference, it was agreed that we would all go to our homes and await developments.

Fighting escalated all over the city. Thousands were killed that night! Sukhoi SU-7 Russian swept-wing supersonic fighter aircraft were dive-bombing the palace. An Afghan was heard to say that Afghans would not be flying those planes.

In our own home, I saw a tank shell rocketing past our boys' bedroom window, over the one-storey house of our neighbour's home. Our bedrooms were upstairs. I said to Ruth, 'We must get downstairs ... now!'

Our house was a modern two-storey, open-plan building. The kitchen / dining room was the lowest open space in the house. We tucked ourselves under the dining room table—David (just 6, birthday 3 days earlier), Andrew (3), baby Carrie (1), Mum Ruth, and Dad Murray—placing mattresses around the table.

A soldier, or someone with a presumed AK-47, was just outside our back door, a few yards from the house. He was firing intermittently through the night. Thank God, he didn't come over the wall and into the house!

There we were, all night! It went on hour after hour. Our phone had gone dead in mid-evening. Carrie cried at times, and no wonder! But my wee family was magnificent during hours of great danger and uncertainty. Constant shellfire, so many explosions ... and a man a few yards away (perhaps 20 feet) who, by his intermittent use of his AK-47, was probably scared stiff. That made him all the more dangerous!

In the following days, we discovered that we had been in 'no-man's land', between warring factions.

We collected our passports and other important documents, ready to evacuate if an opportunity presented itself and became necessary.

Ruth had a positively spiritual experience that night. She later described an amazing peace. All around us were enormous explosions, tank shells, and automatic gunfire.

The night passed ... and we were still alive!

Let Ruth herself tell her own story of that night:

Protection Under Fire. It is April 1978. Suddenly, we were in a war zone!

At this very time, I (Ruth) had the most extraordinary sense of peace that I have ever experienced in my life, before or since.

Without doubt it was 'The peace of God which passes all understanding'. (Philippians 4:7 KJV)

All through that night, every time the house shook, I heard, 'God is greater than this!' 'God is greater than this!'

I started packing passports, clothing, basic essentials, ready for evacuation.

No doubt at all. It really was 'the peace that passes understanding'. Straight from God. One night only. Next day it was over; the occupying force remained, atrocities began to happen, but, thank the Lord, we had been kept safe.

DR ANISA AND THE WOUNDED SOLDIER

At some time during the evening of the fighting, and before our phone was cut off, Dr Anisa, one of our fine ophthalmologists-in-training, phoned me from the NOOR Eye Institute asking for advice. Dr Anisa had been our resident on duty on the night of the coup d'etat. A soldier, wounded in the fighting, had come into NOOR because of a gunshot injury to his leg. Dr Anisa explained, 'When I try to remove the bullet, it bleeds profusely ...'

'Leave the bullet in the leg, at least until the morning. Then you might try again. There should be less bleeding. Give him an antibiotic and fluids, if necessary, intravenously.' Then I added ... 'It would be quite difficult for me to come up Darulaman Road to help you!' There was fighting up and down this long and broad road leading from our home to the NOOR Eye Institute.

'You mustn't think of it!' was the urgent but thoughtful response from Dr Anisa. 'Don't come! It's far too dangerous!'

I accepted her good advice.

The next day, Dr Anisa successfully removed the bullet from the soldier's leg. Later, she presented the case notes card to me, with the bullet attached. I confess I still have those case notes, with that bullet sellotaped to the card!

Morning dawned, it seemed very slowly. We began to look outside. The soldier at the back of our house had gone. I went out to the garden in front of the house and met up with our next-door neighbour, who had ventured outside at the same time. We shared a few words and as much reassurance as we could muster.

Thoughts began to surface—thoughts of concern about our team members, our many friends from different countries, and, of course, our Afghan colleagues and friends. How could we find out what had happened? When should I go out and begin searching for friends and colleagues? Overnight, our phones had been cut off.

Then, to our delight and relief, a very concerned man came striding down our road. This was the road to the US AID compound and beside Habibia School. Jonathan Lee braved the aftermath of the horrendous conflict, leaving his own family to search for us. He was so concerned about what he might find on arrival at our home. Our house was a few hundred yards from the homes of most of our international team, and so, in a sense, we were more isolated.

Jonathan had some news of our team and was unaware of any of the families having sustained injury, or worse.

Later that Friday morning, Ruth and I drove into the centre of Kabul. There were 'knocked out' tanks skewed across the roads, demolished buildings, debris everywhere, and an eerie silence pervading the city! Some tanks, strategically positioned and clearly 'active', had garlands hung on the gun barrels.

Ruth surreptitiously took hasty photos, with her husband muttering urgently, 'Hurry up! Get down!'

The next day, Saturday, was the beginning of our working week at the NOOR Eye Institute. As I travelled to the hospital, it was quite extraordinary to see many Afghans cycling or walking to work. The routine was continuing in the capital city, despite so much death and devastation!

It seemed that our staff of around 130 Afghans and their families had survived the fighting. Thankfully, there were no physical injuries for our foreign team either. We arrived at the NOOR Eye Institute on that Saturday morning, 29 April, trying to take stock of the situation and, in some way, re-establish routine patient care.

AN UNEXPECTED PATIENT

Not many patients came to our clinic that morning. But one young patient did appear with his mother later in the day, just as we were leaving the hospital earlier than usual, in mid-afternoon.

On Wednesday, 26 April, I had seen and examined a young lad, aged about 11 years, who attended with his mother. His mother was President Daud's daughter. This boy was a grandson of the Afghan President. Having seen the young boy on the Wednesday, I had asked his mother to bring him back the following Saturday, in three days.

As I was walking out of the hospital that Saturday, to my absolute astonishment, there, waiting to see me, was the President's daughter and grandson. They were both crying. I stopped abruptly! The only words I could think of and initially say were 'You came!'

I examined the lad in the private clinic. Further details were recorded on this, his second visit. Frankly, the main task was somehow to express some care and compassion for a very distressed mother and her son.

It was truly remarkable, particularly as we later discovered that President Daud and most of his large family had been killed on that night of the 27 April!

GOD SPEAKING IN THE CRISIS

It was the first anniversary of the Saur Revolution, which had taken place on 27 April 1978—at least, we were told to call it a 'revolution' by the new communist authorities.

We were further instructed by the authorities to have a party at the NOOR Eye Institute recognizing and celebrating the revolution of April 1978. Most of our 130 Afghan staff did not want a celebration of any kind! Certainly, the 25 or so members of the foreign team at NOOR did not want to celebrate.

One of our foreign team came to me as Project and Medical Director, saying that he was so angry (we all were!) and wanted to write a letter denouncing this travesty! He said, 'I realize that I and my family may need to leave the country if I write this letter.'

This man was one of our great team members and a very dear friend.

'If you write the letter, we may all need to leave the country,' I responded.

The letter was not sent and, as far as I know, was not written, but I understood and totally identified with the anger.

Some more background information, as it affected us and our work, may be helpful here. Political activists were becoming more bold and intrusive in the hospital.

On one occasion, a rally and demonstration in the NOOR hospital grounds which saw staff members obliged to attend was addressed by the Minister of Commerce. I stood at the back of the gathering of well over 100 staff. As the Minister harangued the attentive crowd, it was noticeable that quite a number of staff raised their clenched fists, particularly when there was any shouting or cheering. However, what struck me very forcibly was the considerable number of staff members who were brave enough *not* to raise their fists during the diatribe. Everything was being observed by the 'heavies'.

Outside of NOOR, amongst the general population, there was great anxiety and fear. Soldiers would break into homes at night and all the men of a family would disappear, never to be seen again!

Mothers were desperately worried that their young sons looked older than their actual ages and would be impressed into the army.

But on this day, we had been effectively commanded to have a party.

What was I to do? The next morning, I was to speak briefly at our weekly prayer meeting with the foreign team. How should I direct our thoughts? I could easily lead them into furious frustration, or something else.

I decided to bring these heartfelt and weighty concerns to God in prayer. Soon I was on my knees. Then I found myself on my face before God.

Inside I was so angry! How could we be coerced into a celebration? This was my spirit and my heart as I asked, 'Lord, show me how to handle this situation. It's so wrong!'

Quite suddenly, God spoke to me! It didn't seem to be an audible voice, although it could well have been. Clear as could be, the voice spoke into my thoughts the words of Jesus recorded for us in Matthew's gospel: 'Pray for those who despitefully use you, bless and curse not' (paraphrased from Matthew 5:44).

I was so angry and frustrated, and this 'word' was truly startling!

In an attempt to be obedient to God's word to me, I started to pray for those in authority, some carrying out horrendous atrocities, and others, who had disrupted the care of our patients, making our work and calling subordinate to their political ends. I kept praying for the Soviet soldiers who had entered Afghanistan, instigated the coup, and were crushing any resistance in those early days.

Quite suddenly, after 10 to 15 minutes of praying, an extraordinary experience! Wave upon wave of the Love of God began to flow over me and through me from head to toe, time after time!

This lasted for a few minutes, perhaps longer. Time was irrelevant. I was utterly transformed! From an angry, frustrated man, there was the God-given experience of overwhelming Love, followed by Peace and Joy!

This was real! This was true! This worked!

I began to realize even more of what Jesus Christ has done for each one of us. His own situation had been so utterly unjust, yet He gave Himself so that we could be set free!

In retrospect, we, the foreign team, always had the prospect of leaving Afghanistan, whether we had or had not forgiven and prayed for those who had wronged us.

So much tougher for our Afghan friends, to forgive and to pray blessing on those who have done us wrong. Certainly, it is one way of bringing healing to our own souls, to our minds, and even to our bodies. This was my personal resolution and conviction and does not, in any way, condone or gloss over atrocities or evil acts perpetrated by any party in a distraught and devastated nation.

NOOR HERAT OPHTHALMIC CENTRE (HOC)

On 1 July 1979, the NOOR Herat Ophthalmic Centre was opened in north-west Afghanistan. A 35-bed facility, it was the first of the satellite eye hospitals of the NOOR Project. The main teaching hospital was the 100-bed NOOR Eye Institute in Kabul.

The significance and importance of this new eye clinic was enormous for eye care in a country where some said that 90% of Afghans had eye problems.

AN UNUSUAL PLATFORM PARTY

The day of the formal and official opening of the Herat Ophthalmic Centre arrived. The platform and room where the ceremony took place was packed with officials and dignitaries.

I have never seen so many AK-47s in a concentrated space, wielded by military guards! These weapons had become a consistent feature of any similar ceremonies or official functions.

My colleague, George, was sitting beside me. George was the Executive Secretary of our Programme in Afghanistan. He turned quietly in my direction.

'Murray, when the shooting begins, I'll get straight under the chair!'

'Thanks, George. That's good to know!'

Dr Mike Frederiksen had been appointed Medical Director of the NOOR Herat Ophthalmic Centre. His team had been formed and was ready to move from Kabul to Herat. When NOOR–HOC opened, the foreign team, as recorded in the 1979

Annual Report to the Minister of Public Health, included Dr Mike (Medical Director, USA), Tom (Optometrist, USA), Jenny (Nurse, UK), Rosemary (Nurse, UK), Eppi (Nurse, Finland), and Isabel (Administrator, UK).

As Director of the NOOR Project, it was my responsibility, together with Mike and our senior colleagues, to get the NOOR–HOC programme underway. Also, it was both a requirement and courtesy to inform the Ambassadors of the countries represented in our teams that their citizens were, in one sense, 'going out on a limb' to Herat.

Our western Ambassadors can usually only advise, though sometimes they can give very clear and emphatic advice in explaining their views, based on the information they receive. This is what happened in my conversation with the British Ambassador.

Ambassador Crook advised me that he was very concerned to hear that the new ophthalmic team was leaving to establish the work in the Herat Ophthalmic Centre.

'I have information which has reached me in the last few days which makes me very concerned for the safety of your team in Herat!'

The team was extremely keen to go to Herat. What should I do? I called the Herat foreign team together. I told them that I had spoken to the British Ambassador and what he had shared with me, although he would not elaborate on the reasons for his concern.

'I have decided to keep you all back from opening the hospital and starting the work for one month. If, after a month, there are no further significant developments, we should be free to begin eye care in Herat.'

The team was disappointed, but a decision had to be made, which I hope they understood. Sometimes the buck stops!

A month later, with no further word from Ambassador Crook, I phoned our senior British diplomat.

'The situation seemed to have improved up until a few days ago, but now, again, Murray, I can't say I'm happy about the team going to Herat!'

I had to explain to Ambassador Crook the decision I had taken a month earlier because of our previous conversation and his advice, but that the team now planned to go to Herat.

'I'm concerned to hear that, Murray! You will appreciate that I will need to inform London of your decision.'

This is where I would explain to groups and churches that their prayers are so vital.

Not easy for the Ambassador either. These are some of the realities of living and working in a war-torn country.

There were many other obstacles and dangerous situations that the team would face in the months that followed. Yes, and tragedy also, which had already occurred.

DWIGHT AND WINNIE

The engineer in charge of construction of the NOOR–HOC had been Dwight, who, together with his wife, Winnie, formed a wonderful team. This very special couple from the States covered all their activities with prayer. It meant that they were always quietly wise and God-orientated in their advice and leadership.

In 1978, during the construction of NOOR–HOC, we received the tragic news that Dwight and Winnie had been in a road accident while driving between Kandahar and Herat. Dwight did not survive the accident, and Winnie was severely injured.

We hired a small jet, flew to Kandahar, and brought Dwight back to Kabul with Winnie. Winnie needed great care, both medical and nursing, because of her injuries.

Dwight and Winnie's sons came immediately from the United States.

This inspiring couple had given themselves, in every way, to the people of Afghanistan. Their love for Afghans shone through their lives.

There were rumours that the accident had been a set-up, a deliberate and planned incident; but whatever the truth or otherwise, there was no bitterness evident, and Winnie, following some extended time of recovery, was soon back visiting in both Afghanistan and Pakistan.

'LONDON! BBC!'

Afghan freedom fighters, the mujahideen, were gathering strength throughout the country. Afghans are natural warriors and deeply resented the communist takeover of their country in late April 1978, backed and supported by the northern neighbours.

The situation in Herat was fraught with conflict and danger. There was fighting going on in the streets of Herat, and the Herat team was advised to move together to a safer location and house.

Rosemary, our ophthalmic nursing sister, now with the team in Herat, was walking near to the group, making her way to the new safer house, when suddenly, a man, dishevelled and with glazed eyes, appeared out of nowhere! He was wielding a large knife! There was fresh blood down his front.

He went straight for Rosemary! Did he think she was a Russian?

Rosemary was inspired! God clearly gave her the words in those few seconds. It was a matter of life or death!

She spoke straight to the man. 'London! BBC!'

The man stopped abruptly! He stared at Rosemary and then allowed her to walk on freely up the street, to safety!

I should mention here that it soon became an offence to listen to the BBC World Service, which we all did. Many Afghans had their own radios, even the Kuchis (nomads) sitting in front of their tents.

The *Kabul New Times*, which was the English newspaper, had a front-page article which described the BBC as 'that lie-generating machinery' from the West. Certainly, in those days, I considered that the BBC was our best export from the UK, giving careful and accurate-as-possible descriptions of situations, which we listeners very much relied on.

After many years of dedicated service to eye care and the people of Afghanistan, Rosemary would later receive an MBE from the Queen.

CHRISTMAS EVE INVASION

The communist takeover and coup d'etat in Kabul took place on 27 April 1978.

The Soviet invasion began on our Christmas Eve, 24 December 1979.

Jenny, one of our team in Herat, described the Soviet tanks and all kinds of military vehicles pouring from the north, through Herat, and onto the road to Kandahar. Jenny said they watched from their houses or rooftops as convoy after convoy passed through Herat for two to three days!

Afghans were watching, utterly distraught! Many were crying!

Some years previously, a colleague asked the Soviets—who were constructing the two major roads from north to south, in the west of the country and in the east (over the Salang Pass and Tunnel at 12,000 feet)—why the roads were constructed with reinforced concrete.

He did not receive an adequate reply. Speculation was always there that someday these two arterial roads would be used for the transport of heavy military vehicles. And so it proved!

HOSTAGES, OR WORSE?

Returning from the UK to Kabul in late August 1980, I was greeted with the news that our Herat Ophthalmic Centre foreign team had been taken by the mujahideen and held overnight at some location near to Herat. While our team would have known, or at least hoped, that the mujahideen understood that our sympathies were with the Afghans, whose country had been invaded, in this extraordinarily tense situation, with men and boys in war-like mode and chronically exhausted, what might happen?

Dr Mike and the team, a number of whom were fluent Farsi speakers, heard the mujahideen discussing whether they should kill these foreigners! Thank God, they were released the next morning and contacted Kabul.

I joined the group flying in a small jet to Herat.

When we arrived at Herat airport, we met with the NOOR–HOC foreign team, who had evacuated from the hospital and assembled at the airport.

Soviet soldiers were everywhere and very much in evidence at the airport.

THE KINDNESS OF A SOLDIER, AND A BAR OF SOAP

A poignant moment during the time at the airport was a request I received to examine a child. The little girl had a very active conjunctivitis. It was a straightforward examination, and we were able to give advice and prescribe antibiotic eye ointment.

As part of the care of the child, it was important to have clean hands, to scrub up, before and after examination. I went to the rather dirty wash and toilet area in the airport, but there was no soap. A soldier was watching me looking for soap. Then he walked towards me, and in his hand was a bar of soap. He gave it to me. I said 'Besyor tashakor!' ('Thank you very much!').

After examining the child, I looked for that soldier but didn't find him, and we were in a hurry to leave the scene.

Then I realized the soldier was probably an Uzbek, but he was a Soviet soldier. He had seen my need and, indirectly, the child's need. With a kind heart, so opposite to all that was happening around us, he had offered his practical support—his own bar of soap.

Because of the ethnic bonds between Uzbeks and other citizens of the southern Soviet territories, and reports of these soldiers fraternizing with Afghans, who might be Uzbek also, it was rumoured the Soviet army may have reduced the numbers of these men and introduced more soldiers into Afghanistan from the eastern European countries of the USSR.

As we were about to fly out with our Herat team, we were faced with a hard decision. A badly injured man was lying on a stretcher and appealing to us to take him to Kabul for medical care.

There were other injured men at the airport watching us, also hoping for some kind of help in their distress.

Our jet was small, and already we were over-full with team members, air crew, and ourselves. I did and said what I could to explain. Really, there was a concern also that these desperate Afghans might even try to rush the plane!

This may have been the only time in my medical life that I have turned away from a patient who was asking for my help.

TOM AND LIBBY

Tom and Libby were a great American couple! Tom was our optometrist and dispensing optician at NOOR, where, with our other optometrists, an outstanding department could often provide spectacles/glasses on the day of refraction.

Some weeks later, the huge issue of resuming the work in Herat loomed large. Tom and Libby were to be part of that team.

Libby had written very frankly, and understandably, about the apprehensions she felt for their three young daughters in the midst of conflict.

Knowing that Libby had spoken honestly about how she (in common with all mothers) was affected when the shooting began, I resolved to take the decision of returning to Herat away from Tom and Libby. I wanted to protect them from the decision that each potential team member was making.

'Tom and Libby, I'm not allowing you to go to Herat, at least, not in the meantime.'

Tom and Libby were disappointed. Others were grateful. The second in command at the United States Embassy thanked me for keeping Tom and Libby in Kabul. Then other views and opinions began to surface. Further, Tom and Libby began to 'lobby' me, at every opportunity. 'Murray, we really want to go to Herat. We really believe that God wants us to go to Herat!' (That is always a tough one to handle).

They both continued to ask me and say how much they wanted to go to Herat. Tom was very laid back, an ideal man in a crisis, but I wanted to protect Libby. With all of the genuine and consistent efforts to persuade me to change my mind, I eventually decided to allow Tom and Libby to go to Herat.

'I'm documenting all of the circumstances and your own preferences and convictions, Tom and Libby. I do appreciate how much you really do want to go!'

Of course, we had to advise the United States Embassy. It was an added burden for them. Dr Mike, the Medical Director of the NOOR–HOC was also American.

When the news of the decision to allow Tom and Libby to go to Herat spread abroad, and opinions were expressed, I even had a phone call from Canada! The gentleman, not a member of our team or NOOR, just a well-meaning expat in Afghanistan on home leave in Canada, was furious with me and said so, in no uncertain terms!

It meant so very much to me, some weeks later, when Libby shared with me something of her conversation with Tom as they flew out from Kabul airport, on their way to Herat.

'Murray, Tom and I were talking in the plane as we flew to Herat, after you had allowed us to go. Your approach to our going had been so full of concern for us. I said to Tom ... because Murray is in Kabul, I believe we will be safe!'

You will understand the reason and the need to share with praying groups in other parts of the world, asking them to pray for God's wisdom and direction in decision-making.

Later in this book, and many years later, there is another story. Very sadly, we lost our dear friend Tom, with other dedicated workers in his team. It was 2010, and he was leading an eye camp team in Nuristan, eastern Afghanistan. On their way home, they were attacked, and Tom and nine others of his team were killed by a group of warring Afghans.

A LETTER TO THE MINISTER OF PUBLIC HEALTH

In August 1980, I had returned from some time in the UK, this time without Ruth and the children. It became painfully clear that party activists were intent on disrupting our service to the people of Afghanistan. At least, it seemed that all was subordinate to the whims and ideology of these angry men.

We came in to the Hospital one working day to see a huge banner which had been slung across our main entrance hall. It read,

DEATH TO THE IMPERIALISTS, THE FEUDALISTS
AND THE
MESSENGERS OF SATAN

Communist party members had taken over our gatehouse at the entrance to our extensive grounds and 100-bed eye hospital. They began 'vetting' patients who arrived at the NOOR Eye Institute for medical or surgical care. 'Where are you from?' 'How did you get your injury?' 'What is your allegiance?' 'Who are you fighting for?'

Patients might be redirected elsewhere or even arrested!

Political meetings began to be called during the working day. Medical care was profoundly affected.

This meant that there was an increasing requirement to develop a diplomatic role in extremely tense situations. There was a possible advantage in our discussions and negotiations, in that our service was seeking to meet some of the enormous medical needs throughout the country.

I decided to take up the matter with the Minister of Public Health, who was a fine and genuine man, a respected colleague, and a patient of mine.

The following revealing letter (in part) was sent to the Minister of Public Health by NOOR senior staff on 9 September 1980.

To: The Minister of Public Health
Democratic Republic of Afghanistan

Your Excellency

We respectfully bring to your attention some
recent events seriously affecting the medical
services and administration within the NOOR
Eye Institute. These matters are conveyed
to you in a spirit of concern for the effective
implementation of our programme according
to our protocol agreement with the Ministry of
Public Health.

Previously, we requested the return of our
gatehouse so that its original function could
be resumed, that is, a place of shelter for our
gatemen who work long hours on behalf of the
hospital. This request has not yet been granted.
Further, the personnel occupying the gatehouse
have increased their activities and influence
within the NOOR Eye Institute, such that
normal medical and administrative services are
now being disrupted in a most disturbing way.

As you know, our position here in Afghanistan
is non-political, and we seek only to serve the
people of this fine country through an effective
programme of ophthalmic care. We fully
understand that Party activity is part of the
function of government in Afghanistan and in
no way do we presume to comment in regard to
these matters ... However, as medical colleagues,

we consider it our grave responsibility to convey to you matters ... which we believe you will readily agree have become intolerable.

These matters are enumerated in the form of requests for your anticipated action.

1. Decisions authorising or denying access to patient care should be the business of official NOOR personnel only.
2. Any and all non-medical meetings should be outside regular hospital working hours. Four accident patients, including two cases of alkali burns, were not seen promptly because a meeting was in progress.
3. All poster space in the hospital premises is reserved for illustrative material, prevention of eye disease, instructions to patients ...
4. All medical record cards ... handled only by NOOR staff.
5. Interviewing of patients ... only by medical personnel. In the exception of criminal injury, it would be appreciated if the police would notify a senior doctor before interviewing ...
6. Only patients, or medical staff, should use hospital beds for sleeping.
7. Official hospital transport and hospital food ... only for NOOR personnel.
8. Decisions regarding hospital staff duties, and the use of resources only by official and qualified NOOR staff.
9. Our second telephone line is returned to us.

10. We request, finally, that should the authorities require to apprehend a member of our staff, this is carried out, outside of the total hospital premises. A staff member was recently apprehended from the operating suite by four men in street clothes entering a sterile area while surgery was in progress. One of these men was smoking a cigarette in the operating suite while an anaesthetic was being given. Two of these men also demanded immediate access to the lockers in the ladies changing room.

We know you will understand our motivation in making these requests ... no desire to interfere in other matters that are not our affair ... a very unsettled staff at the NOOR Eye Institute, to the detriment of patient care and potentially to the disintegration of any effective service.

As your medical colleagues, you understand the responsibility we feel that the highest level of medical ethics is clearly evident in our hospital. Further, we are obliged to say, we are very concerned in regard to the feelings and decisions of our International Executive Committee which meets in two months. We very much hope, and indeed anticipate, that we shall be in a position to inform them of a speedy response to the requests we have listed in this letter.

Respectfully

The private response of the respected Minister was very informative: 'I have no real power in the Ministry or politically. The Second Deputy Minister is in the Politburo. That is where the power lies.'

My excellent Canadian colleague, Richard, and I arranged a meeting with the First and Second Deputy Minsters of Health. We met with these important gentlemen in the Ministry.

In God's providence, shortly before our meeting, children of both of these Ministers came to our Hospital as patients. It meant we had a slightly different relationship with these men.

We had a good meeting, during which Richard and I laid out our concerns and objections, citing patient care as our responsibility and priority and that this care was being jeopardized.

We finished the meeting by telling the Ministers that we pray for them and would pray for them. This might not have been entirely unwelcome news for these two men, whose response indicated some surprise but an element of appreciation.

The banner in reception came down.

The men who had commandeered the gatehouse were removed.

Relative normality and good patient care returned to the NOOR Eye Institute.

However, we became aware that although we had objected on the grounds of the effect on our medical care and service, for those perpetrating these disruptions, everything and everyone must be subordinate to their ideology and politics.

We were viewed, thereafter, by some, with increased suspicion.

CONFRONTATION WITH A TANK!

Tom and Mary-Jo were cut off by the fighting in Kabul. They had been meeting someone at Kabul Airport, which is on the north side of Kabul, but could not make it back to their home in Karte Char, on the south side of the city.

Tom was Headmaster at Ahlman Academy, where Ruth taught music and our three—David, Andrew, and, later, Caroline—attended. In fact, Ruth had also gone to the Airport and had not yet managed to make it back to our house in Karte Seh.

My phone rang. 'Murray, Tom here. Mary-Jo and I are cut off and can't get back home. We're phoning from the US Embassy. Our son, Mike, is in our house, on his own, and we can't get through to him because of the fighting!'

'I'll go and pick him up and bring him to our place. Then we can make contact later.' I jumped into my car and headed towards a small bridge crossing a large tributary of the Kabul River. The bridge was called the Red Bridge.

As I drove over the bridge from Karte Seh to Karte Char, there were signs of military activity, with disturbance and apprehension on the streets.

Mike was looking out for me. He was 17 years old.

Mike climbed aboard, and we headed back towards the Red Bridge. But the situation on the ground had changed. Straddling the Red Bridge, and facing our approaching car, was a large Soviet tank! I drove up to within a few feet of the tank. If we could just squeeze past the tank on the bridge, my house was only a few hundred yards away.

An agitated Afghan soldier was hovering around the front of our car. I wound down my window. 'Ijaza as? Khana-yi ma unja as!' ('Is it permitted? My house is over there!'). I indicated the direction on the far side of the bridge.

The Afghan soldier, holding his AK-47 menacingly, actually beat the bonnet of my car with the flat of his hand a number of times!

'Buro! Taraf-i unja!' ('Go! That way!'). He indicated the wrong side of the river. He would not let us pass!

What really impressed us was watching the tank gun barrel swivelling towards us until Mike and I were gazing up the gun barrel that was pointing directly at us at a distance of a few feet! In sharing this story, I usually say that, at this point, I did what I was told!

We drove along the wrong side of the river. When we reached the next bridge, a broader one, another tank and soldiers there ignored us. I drove on, and Mike and I reached our Karte Seh home safely.

Later, thank God, our respective families were happily reunited.

JET FIGHTERS AND HELICOPTER GUNSHIPS

Our lives in Kabul were characterized by a constant drone of aeroplanes overflying the city, whether helicopter gunships (going out, or coming back having dropped their payload), military transport planes, or jet fighters. On the night of the coup d'etat, jet fighters were dive-bombing the palace in central Kabul.

Occasionally, aircraft would scatter propaganda leaflets which drifted into our yards and homes in and around Kabul.

A CRASHED JET NEAR TO OUR HOME

While we know that there are those worldwide who will become rich during times of war, usually by nefarious and callous transactions of weaponry, reflecting their greed and indifference to humanity, this brief story shows a certain and innocent initiative by a young Afghan boy, probably about 14 years old.

A jet fighter was flying dangerously low near to our house in Karte Seh. Was it out of control? Within seconds, there was a screeching and horrendous explosion on the ground, with debris and dust rising, all too close for any comfort!

A long pause of relative stillness followed. Then an eerie silence.

About 15 minutes later, there was a loud banging on our front gate. I went to the gate, conscious that we were in the aftermath of a highly significant incident and that there might be further nasty consequences!

When I opened the gate, there was a young Afghan boy

holding out a large, crumpled fragment of silver-coloured metal, which was still quite hot! It was about one foot in diameter.

'Doktar Sahib! I az tayora amada! Bara-yishuma mefrosham?' ('Doctor Sir! This came from the plane. I'm selling it to you?'). I declined his very interesting offer. Any fragment of a jet fighter that size could not be taken anywhere!

ANOTHER NARROW ESCAPE!

Another incident involving fighter jets flying over Kabul came to light months after the event.

Ruth and I were at a reception in one of the Embassies in Kabul. We were introduced to an Afghan with a serious manner and expression, who, like most of the men present, was wearing a smart suit and tie. Apparently, he had been a pilot in the Afghan Air Force.

When I explained that I was Director of the NOOR Eye Institute in Kabul, he said that he had a story to tell us.

'On the night of the revolution and fighting, I was in my jet, flying over Kabul. I radioed to my base enquiring about targets that I should hit in the city. I had a particular large building in my sights, on the south side of Kabul.

"'Identify and confirm that I'm to rocket this building on the south side of Kabul, just off Darulaman Road!'"

He explained that the base replied urgently.

"'No! That building is not the target! Repeat! Not the target! The building you have in your sights is the NOOR Eye Institute!'"

I responded with a rather wan smile and expressed my gratitude that he was clearly a very good pilot who considered it important to be accurate in his flying requirements and his military responsibilities!

'PASS FRIEND'

The NOOR Eye Institute had about 130 Afghan staff and usually around 25 foreigners from a variety of countries: UK, USA, Finland, Sweden, Germany, Canada, New Zealand, The Netherlands, and others.

We tried to create a happy and effective work environment. I arranged for all the women on our staff at NOOR to have a head scarf, designed with the NOOR logo, in the recognized light blue colour of NOOR. All the men of our staff were given a necktie with the NOOR logo, again in light blue. These had been designed and produced in Glasgow, Scotland.

A further innovation was to design and produce a NOOR Eye Institute key ring. This handsome key ring was expertly produced in London and, subsequently, presented to each member of staff.

Many months later, I heard an encouraging story of how a NOOR key ring had helped a staff member travelling in the mountainous regions of central Afghanistan. It might even have saved his life.

The story concerned an Afghan NOOR team member who was stopped by a warlike group of Afghans, in a remote region of central Afghanistan. They demanded his credentials and evidence of who he was and where he was going. It was a truly nasty situation and so very dangerous!

Nothing he said or did, or any papers, satisfied his captors. Then, in a last effort to appease his assailants, he pulled his NOOR key ring from his pocket.

The situation was transformed! They looked at his key ring and accepted that he was a genuine NOOR Hospital staff member. We understand that the formerly hostile group ushered him on his way, with words such as

'Pass friend! Go in peace!'

UNUSUAL PATIENTS IN AFGHANISTAN

Every patient is an individual human being who requires and deserves our devoted care, whether rich or poor; famous or ordinary; old or very young, including the unborn child; beautifully dressed or in rags ...

My respected colleague Dr Jock taught me many lessons. While in a clinic in Afghanistan, Jock was examining an old Afghan man in rags and tatters, who had a foul body odour. (An ophthalmologist gets very close to his patient). Immediately, God spoke into Jock's thoughts: 'You did it to one of the least of these My brethren, you did it to Me' (Matthew 25:40).

CULTURAL DIFFERENCES

Certain cultural differences are important to recognize. A rather unpleasant example which I have described and used often to illustrate these differences concerned an older man whom I was examining on the slit-lamp microscope.

The examiner looks through this binocular microscope, level with the patient's eyes. The distance between the patient and the examiner is about 8 inches (20 cm).

This particular Afghan patient had a real problem with catarrh! He decided to clear his nasal passages by outrageous and noisy sniffing and inward snorting, without moving his head from the chin rest. I was a few inches away, and it was extremely unpleasant for my delicate Western preferences. How offensive!

But hold on! What would I have done in the same situation if I had my own problem with catarrh? I would have apologized to the examiner, excused myself, turned delicately to the side, and extricated a piece of cloth from my pocket. Then I would *deposit* the offending nasal secretion into the cloth ... and I would *keep it*! That particular 'polite' procedure is very offensive to Afghans, and in many other countries.

An early and important lesson to learn was that not all of our ways, habits, and traditions are necessarily the right and best ways.

THE MARK OF THE BEAR

An unusual patient, at least for me, was the victim of a bear maul. This middle-aged man had travelled to Kabul for three days from Nuristan, in the mountainous region of eastern Afghanistan. The extensive maul began at the back of his head, and the claw furrows, more or less in parallel, extended across the top of the head, reaching the forehead and then on to the middle of his face. His eyes were 'intact', but one claw had severed the lateral rectus muscle of his right eye.

Astonishing that he had survived the attack! Then, to survive the blood loss (scalp wounds bleed profusely) and journey, by whatever means, between 100 and 200 miles to reach Kabul and our NOOR Clinic and Hospital.

There was one Afghan plastic surgeon in Afghanistan at the time, who kindly joined me in the operating room. Since the right eye was involved, I began stitching the face, and my colleague started at the back of the head. Eventually, after a considerable time, we 'met in the middle', having placed well over 100 sutures.

Initially, I worked on the right eye. As expected, the severed lateral rectus muscle had retracted into the depths of the bony orbit and could not be located. Certainly, he would have double vision when looking to his right, but he would learn to some extent how to cope with his diplopia (double vision) even by putting a patch over one eye.

Working in Afghanistan, you tried to accomplish all you could at the first and perhaps only visit, as often patients would disappear into the mountains or away to desert places, never to be seen again.

A SOLDIER IN TROUBLE

On two separate occasions, soldiers came to our outpatients' clinic at the NOOR Hospital. They were in the Afghan Army during the time of the Soviet occupation of Afghanistan. Each time, I was asked to examine them.

The first soldier had very irritable, dry eyes. His head was bowed, and his vision was much reduced. This was the consequence of very severe trachoma, which had typically affected both eyes over many years. Trachoma, caused by infection with *Chlamydia trachomatis*, can cause gross scarring of the eyelids, conjunctivae, and corneae.

His complaint? He told me that the officers in the Army were beating him up because he wasn't saluting them. He explained, 'I can't see who is an officer and who isn't an officer. So, they beat me up!'

I examined my soldier patient in detail. At the end of the examination, I wrote on his case notes, 'This young man should not be in the Army.' It was the kind of comment that I would expect to make in any situation back in the UK, although, of course, that particular clinical situation wouldn't have arisen.

Apparently, the request for an examination of the soldier came from Afghan Army Generals and Medical Officers through our Hospital President, Dr M. H. Sherzai.

A few days later, Dr Sherzai called me to his office. 'The Generals are really angry with you! They say that it is not your decision whether a man is in the Army or not!' He paused, looked enquiringly at me, and said, 'What did you mean by your comment?'

Rather facetiously, I replied, 'Let me put it this way, Dr Sherzai. The Generals should not put a gun in this soldier's hands; he will shoot his friend!'

Dr Sherzai smiled and told me that he would let the Generals know.

Our American Optometrist, Chip Parker, had said to me, 'Murray, you must do something for this man!'

We were able to conserve the minimal tears that still existed on the surface of the soldier's eyes by cauterizing the lacrimal punctae at the nasal aspect of each of the eyelids. Both eyes were transformed and began to open and gradually 'quietened'. He could see again!

THE RADAR OPERATOR

The second soldier I examined at NOOR had most interesting and even confusing clinical features and presentation. He had an advanced cataract in his right eye and evidence of damage and inflammation of his peripheral (temporal) retina in the left eye.

I asked him, 'You're a soldier. What do you do in the Army?'

'I'm a radar engineer. I've been operating the radar systems in military tanks. It was after very intensive work for about 20 days that I was aware of poor vision, particularly of my right eye.'

Apparently, the radar screen was slightly to his right, as he sat there for many hours. Then it dawned on me. I was seeing a radiation cataract in the soldier's right eye and radiation retinopathy affecting the peripheral retina of the left eye. Of course, at that time I could only report my findings to the senior Army Officers. A very sensitive political situation.

But I can write about it now!

AFGHANS FIGHT EVERYTHING!

The most unusual patients I examined in Afghanistan were undoubtedly the fighting cock and the fighting dog!

The fighting cock was brought into the clinic by the administrative staff. An outpatient's card had even been filled in.

NAME: Cock Bird   AGE: 2   ADDRESS: Kabul

Dr Herb saw our feathered patient and called me to the clinic to see the eye patient. Sadly, we could do nothing for the injured bird. The nasty peck to one eye had left a severely damaged cornea.

I was in our outpatients' clinic at the NOOR Eye Institute. A staff member interrupted me and advised me that there was a large fighting dog outside in a taxi, with an eye problem. Would I go and see the suffering animal?

The Afghans fight everything! A common sight on a Friday was huge crowds of yelling men on hilly land that might form a natural bowl, with the canine contestants engaging with each other in an enclosed arena.

I went out through the front entrance of our fine hospital. A taxi was parked there, and on the back seat was one of the largest dogs I have ever seen. The ears and tail were cropped, as this was a dog for warfare! The baleful eyes engaged mine as I walked carefully towards the car.

The back window was slightly lowered. This poor dog had a roaring conjunctivitis. Both eyes were very red and inflamed, and one eye was discharging copious pus. This was a patient in real need. I stretched out a hand towards the window and the huge dog behind the window. I said something utterly inappropriate, such as 'Good dog!' and 'Koochi-koo!'

The dog took off and launched itself directly at me, hitting the window with his slobbery snout and snarling mouth! Mercifully, the window held.

A quick decision was required. I backed off very sharply! 'Chloromycetin eye drops, four times a day ... or perhaps hourly?'

My patient never returned after receiving the prescription for Chloromycetin, and I like to assume that the conjunctivitis was cured!

Part Six

DIPLOMATS AND EMBASSIES

CHINESE AND OTHER DIPLOMATS

Diplomats from a variety of countries came to our private clinics at the NOOR Eye Institute. This meant that because we were entirely apolitical in our practice of medicine, we had a number of invitations to receptions and functions in different embassies.

A GLITTERING RECEPTION!

Ruth and I were invited to the most grand and flamboyant reception at the Chinese Embassy. It was 1979, and the reception was to celebrate the 1949 Chinese revolution and communist takeover of the country, through Mao Tse-tung, 30 years previously.

Military attachés from the various embassies were there in full regalia! It was quite a display of country presence and diplomacy from all around the world.

Some of my friends in Kabul, who knew that I was born in Shanghai, told me that I should be careful not to mention the place of my birth. They teased me that the Chinese authorities would require me to do army national service if this were known! All good fun, but I certainly did not mention to these, my erstwhile Chinese compatriots, that my family had left Shanghai in 1949 *because* of the revolution, moving to Hong Kong, where we settled for some months before returning to the United Kingdom.

Usually, I didn't ask diplomats about their political situations, tensions, and concerns. After all, they had these discussions and pressures all the time. Indeed, they sometimes had more than one reception or function in an evening. However, at this Chinese Embassy reception, I was chatting with a very senior American diplomat. The Ambassadors of the Western Embassies had been withdrawn after the Soviet involvement and entry into Afghanistan. Unusually, I asked if it was true that the incumbent Afghan President, Hafizullah Amin, had been making quiet overtures to the West.

In the weeks before this conversation in the Chinese Embassy, an Afghan delegation, led by the then President, Nur Mohammed Taraki, had visited Moscow. Apparently, the delegation was told that Hafizullah Amin was not in the favour of Moscow and should be 'removed' from the scene! The Soviets wanted Taraki to 'eliminate' Hafizullah Amin on his return to Kabul. However, Amin got wind of this plan, there was a shoot-out at the palace on their return, and Nur Mohammed Taraki was killed.

Our first knowledge of the shooting that evening was a phone call from the German Embassy to our senior German administrator, Albrecht Hauser. We were in our church building near the Darulaman Road when the call came to Albrecht, advising us all to go quietly to our homes and await developments.

Suddenly, the pictures of President Taraki were taken down in official offices and government buildings. About six weeks later, the newspapers said that he had died of pneumonia.

Unfortunately for him, the man who had assumed power as President and Prime Minister, Hafizullah Amin, was not the leader that Moscow had wanted.

My conversation with the American diplomat was abruptly curtailed just as he was advising me that Hafizullah Amin had indeed been quietly approaching Western diplomats. The reason for our sudden change of conversation, and even expressions, was the arrival and approach of the Soviet Ambassador. Ambassador Pusanov appeared, shaking our hands, with his entourage in tow!

President Hafizullah Amin was killed during the Soviet invasion at the end of 1979, having been in power for about three months. 'All who take the sword will die by the sword' (Matthew 26:52).

At another time, and another reception, I recall an intense conversation in the British Embassy. At least, the man I was speaking with was fairly intense. It turned out that he was the third-most-senior diplomat in the Chinese Embassy. He asked question after question, wanting to know my views and opinions on a number of issues. I found myself giving guarded replies because I was picturing him writing up his report on returning to the Chinese Embassy the next day. I realized, as did the Chinese diplomat, that I and my colleagues had the privilege of working with and alongside our Afghan colleagues and friends, whereas diplomats were always on diplomatic duty. We might have certain insights into some situations, but it was wise to be guarded!

Chinese diplomats based in Kabul came to our eye clinics, usually in groups of four or five. They were seen and examined either by Dr Herb or by myself, depending on who was 'on duty'. On this particular day, Herb was examining some of a small group of Chinese diplomats. I came into the private clinic and, on seeing our Chinese friends, greeted them with 'Good morning!'

Herb exclaimed, 'You know these gentlemen, Murray. You were born in Shanghai. Do you know any Chinese?'

My reply: 'My mother taught me how to sing "Jesus loves me" in Chinese!'

'Let's hear it!' said Herb.

There in the clinic I sang, *Jesus loves me, this I know, for the Bible tells me so ...*

They, the diplomats, were very diplomatic in their appreciation. Then the interpreter said to Herb and myself, 'Gentlemen, you speak about prayer as though you were breathing ...'

It was a gracious comment which had a depth of understanding and appreciation from a fine representative of China.

A NORWEGIAN FILM FESTIVAL AND A LAST MEETING

The Norwegian Ambassador was a patient of mine. Ruth and I were invited to a film festival organized by the Norwegians.

The significance of our being at the film festival was an unexpected meeting during the interval with our former language teacher, Mohmand. We had not seen Mohmand for a long time, for many months.

When Ruth and I were asked to be Mary and Joseph in the church pageant at Christmas time, 1969, Mohmand told us that he knew and loved the Christmas story.

Later, Mohmand was promoted in the Ministry of Agriculture, where he had very real pressures and even persecution, which he often described to us. Despite this, he rose to become Minister of Agriculture. The reason? He did not allow any form of giving or taking of bribes in his Department. Those in authority, including different communist factions, recognized him as a man of complete integrity whom they could trust!

However, he had many enemies, and his life was always in danger. On meeting him at the Norwegian film festival, he said to me, 'It's a miracle that I'm still alive!' He couldn't spend time talking with me; it was too dangerous.

We gripped each other's hands briefly, murmured a few words, and committed each other into God's keeping.

Mohmand and his family later went to the United States, where our dear brother and man of God died peacefully. He was a gentle man whose face shone!

A COMMAND AND A REQUEST

In all walks of life, but perhaps particularly as a medical professional, there can be a mix of the trivial and amusing, suddenly becoming deadly serious and even tragic! This was my and our experience over an hour or so on one day in Kabul, Afghanistan.

Our dog, Beanie ('Bini'), was a gentle and lovable boxer. 'Bini' is the Farsi word for 'nose'; thus, with a pushed-in face, the name seemed appropriate. Dogs are generally considered to be unclean in Afghanistan, and so Beanie had to live in our yard outside.

Beanie had an occasional pointless habit, an aberration! Without any warning, he would begin to turn, at speed, in a tight circle. If we saw this happening, our usual comment was to groan, 'Oh, no! Here we go again!' After perhaps six or seven circuits, Beanie spun off and leapt up and over our high wall which surrounded the house and yard.

On this particular evening, I was away from home and returned to find Ruth waiting to tell me about two pressing issues.

'First, Murray, Beanie has gone over the wall, and I couldn't leave the house to search for him. Second, there has been a very unusual and formal phone call. They're calling back.'

I rushed out and, after a few minutes, found Beanie and led the irresponsible canine back to his yard.

Sure enough, after a further few minutes, the phone rang. A very formal voice, speaking good English, said, 'Dr Omar, Minister of Public Health, has commanded me to request that you come immediately to the Jamhouriat Hospital in central

Kabul, as there has been an incident affecting a staff member in Dr Omar's Office. Can you attend right away?'

'I'll come immediately!' I said. I arrived in my car at the Jamhouriat Hospital. Dr Omar, a very fine Minister, was about to leave in his limousine. We exchanged a few words, with the Minister explaining what had happened.

The Minister's Secretary, a young man, had been carousing with two men friends some hours previously and had apparently consumed some wood alcohol (methanol). Only the Secretary seemed to be in a hospital bed in an upstairs ward. I didn't know where the other two men were.

The senior physicians of the Jamhouriat Hospital were in attendance, with an entourage of doctors, all in white coats. They were standing in a semi-circle of medics near to the Secretary's bed.

As the visiting eye specialist, I briefly greeted each doctor on arrival and shook hands with 8 or 9 medics before going to the bedside to examine the patient.

The Secretary was unconscious. I examined his eyes, although in one sense that was something of a formality. His general condition and unconscious state was the prime concern. In fact, he died very shortly thereafter.

The reason the Minister of Health, Dr Omar, asked me to see his Secretary was because those who have drunk wood alcohol, if they survive, may develop optic nerve atrophy—that is, irreversible damage to the optic nerves, which are extensions from the brain that enter the back of each eye and can be visualized as the 'optic discs' when we look into the eyes with an ophthalmoscope. This damage takes time before it becomes apparent, although the effect on the optic nerve may occur in a matter of hours.

When I examined the Secretary's eyes, as anticipated, I found nothing of note, and it was clearly only possible to wait and see what would happen.

Later, I heard that one of the other two men also died. The third man survived, apparently without any residual defect or disability.

Many years later, one of the Afghan doctors in that 'entourage' became our very excellent family doctor and friend in Glasgow, Scotland. He told me that the first time we had met was in the Jamhouriat Hospital, Kabul, as I formally greeted my medical colleagues on that particular day.

THE AMERICAN AMBASSADOR

As an international team, we had many contacts with our respective embassies and their diplomats. Sometimes more formal occasions were required, as foreign nationals living and working in Afghanistan. At other times, there were informal invitations for dinner, and even fun times, such as the tennis tournament at the British Embassy. Many of these foreign colleagues or their families, were patients of ours at the NOOR Eye Institute.

AMBASSADOR ADOLPH 'SPIKE' DUBS

One senior diplomat we met was the newly appointed US Ambassador, Adolph 'Spike' Dubs. Ambassador Dubs visited the NOOR Eye Institute, and it was a privilege to show him around our 100-bed eye hospital. Later, I received a letter from Ambassador Dubs expressing very warmly his appreciation of what we were seeking to do in our beloved Afghanistan. I still have that letter.

An invitation came from a US diplomat and his wife, for dinner. When we arrived on the appointed evening, there was another younger diplomat and his wife, and Ambassador Dubs (whose wife and daughter were to come to Kabul later for a short visit).

It was so enjoyable! The chat, the banter, the serious conversation.

At around 8.30 p.m., one of the young men said, 'Sir, we should be thinking of going to our homes. Our 9.00 p.m. curfew is in half an hour.' The US Embassy had their own curfew deadline for all Americans in the country.

Ambassador Dubs responded, '9.00 p.m. Who made that rule?'

'You did, sir!' was the quick reply. 'Ah, well! We'd better do that then!' smiled the Ambassador.

Some months later, we had the always distressing sight and sounds of an ambulance racing past our house en route to the US AID compound and the American Dispensary. Later we heard that the man carried in that ambulance was Ambassador Dubs. He may have already died.

It was 14 February 1979. There had been some kind of set-up. Ambassador Dubs had been abducted by a group of Afghans in central Kabul. He was then forcibly taken to the nearby Kabul Hotel. Who were these people? Who had instructed them to carry out this crime?

The group, with their captive, were under siege in the Kabul Hotel. A military attaché from a Western embassy told us later that he had watched while senior soldiers of the invading and occupying force directed Afghan soldiers to launch an attack on the Hotel, flushing out and killing all the abductors, and mortally wounding Ambassador Dubs.

Was this a genuine attempt to rescue Ambassador Dubs? Or was the actual target the Ambassador himself? Perhaps their own Afghan soldiers and abductors had been sacrificed to reach and murder this fine man.

Part Seven

LIFE IN WAR-TORN AFGHANISTAN

ON BEING SCOTTISH
IN AFGHANISTAN

It came as a real surprise to discover that the Afghans have many jokes about the Scots being tight with money! When they realized that I wasn't offended by these stories, they began to tell me some of them.

Classical and typical, here is one example:

A Scotsman and his wife and four children hail a taxi and request a lift from Kabul to Khair Khana (a village a few miles from Kabul). 'How much will it cost?' asks the Scotsman. 'For you and your wife it's 200 afghanis, but I'll take the children free.' 'In that case', replies our Scot, 'You take the children. My wife and I, we'll walk!'

Going into the bazaar was always interesting. You could pick up coins which could be hundreds of years old. Invariably, you were given an inflated price because you were a foreigner. At this point, I would say 'Ne! Ne! Khub nes! Ma Scotlandi astum!' (No! No! It's not good! I'm a Scotsman!)

The shopkeeper usually looked amazed, then smiled. He reduced the price!

Two Partick Thistle Supporters

From our earliest times in Afghanistan, my mother would send out sporting newspaper cuttings on a Monday morning, after weekend games, mostly from *The Glasgow Herald* and *The Bulletin*. After the Soviet intervention into Afghanistan, newspaper cuttings were highly sensitive. But the authorities seemed to accept that the eye doctor's cuttings were only about sport.

Years later, my sister, Margery, was in contact with me from Bearsden, Glasgow, telling me that I had been mentioned in *The Herald*, in 'Letters to the Editor'. I asked her if it was about rugby, as our older son, David, had been doing well in his rugby, and sometimes papers or programmes had referred to my own rugby of a different era. But no, nothing to do with rugby.

Partick Thistle is a professional football (soccer) team based in Glasgow. Partick Thistle supporters had been writing to *The Herald* from around the world. One such supporter wrote from Singapore. He described how, years previously, he had visited Kabul in Afghanistan and heard there was a Scottish doctor at the eye hospital. He decided to visit.

J. D. Douglas wrote,

> Finding myself friendless in Kabul just before the Russians moved in to Afghanistan, I heard of another Scotsman there, an eye specialist, and went to his hospital to meet him.
>
> We shook hands, and I put my cards on the table right away with: 'Before you say anything, I want you to know I am a Partick Thistle supporter.'
>
> 'So am I,' he responded warmly, and we shook hands all over again!

There we were, in the middle of the enormous land mass of Central Asia, two Partick Thistle supporters, in Kabul, Afghanistan, shaking hands!

I hope this is of some encouragement to Partick Thistle!

Our working week in Afghanistan was Saturday through to Wednesday, with Thursday and Friday our 'weekend'.

One Saturday early evening, after a day's work at the NOOR Eye Institute, I was soaking in a deep bath and had turned on the radio at the BBC World Service. Unexpectedly, I heard a broad Glasgow accent. 'He's beltit a long ball doon the right wing ...!' These early Saturday evenings became a sporting fixture hugely anticipated and enjoyed!

A TAKEOVER BID?

My love and involvement in sport was a real help in highly sensitive situations.

Some months after the Soviet incursion into Afghanistan, I received an urgent call from the NOOR Eye Institute. A visiting group of Soviet officials had appeared at the Hospital and wanted to view the facilities. I raced up to the Hospital and went into our Hospital President's office.

'We are here to provide help for the Afghans, also through medical care' said one Soviet official.

'I'm so glad you're here to provide care and assistance, also through medical care', I replied. The atmosphere was rather tense and unreal.

Later, our Afghan staff told us that the Soviets had wanted to take over the NOOR Eye Institute.

A RUSSIAN OPHTHALMOLOGIST AND A BOXER

Nearly three hours on, after showing the delegation around our 100-bed eye hospital, we were walking out of what we called the private ward. Here, Afghans who could pay gave the equivalent of around £14 (about $18) for all the requirements of their cataract surgery and post-operative care. The great majority of Afghans were treated entirely free.

One of the visiting Soviet specialists, possibly an ophthalmologist, was young and extremely fit looking. I glanced towards him and asked, 'Sport? You look strong and fit!' He responded with one word—'Box!' I was impressed. He hadn't a mark on his face!

GLASGOW CELTIC!

The young Russian interpreter was pleasant, if slightly cocky! We came into my fairly spacious office. Someone had given me a poster of a cat wearing a kilt, because I'm Scottish. I had placed it on the wall.

'You see' I said to the interpreter, 'I'm Scottish!'

He looked at the poster, then at me, and said two words: 'Glasgow Celtic!'

The atmosphere relaxed immediately. Thank you, Celtic!

Later, my interpreter friend would come into the hospital and we would tease each other. 'Dynamo Tiblisi beat Liverpool!' he taunted one time. In fact, he would come into our Hospital to pick up literature left by Chinese diplomats who were patients of ours. That is another story!

THANK YOU, SCOTLAND!

I was in the Ministry of Health with my Afghan counterpart and President of our NOOR Eye Institute, Dr M. H. Sherzai. There were about eight or nine officials around a conference table, preparing to discuss financial issues, which usually require a deep breath for all concerned as we enter into conversation and discussion.

Suddenly, my respected colleague Dr Sherzai informed the company, 'You know, Dr Murray is Scottish!' The inference was clear—they should expect shrewd deliberations on these financial matters.

Smiles cracked their somewhat stony faces. The officials visibly and dramatically relaxed! We speedily concluded our business in a professional but warm atmosphere.

An Afghan official with whom I was in conversation asked me an obvious question. 'Are you English?' I knew he meant British. This is a very common misconception when travelling in other countries, which can irk Scots—and, probably, Welsh and Northern Irish!

I decided to reply, without any explanation, with a clear 'No! I'm not English!' To my surprise, my Afghan colleague commented, 'That's fine then!'

It will not be difficult for my reader to recognize that I am a patriotic Scot, but also proud to be British! These are entirely compatible!

PROTOCOL AND THE LOCH NESS MONSTER

Before the Saur Revolution, Mohammed Naim, brother of Afghan President Mohammed Daud, came as a patient to the NOOR Eye Institute. He had been President Daud's special representative to the United Nations. I examined him in our private clinic.

During the course of the examination, I decided to mention to my eminent patient that I am Scottish. Immediately, he asked me to tell him about the Loch Ness monster! Amazingly, I was well informed, because I had just read a book about the monster while in Afghanistan. I also told him that, more than once, I had driven the length of Loch Ness, a long loch (or lake) in the middle of Scotland, with my camera very much at the ready, hoping to catch a glimpse of the elusive Nessie!

RESTRICTED TRAVEL

After the Saur Revolution (the coup d'etat of 27 April 1978), it became more difficult for Afghans to travel outside of Afghanistan.

As the mujahideen were gathering strength, in 1978 and beyond, in opposition to whichever ruling communist party was in power, travel also became increasingly difficult, and sometimes dangerous, inside the country.

Official restrictions began to bite and soon had an effect on our medical care and services, especially if a patient had a recommendation to travel abroad. Occasionally, medical consultants in Afghanistan might recommend a particular hospital, clinic, or specialist in another country, for further advice and treatment. For example, patients might travel to London or other centres of excellence—but, of course, only if they could afford the travel costs and professional fees.

My predecessor as Project and Medical Director, Dr Herb, referred King Zahir Shah to a well-known retina specialist in London. There is reference earlier to the coup d'etat of 1973, when King Zahir Shah's eye problems may have played some part in ending the royal dynasty, bringing in the Republic under the King's cousin and brother-in-law, Mohammed Daud.

PLEASE GET US OUT, DOCTOR!

Most patients could not even think of travel abroad. Only the few. One such family came to us for advice and treatment. Two sisters, both in their early twenties, had the inherited condition retinitis pigmentosa. This condition, to which I've referred earlier, affects the retina of each eye and is progressive.

The father of the two girls came to me. They were a fine-looking family, tall and striking.

'Doktar Sahib, I'm not a political person, and so the new authorities are not interested in me because of my politics. But I have wealth. As a rich Afghan, they will come in my direction once they have dealt with others with political and ideological differences. I want to get my family out of Afghanistan! Can you help me?'

These requests came to us from time to time. Or, sometimes, we made our own recommendation that a patient travel abroad for further advice and care. At no time did we consider or were asked to fabricate a medical condition.

The official guidelines for a patient travelling abroad for a medical consultation were very clear and specific. The patient was to be examined by three doctors: two Afghans and one foreigner. But my Afghan colleagues were apprehensive about signing anything on behalf of this family.

A further, almost ironic, difficulty was that the only centre worldwide then claiming some success in treating retinitis pigmentosa was in Moscow! The family did not want to go in that direction!

I had been introduced to this family by our excellent engineer and senior maintenance consultant, Weine, from Sweden.

For a few weeks, I had the case notes of the two young women on my desk, in my office. One morning, Weine came into my office. 'Murray, that family has escaped over the border, out of Afghanistan! They're safe!'

It was a real pleasure to pick up the case notes and write in the top right-hand corner of each, 'File please!'

A MOVING EXPERIENCE

In any situation or life experience, humour alleviates so much pressure and anxiety. This very much applied to our extraordinarily volatile situation in Afghanistan.

Our own work and service was with the National Organisation for Ophthalmic Rehabilitation (NOOR). Once each year, our International Board would convene, usually in Kabul, unless the security situation was too uncertain for a group of Board members to converge in one place at one time.

On the occasion I have in mind, the members of the Board were meeting in Kabul, a gathering of about 28 members, who were leaders of their own organizations and NGOs, from many different countries: Europe, North America, Australasia, Asia.

One of the Board members was Robbie, from Edinburgh, who, with his wife, Dr Jean, had served in Asia for many years.

Robbie was probably about 60, with white hair. He was a man of great resilience, humour and abilities. In Scotland, we would call him a 'lad o' pairts'—and pleasant with it!

Unfortunately, Robbie had a problem. On this particular day, he was suffering from the 'Kabul trots'! These gut problems were, in many ways, routine experiences for us all. As Robbie was incapacitated, he was lying on a couch in the boardroom, still trying to contribute to the deliberations.

The chairman was my colleague, Dr Jock, who was sitting at the far end of a very long table, on each side of which were Board members. At the other end of the long table, we, the workers (those based in Afghanistan) were seated, very close to the boardroom door.

Our chairman was summing up a point of discussion and declared, 'There is a state of flux!'

Coinciding with this statement from the chair, Robbie was already awkwardly rising from his couch and heading towards the door, for obvious reasons. As Robbie passed us, the workers, the chairman had just made his pronouncement.

'Yes, indeed!' murmured Robbie wearily. 'A state of flux!' Robbie disappeared through the door. We, the workers, enjoyed a brief few moments of spontaneous laughter, which brought proceedings to a halt, at least momentarily.

Robbie, poor man, was away for quite some time, probably at least 20 minutes. Then a quiet tread, an opening door, and Robbie was heading back towards his place on the couch. At the very same time, our chairman made another significant pronouncement. 'The motion is passed!' Robbie, passing us, the workers, murmured clearly in our hearing, 'Yes, indeed! The motion is passed!' Gales of laughter erupted at our end of the table, which totally disrupted proceedings, with all the delegates gazing towards our end of the table, with enquiring smiles. Our dear Robbie had maintained his glorious sense of humour throughout and was already settling back into his comfortable resting place on the couch, at least for a time!

SOMEONE TELLING STORIES

The President of our NOOR Eye Institute, Dr Sherzai, called me into his NOOR office one early morning. 'Did you know that you have an informer in your church? There are reports that you prayed in your church for Dr Omar, the former Minister of Public Health. Is that true?'

'I certainly don't have any knowledge of anyone giving any such reports about the church. Nor do I recall us praying for Dr Omar,' I replied. Dr Omar had lost favour with the political authorities and later left Afghanistan and travelled to a Scandinavian country.

I continued, 'But our Bible does teach us that we should pray for those in authority over us.'

'That's very good! Very good!' said Dr Sherzai. 'Tell your people that they should pray for those in authority, but do it openly. You should understand that those who work for you in your homes, your cooks and househelps, are required to report to the authorities about your activities.'

He developed the theme. 'When your people say their prayer before eating food, make sure they pray for those in authority, and if your people are able to speak Farsi, get them to pray in Farsi so that it is better understood by your employees.

'But' he said, 'You have someone telling stories about your church.'

I shared this information with members of the church board, also suggesting that we advise our people to pray openly for those in authority.

In discussion, the church board considered a young woman who would appear at many functions seemingly, at times, quite inappropriately. This girl was Afghan and Turkish. The

'Authorities' did not allow Afghans to attend our Christian church.

It was decided that two of the ladies of the church board would speak to her. They met with her and discussed the delicate situation. After some discussion, they felt they should suggest to her that she stopped coming to the church.

Had they been right to do this? Then the young woman came out with a revealing statement!

'But if I don't come to the church again, what shall I say to the police every Thursday?'

A FROSTY NIGHT IN KABUL

It seemed that we could rely on winter snows falling by our Christmas time in Kabul. Beautiful snowflakes, so big and gentle, quickly provided a carpet of snow. Kabul itself is at 6,000 feet. The country has been called the Switzerland of Asia. The coldest night in our experience was minus 28 degrees Celsius (minus 18.4 degrees Fahrenheit).

One cold and frosty evening, just before Christmas, our church choir was to sing the Cantata *Love Transcending* by John W Peterson. We gathered in the ballroom of the Intercontinental Hotel, a choir of many different nationalities. Crowds of people, also of many nationalities; our Afghan hosts; ambassadors and diplomats from many countries; and representatives of nongovernmental organizations began to stream in. It was a pack-out!

My ophthalmologist colleague, Herb, was our excellent conductor. Ruth and my Canadian secretary, Carol, sang a duet. I sang a solo, the wonderful Christmas carol 'O Holy Night', written by the French poet Placide Cappeau, and set to music by Adolphe Adam in 1847.

> O Holy night, the stars are brightly shining
> It is the night of the dear Saviour's birth
> Long lay the world in sin and error pining
> Till He appeared and the soul felt its worth

The joy of that evening singing praises to God on a very clear, cold, and frosty night with the stars twinkling in the heavens above us in Kabul, Afghanistan, still remains with us after 40 years!

'ANGELS AREN'T DANGEROUS!'

Away back then in the late 1970s, our children were still small. David was 6, Andrew just 4, and Caroline 2 and a bit. We decided that David and Andrew should come to the Intercontinental, but Caroline was too young. Our good friends Dave and Julie kindly agreed to be babysitters in our home in Karte Seh.

After the special Christmas celebration in the Intercontinental, there was to be a party for the choir and families. By this time, Andrew was drooping, hardly keeping awake. We decided to hand Andrew in to the care of Dave and Julie, and we went on to the party with David.

On our return home, after the party, Julie said that Caroline and Andrew were fine but that Andrew had insisted on a bedtime story before being tucked into bed. As Julie began her story of choice, she said that his head was drooping down but that he just about roused himself enough to hear the story.

Julie chose the story about the angel Gabriel visiting the young Mary in the city of Nazareth to tell her that she was going to have a baby. The angel said, 'Do not be afraid, Mary!' Andrew 'surfaced' a little and asked Julie, 'Why did the angel tell Mary not to be afraid?' Julie, a good and lively storyteller, responded, 'Well, Andrew, if an angel appeared in front of you, wouldn't you be afraid?'

Andrew replied, 'No! I wouldn't be afraid. Angels aren't dangerous!'

'RUMOURISTAN'

For many months, and even years, after the coup d'etat of 27 April 1978, the entire cultural and social life in all the varied populations and different people groups in Afghanistan was permeated with so many rumours. A destabilized and exhausted country could not cope with the uncertainties that existed.

A member of our foreign team believed that the portents were not good. Indeed, they were dire! The difficulty for our team was that these anticipated dread events were being passed on, and this was causing alarm and even fear.

Ruth and I invited our colleague for a meal. One thing is certain, for him these anxieties and fears were very real. Sure enough, within a short time our visitor was talking of 'rivers of blood' and similar frightening expressions! After our meal together, our friend, who was a diligent team member, expressed thanks and returned home, probably well before the curfew.

When we were alone together, Ruth and I turned to each other in some consternation. Ruth exclaimed, 'I feel awful!' 'So do I!' was my response. We had never experienced such a sense of dread either before or after that evening in Afghanistan, or anywhere else! It had come heavily on us both!

Now, whether it might be considered that the 'power of suggestion' had produced this reaction and fear, or some spiritual influence had affected our minds and emotions, let me share how we dealt with our most unpleasant experience.

Recognizing what we personally considered to be a spiritual influence or attack on us both, we 'came against' these entities and forces in the name of Jesus!

We also exercised another very significant dimension in prayer on this troubling occasion. Both of us prayed in tongues. We prayed in the Spirit.

It was a fearful oppression on us, and the lift-off was dramatic and immediate! The fear vanished, and we enjoyed extraordinary peace, comfort, and reassurance. That fear never returned. Thank you, Lord!

RABIES?

A tributary of the Kabul River flowed near our house in the Karte Seh district of Kabul. On the opposite bank, was the Kabul Zoo. We heard that an animal in the zoo, probably a deer, had contracted rabies and died.

TORTOISESHELL TARA

Tortoiseshell Tara had been a British Embassy cat but was now one of our household pets with Beanie, our boxer dog; Sophie, the dachshund; and a happy community of twelve French chickens, originally given as chicks to Caroline in a baby shower.

Soon after the news of rabies nearby, Tara was sick and started to stagger awkwardly. She had suddenly became very ataxic! Was there a rabid dog in the area that had bitten the deer in the Zoo?

With three small children, the prospect of a nasty round of immunization, involving a regimen of vaccination for each child, was a ghastly thought!

I called an Afghan veterinarian to see our cat. After examination, he said that he would give an injection to Tara and that if the cat died within 24 hours, it was likely to be rabies.

Tortoiseshell Tara died a few hours later! I realized that although Tara died within 24 hours, the cause might be some condition or infection other than rabies.

But what should we do? We couldn't take any risk with our much loved children.

Then, wonderful news! A Polish expert in rabies was visiting Kabul and was based at the University. There was no one else in Afghanistan who specialized in the field. I made contact.

Within hours I drove across Kabul to the University, with a sadly stiffening cat lying in her basket. The Polish professor received Tara and told me he would be taking a specimen of the cat's brain for microscopic examination to identify the rabies virus if it was there. He would get in touch.

The next day, we had a phone call. 'This cat does not have rabies! You and your children are entirely in the clear!'

Thank God for that expert from Poland and the timing of his visit.

IN AND OUT OF PRISON

During our time in Afghanistan, there were many stories of Afghans being forcibly taken from their homes. There were reports of night-time attacks without warning, when soldiers crashed into these homes and the men and boys of the family were taken, never to be seen again. Young boys were enlisted to fight.

In the infamous Pul-e-Charkhi prison, near Kabul, there were reports that many thousands had been executed. At least one mass grave dating from those years was found in 2006.

A CALL FOR HELP!

Ruth and I lived with our children in a house near to the US AID complex, in the Karte Seh district of Kabul, just a few yards from the main Darulaman highway.

One morning, there was a banging on our front gate. Our lovely, young newly married neighbour, Mirjam, was standing there in floods of tears!

'They came in the night and took my husband away!' she sobbed. Ruth and Mirjam knew that this was almost certainly 'the end'! Or was it? No one, in our experience, had been taken in the night and been returned.

Ruth's Farsi was not perfect, but perhaps enough? She put up a brief prayer for wisdom and then said to Mirjam, 'Shall we ask God about this?' Ruth suggested something that we had often done together in prayer when facing a difficult, even impossible, situation. We would hand the problem over to the Lord.

'Mirjam' said Ruth, 'How would it be if you and I take our problem to Jesus and ask Him to help us? As a symbolic gesture of "casting our cares on God", we can take this cushion, put our problem "on the cushion", and hand it over to Him, asking for a miracle. Are you ready to do this with me?'

'Yes!' she said. So they did!

Only a few days later, there was another rapid rat-a-tat on our front gate. It was Mirjam. 'Khanum Sahib! God be praised! He has come back to me!'

ANOTHER MIRACLE

Not so long after this, Ruth discovered another friend in tears. They were both in the American Thrift Shop at the time. Ruth's friend was also from Britain, but her husband was Afghan. Their children were at the same school as ours.

'What's happened?' Ruth asked. 'They took him!' she cried. 'Let's pray!' said Ruth. So they both prayed, standing together in the corner of the Thrift Shop. Amazingly, it happened again! He came back!

ISABEL'S VIRAL KERATITIS

In July 2019, Ruth and I enjoyed a meal with good friends who had been with us in Afghanistan. Isabel (Scottish) and Jan (Dutch) had met in Afghanistan, married in Edinburgh, and are now based in Inverness, Scotland. We had seen little of Jan and Isabel in the many years since we had been in Afghanistan.

Two hours of delightful sharing of memories included Isabel asking me if I remembered her chronic eye problems in Afghanistan and the outcome and solution to her severe eye infection. I asked her to remind me about the details, and she has kindly written what follows:

HEALING OF MY EYES

For a period of about seven years during the 1970s, I had trouble and intermittent problems in both eyes. Working and living with a medical team concerned specifically with eye care gave access to all one could ask for …

Dr Herb was the first to diagnose infection with a *Herpes* virus. It was very painful, especially on opening my eyes in the morning. I learned that this was caused by tiny blisters or ulcers forming on my corneas. Sometimes I had drops, sometimes ointment and then at times I went around like a sheikh whose turban had slipped. (Editor's note: This *Herpes simplex* virus is the one that most of us have experienced as a 'cold sore', usually on the face).

As time went on, various ophthalmologists joined in, including visitors from the States. A couple of times my corneal epithelium was removed, an attempt to remove the virus in the epithelial cells. (Editor's note: There was no acyclovir (Zovirax) available in those days).

However, problems continued to occur prompting yet another visit to an ophthalmologist. It was Dr Murray who examined me at that time. His clear statement was, 'Isabel, we can't do anything more for your eyes but have you ever considered prayer?' That morning, it had crossed my mind, so I was very happy to go ahead. He suggested that I go to his office until he had finished the clinic and that he and his PA, Mary, would pray for me. They simply laid hands on me and prayed for healing. That was it. Next day my eyes flared up and were so inflamed, worse than ever, but the following day it was gone and I have not had any trouble since!

In recent years, when ophthalmologists have examined my eyes they have assured me that there are no scars to be seen anywhere on my eyes. I have no doubt who took care of me. Jesus is His name! I write this more than 40 years later!

Isabel was Senior Administrator at the NOOR-Herat Ophthalmic Centre, establishing, with others, this vital medical service in north-west Afghanistan. Isabel received a very well-deserved MBE from the Queen.

FOUR ANCIENT COINS

It was the end of four rather lonely autumn months in Afghanistan, without Ruth and the children. I was to return home in time for Christmas. The year was 1980.

A few days before leaving Afghanistan, in December 1980, I decided to visit the Intercontinental Hotel situated high on a mountainside, overlooking Kabul. The Hotel had been constructed by Taylor Woodrow (UK) some years previously, apparently in record time. We had visited the Hotel several times. They sometimes had an excellent buffet on offer for the equivalent of £3 a head.

When I arrived, the depleted staff made a great fuss of me. I was given a bottle of Coca-Cola to drink. It seemed they had only eight residents in the Hotel. Clearly, in the uncertain circumstances, with an occupying power, tourists were not visiting Afghanistan.

The shopkeeper, whose boutique was in the main reception area, chatted quietly with me. 'Doktar Sahib! I'm escaping in three days, either with a government passport or a mujihadeen passport. Come into my shop; I'll tell you what is *genuine* in there!'

He was referring to antiques. Some Afghans were rather good at 'making' antiques. 'New' guns with wooden stocks might be dipped in sewage to give them an 'antique' look! Years later I discovered that the lapis lazuli cufflinks I enjoyed for five years were actually plastic.

But my shopkeeper friend was going to offer me genuine articles. In this case, very old coins.

I was interested. He showed me four quite small silver-coloured coins. 'These coins are 600 years old!'

'How much do you want for them?' I asked.

'200 afghanis for each one.' This was about £2 each. The deal was struck. He was happy, and I was happy!

On returning to Glasgow, and after some weeks, I decided to ask for advice about the coins from the Kelvingrove Museum and Art Gallery, near to the University. They had an excellent service providing assessments and free advice about antiques.

After some days, the formal document arrived in the post. 'Your informant was inaccurate. These four coins are from the time of Christ or before!'

I hadn't looked carefully at the silver coins, in all the busyness of preparing to fly home. But, faintly, there was evidence of Greek lettering on the coins. Alexander the Great, from Macedonia, had travelled with his Greek armies to the northern areas of Afghanistan in the year 328 BC. In 327 BC, he had married Roxane, the Persian princess, in Balkh, a city long since in ruins. We had visited Balkh a couple of times.

No wonder some have called Afghanistan the crossroads of Asia. Landlocked, it seems that Afghanistan has had no respite from invaders from the west (The Greeks and the Persians), the east (Genghis Khan and the Mongols) and the north (Russia / Soviet Union). Of course, Afghanistan was central to the 'Great Game', so many years of tension and confrontation between the Russian Empire in the north and the British Empire in India, to the south. Or, if outside invasion was temporarily in abeyance, Afghans would war with Afghans! In that sense, one might describe Afghanistan as having a 'rich' history. What is fascinating is that one can locate unspoiled artefacts, freely available in the bazaar, or even from the ground in ruined dwellings.

I have some copper coins from the Kabul bazaar and, also, similar copper coins brought to us by our babysitter, Shah Gul.

She had found them in the dirt floor of her mud house, under the bed! I took these to the bazaar to ask their value, as we wanted to be sure that we gave Shah Gul more than their value. These same copper coins were categorized into two separate groups by the Kelvingrove Museum and Art Gallery, as 17th and 18th centuries, and 1st to 5th centuries!

I should point out that I did declare the four silver coins to the customs official at Kabul Airport when flying to the UK but was allowed to take them with me.

THE CASE OF THE
MISSING PASSPORTS

We usually had good experiences in attending different offices to obtain administrative documents, necessary in any country, particularly as a visitor. Our Afghan friends and officials were almost invariably courteous in dealing with our administrative needs.

In many instances, it should be said, there was a real advantage in being an eye doctor. So many Afghans have eye problems, and someone—young or old, or in-between—in the officials' families would want and need to see an eye specialist. Many had already attended the NOOR Eye Institute.

I came into the Passport Office with our two passports. I was asked to leave the passports with the officials who would arrange for the appropriate stamps, confirming our ongoing residency status in the country.

'Come back tomorrow, Doktar Sahib.' The official's advice and instruction was friendly and clear. 'Your passports will be stamped and ready for you then.'

I returned the following day. There followed a search by two officials for our two passports. The main table on which were numerous papers and scattered passports was a simple structure, with four quite slim legs and a flat tabletop. The officials sat behind the table. 'So sorry, Doktar Sahib! We have your passports, of course, but ... not quite sure where. Please come back tomorrow.'

I returned the next day. Again there was a search underway. My eyes scanned the table, looking for our typical British passports of the 1970s, and then strayed elsewhere, to any other surfaces on which items might be placed. I glanced down to the floor. There, nestling at the foot of one slim table leg, were what appeared to be two little booklets. I bent down for a closer look and there they were! Two lost passports propping up a wobbly table!

Both were efficiently and correctly stamped with permission to stay on in the country. 'Bubakhshan! (Sorry!) Doktar Sahib!' The official smiled his apology. But all was well, and we had made new friends in the process.

THE TRAGEDY OF ERIK
AND EVA ... AND ZIA

ERIK AND EVA

In the late autumn of 1980, after over four months in Afghanistan without Ruth and the children, I returned to the UK for Christmas.

Just after that Christmas, back in Kabul, our outstanding Dutch pharmacist, Erik Barendsen, and his Finnish wife, Eva, were murdered in their home, leaving their two small children alive in their house overnight.

Erik had written a long letter to Ruth while I was in Kabul, thanking her for agreeing to my coming out to Afghanistan on my own. He also gave me another note to carry home which read, 'We'll see you in the morning!'

Who had carried out this atrocity? The foreign personnel of our team in Kabul withdrew from Afghanistan for about two months.

Then an official and formal invitation to return was extended by the authorities in Kabul. The team members returned to Afghanistan. It was never revealed who had committed these foul murders.

ZIA

Zia had a room in the outhouse of the Barendsens' home. This gentle, blind man was arrested with the ludicrous accusation that he had murdered Erik and Eva! He was sent to the dreaded Pul-e-Charkhi prison, east of Kabul, not far from the Kabul Gorge. There were stories of a blind man singing in prison.

The story of Zia needs to be told in full elsewhere. But a few more words about this amazing Afghan should be shared here. Zia was blind from birth. He spoke seven languages and was learning Russian. Ruth was teaching this talented, blind Afghan to play the piano by ear.

Zia had been a pupil in the famous Habibia School for Boys. He was top in a class of 45 boys, and all of his fellow pupils could see! He was the first blind person to graduate from Kabul University.

Zia's last words to me before I returned to the UK in 1980 were 'Get them to pray for us. We look forward to the day when we can meet freely to worship God!'

Later, and I'm not sure of the exact timing or sequence of events, Zia was a prisoner of an Afghan warlord (a classmate of Zia as a schoolboy) who had a personal fortress on the Afghan–Pakistan border. Zia was seen by independent observers having his daily walk in the compound. Then the days arrived when he was not there. It is surely the case that this fine Afghan has gone to his heavenly home.

AGHA JAN, NURSE ANAESTHETIST

Agha Jan was a very special Afghan—One of these people with whom it's a delight to work and bring help and healing to many needy Afghans. A very reliable anaesthetist, he was our mainstay at the NOOR Eye Institute, with the increasing number of surgical procedures requiring a general anaesthetic.

Most of our patients were poorer Afghans, and each one was cared for free of any charge. Agha Jan would care for each one with expertise, friendliness, and compassion.

Sometimes, of course, there were patients who were in positions of status and power. Or, if not a government minister, it might be a member of his or her family, expecting the highest standards of care. Despite the obvious pressures on Agha Jan as a fellow Afghan, it was so encouraging to see how he more than coped in all responsible situations.

I recall having a young girl, aged about seven or eight, who attended what we called the private clinic. She had multiple umbilicated papules on her face but mostly scattered over her chest and trunk. These were typical of a virus infection with *Molluscum contagiosum*.

Her father was an important gentleman in the Afghan political hierarchy. After examination and explanation to the father, mother, and our patient, we agreed to take her to theatre and attempt to clear the offending tiny papules.

Agha Jan administered the general anaesthetic, and I removed each of around 60 papules, using a tiny curette, which took some time.

The recovery of the young girl was speedy and encouraging.

The next morning, there were only tiny, faint red dots scattered over her face and chest. These would disappear over the following weeks.

Another patient, again a young girl of about the same age, presented at the hospital. Her father was the Minister of the Interior. We stressed that all our patients should be given equal care, whatever their status in society. Some, however, were those who were the decision-makers, who made decisions about our permission to remain in Afghanistan. It helped if these ones looked favourably on us rather than otherwise!

This young girl presented with a benign swelling under the temporal conjunctiva of one eye. The diagnosis was a dermolipoma. It was unsightly, and we were asked if it could be removed. My colleague, Dr Herb, warned me, quite rightly, that a dermolipoma could extend deep into the bony orbit and could cause real difficulties in effecting its surgical removal.

Agha Jan administered his usual excellent anaesthetic. I dissected the dermolipoma from under the conjunctiva, and to my considerable relief, the whole offending dermis, fat, and connective tissue tumour shelled out in its entirety.

There is no more rewarding experience in medicine, or surgery, than to have the heartfelt gratitude of happy parents!

Sometime later, Agha Jan appeared in my office at NOOR in deep distress. I sat beside him on the sofa in my office and asked him to tell me what was happening.

He told me that his family was in danger. There was fighting all around where they lived, and no doubt, evil men were using the dreadful situation for their own purposes and even vendettas. Agha Jan and his family lived on a hillside on one of the mountains surrounding Kabul. He knew that he must rescue his family in some way, and undoubtedly, he would do just that!

This man, with a fine and genuine heart and spirit, was an

enquirer and a truth-seeker. It was a privilege to pray with him. I cannot recall seeing any other Afghan man in tears, but as we prayed, he cried.

Later, I heard from others what happened. Agha Jan had gone home to rescue his family and had taken them higher up the mountain to a place of relative safety. But not all of his family were safe. His old father was still down the mountainside. Apparently, he went back down the mountain searching for his father to bring him also to safety, but on his errand of mercy to rescue his father, Agha Jan was shot and killed.

REPORT FROM AN AFGHAN DOCTOR

Some terrible things happened in war-torn Afghanistan during and after the coup d'etat of April 1978 and the Soviet invasion at the end of 1979.

AN ANGEL OF MERCY AND A RUNAWAY TANK

Many years after these events in Afghanistan, one of our Afghan lady doctors, who had been awarded a British Council scholarship to study ophthalmology in the UK, told us the following story. Although Ruth and I met with her on occasional visits to London, she had not shared what follows at any previous visit.

We asked her what happened to her on the night of the coup d'etat in Kabul. She described how she was cornered somewhere in the centre of Kabul, on her own and in mortal danger. There was fighting all around her, no doubt with angry and scared gun-toting fighters, which meant she had to cower in different buildings in the city.

She described how a young man had come to her rescue, kept her as secure as possible, guiding her to different places of relative safety. It seemed this young man had appeared miraculously, and as the situation quietened, he was no longer there!

Some relatives of this doctor had not been so protected or safe. Through her tears she described what happened, weeping as the story unfolded. Reports reached her in London.

A group of her young relatives were in a car in the Shari-Nau district of Kabul, having been at a family party. As they were driving through Kabul, they realized that a tank was behind them, possibly chasing them. When they decided to slow down and stop, drawing to the side of the road, the tank kept going and drove right over them!

Of course, she was grief-stricken and utterly distraught! How can you comfort someone in the face of such sickening evil?

CASTING THE BURDEN!

QUIET TIME

It has become a pattern of life, I submit a good one, to spend time alone with God each morning. Through the years, there have been men and women who have been great examples in their exercise of these times of devotion. My own parents would begin each day with prayer and Bible reading. Ruth's parents were an amazing example to us all. They would rise at 5.00 a.m. and spend time with God, right into my father-in-law's 80s! Our Great Example, Jesus Himself, would 'go apart' to a quiet place to pray to His Father and listen for His words and guidance.

RESPONSIBILITIES AND PRESSURES

The pressures in Afghanistan were considerable. On our return to Kabul in 1975, my senior colleague, Dr Herb, then Project and Medical Director of the NOOR Project, told me that he had been advised that he should go back to the States for two years of rest and recovery.

One morning, I was in my office and about to go the operating theatre to operate on a patient who was being prepped for surgery. A phone call came from the clinic. Would I come and consult on a patient for whom advice was needed? Very soon after that, a call came from the operating room. 'The patient is actually on the operating table, waiting for you to operate!'

Immediately after the second call, I was advised that two VIPs had appeared at NOOR, expecting to be seen by the Project and Medical Director. We were often asked to see government ministers or members of their families. These were the officials who decided if we were to continue our work in their country ... or not!

How should this situation be handled? We had often pointed out to our patients that there were senior Afghan ophthalmologists who were excellent clinicians and surgeons, with vast experience.

1. I called the clinic and advised that they would have to make their own decisions or ask the patient to come back.
2. A phone call to the operating room. I would come as soon as possible.
3. I went and saw the VIPs in the 'private' clinic. 'Early' examinations reached initial conclusions in each case, followed by a request to return in a few days' time for further, in-depth examinations.
4. The patient lying on the operating table was typically patient. Surgery was accomplished in the relative peace and isolation of our operating theatre!

The requirements of running a 100-bed eye hospital, with training programmes for various categories of staff, primary healthcare clinics, surgical theatres, each of which required that actual patient care was an absolute priority; this was rewarding work, but demanding!

All of these circumstances were compounded by the outbreak of fighting and civil war following the coup d'etat of April, 1978.

Also, the increasing conflict and 'theatres of war' in Afghanistan, involving Soviet and government forces and the increasing resistance of the mujahideen, brought their own responsibilities.

The United States Embassy asked me to be a warden for their Evacuation Program. Our house was near to a designated

Evacuation Point at the US AID compound. We reached Phase 2, of four Phases, on a number of occasions. This meant, 'Stay where you are, confirm where your family is, be ready to move.' Usually, this followed reports of fighting in the city or nearby.

THE HEAVY END OF THE LOG

With these pressures to handle, it was so encouraging to know that many around the world were aware of the needs and were praying. Chris, the son of our colleague, Dr Jock, sent a drawing, a cartoon from the UK. He portrayed me trying to lift the very heavy end of a log while, at the other end, the thin end of the log, were a few individuals lying around, ignoring the log! It was a thoughtful cartoon, full of understanding and sympathy. It meant they were thinking of us and also praying.

Those years were the most demanding professional years of my life! But enormously rewarding!

The time came for me to hand over the leadership at NOOR. The ideal person, who followed as Director, was a very fine ophthalmologist, respected colleague, and friend from New Zealand, Dr Russell Lienert.

CASTING THE BURDEN

In Isaiah 40:31, these words:

> Those who wait on the Lord shall renew their strength
> They shall mount up with wings like eagles
> They shall run and not be weary
> They shall walk and not faint

And in 1 Peter 5:7

Casting all your care on Him, for He cares for you

Also, in Psalm 55:22

Cast your burden on the Lord ... and He shall
sustain you

The discovery of a way to hand over to God the pressures of
the daily round, to turn to Him again and again for clear leading
in decision-making. In short, 'Casting the Burden'! This was so
invaluable and refreshing.

1. Come before a loving God in prayer. You might decide
   to kneel.
2. Ask forgiveness for sins because of Jesus' sacrifice for
   each one of us. Commit to Him.
3. Present the problem, concern, worry, 'burden' to God.
   It may be concern about a loved one, a heavy task or
   responsibility, an examination ... You name it!
4. Hand it over to God! Even again and again, until it stays
   with Him! Visualize the burden, sending it on to God,
   or Christ on the cross.
5. 'Casting all your care on Him, for He cares for you!'
   (1 Peter 5:7)

It has become more than a way of coping! Often burdens or
pressures creep up on us. Then, realizing that the anxiety, the
hurt, the pain, has affected us in so many different ways, the
knowledge that Christ has died for us, also to take these burdens
away, is an enormous relief! Cast the burden!

Part Eight

THE NORTH-WEST FRONTIER PROVINCE OF PAKISTAN, AND CHINA

THE NWFP OF PAKISTAN: 1989

In 1989, there were in the region of three million Afghan refugees in what was then called the North-West Frontier Province of Pakistan. Families had come over the border from Afghanistan— all ages, young and old—fleeing from so many conflict zones, hoping for some respite and relative peace. They were housed in a great variety of tents and makeshift dwellings in camps, many of which were near to Peshawar.

SOVIET WITHDRAWAL

In the early weeks and months of 1989, there was another historic date which was very much in the consciousness of all these populations, whether Afghan, Pakistani, or others living and working in the region and, indeed, worldwide.

Soviet armed forces were to withdraw from Afghan soil. The date given was 15 February 1989.

AFGHAN REFUGEES, AND MILK FOR CHILDREN

Dave and Julie, the same great couple who babysat our kids in Kabul, were working in and near the camps, while living in Peshawar. Shelter Now International provided homes and dwellings for the refugees. A particular contribution of the programme was the provision of fortified milk for the children in the camps. Thousands of children received reconstituted milk fortified with vitamins, particularly vitamins A and D. Good and healthy water was used on site to make up the milk, and children, both boys and girls, lined up day after day, each with a metal milk urn, to receive their quota for the day.

Dave and Julie asked us if we would come out to Pakistan to examine the eyes of the refugee children in the camps. It was so good that Ruth was able to join me for three weeks.

Ruth and I were to be based in Peshawar for three weeks. We would be close to the border with Afghanistan over the time and date of the Soviet withdrawal.

Any Afghan boy or girl with a concern about his or her eyes would first get their milk urn filled, then join a queue, girls first and boys second, to have their eyes examined.

Ruth and Julie saw each child first, registered each one, asked about the problem, and recorded their visual acuity for each eye, using the 6-metre (20 feet) vision chart.

Each child then came to my section of the 'clinic' area for examination.

Trachoma, the eye infection caused by *Chlamydia trachomatis*, which can spread rapidly in populations living in unhygienic surroundings and crammed together, with a constant plague of flies, was a consistent finding. We were able to provide tetracycline eye ointment, to be applied over some weeks.

These young patients could be referred to local eye clinics in Peshawar, if necessary.

The refugees came from many backgrounds and parts of Afghanistan. But the vast majority were tribal people—very conservative, religious, and in a foreign land. Dave and I could relate directly to the Afghan men of the team, especially to the team leader, who was an outstanding and principled gentleman, with absolute integrity. Many years later, as I write, Dave has kept in close touch with this very fine Afghan friend and colleague.

However, our wives, Julie and Ruth, both recognized that, in this setting, it was important that they observed the courtesies of tribal etiquette and culture. They were totally covered, from head to foot, with only faces showing. They spoke directly to Dave and myself but never 'directly' to Afghan men of the team—certainly with no semblance of eye contact.

These two women of character still found ways, however, to make their views known and always got on with the job in hand!

To our surprise, at the end of our three weeks, one of the Afghan team leaders quietly and graciously complimented Dave and myself on the dignified, courteous, but effective way that our wives had conducted themselves in their various activities and responsibilities!

During our three weeks in Pakistan, we stayed in Dave and Julie's home. News of our arrival reached the ears of some whom we had known in Kabul.

OUR AFGHAN PARENTS

Away back in 1969, when I brought Ruth to our first home in Kabul, right after our honeymoon, a number of my Afghan colleagues and friends were looking forward to meeting my bride. Two families were so delighted to meet Ruth that the parents of each family, quite separately, said that they would be our 'parents' in Afghanistan! After all, they said, we had left our parents back in the UK.

They even gave Ruth a special Afghan name. 'Shah Naz' means 'Queen of the Charming'!

Our 'parents' of one family were Izatullah Mujaddedi and Aisha, of a very well known religious family in Afghanistan. Soon after our arrival in Kabul, we bought an Afghan carpet from the family, which was our wedding gift from my Aunt Margaret Murray. Later, our employee, Mir Ali, was so thrilled that we were friends with this leading family for whom he had enormous respect.

The particular reason why I refer to the Mujaddedi family relates not only to our shared times with them in Kabul but also the huge significance and timing of our visit to Peshawar in 1989 and the election of the First President of Afghanistan after the Soviet withdrawl.

A little more background ...

In Kabul, we had many deep discussions with Izatullah, sharing insights about the Koran and the Bible. We discussed good and evil, the spiritual forces at large in our world, and the second coming of Jesus Christ.

On one occasion, Izatullah and I were to exchange a Koran and a Bible. We met outside our administrative offices in Kabul. Ruth espied a delightful little stray puppy and was briefly playing with the pup. Izatullah, with his parental but kindly voice of instruction, informed Ruth that he would not give the Koran to her, as she had been touching the puppy, which was 'unclean'.

Izatullah said that he would like us to meet his brother, Sibghatullah Mujaddedi. Sibghatullah was a Professor in the University, deeply religious, and who, it seemed, would like to meet us and discuss the Bible and the Koran.

We met in our home—Izatullah, Sibghatullah, Ruth, and myself. It was an amazing two hours of discussion with an intellectual religious leader and his brother, our 'parent'.

The time came for our guests to leave. Night had fallen. We walked together to our front gate, opened the gate, and were standing, all four of us, outside the gate.

Suddenly, Sibghatullah said, 'Your Bible states that you may tread upon serpents and scorpions but they will not harm you!'

'That's correct.' I replied. (The Bible verse is Luke 10:19).

Sibghatullah bent down quickly. His hand stretched out

to the dusty ground beside our gate. He stood upright, a tall Afghan, and in his hand, held between his thumb and index finger, was a large black scorpion! He was holding the scorpion by its stinging tail. The scorpion's legs spread and contorted in the night air!

Then Sibghatullah carefully placed it on the ground. The heel of his shoe crushed the hapless scorpion into the earth! A vivid and unforgettable picture!

THE NEW PRESIDENT OF AFGHANISTAN

Fast-forward to February 1989, in Peshawar, Pakistan.

Members of the Mujaddedi family were living in Peshawar. They heard of our arrival, managed to find Dave and Julie's phone number, and called us. I spoke with Nafisa, the daughter of Izatullah. 'There is a national and international vote amongst Afghans to choose the new President of Afghanistan, who will initially be appointed in exile, before going into Afghanistan after the Soviet withdrawal. My Uncle, Sibghatullah Mujaddedi, is a candidate. Please, would you and Ruth pray for my Uncle and for the voting?'

I said that we would certainly pray for and about such an important appointment and position.

Some days later we heard that Professor Sibghatullah Mujaddedi had been elected the First President of Afghanistan in Exile by a very narrow margin!

ONWARD TO CHINA

We had been able to arrange flights with PIA (Pakistan International Airways), first to Peshawar, Pakistan, with a stopover of three weeks to work in the camps, then flying on to Beijing, China.

Our contact in Beijing, Carolyn, had been with us in Afghanistan. She was teaching English to Chinese diplomats. Carolyn suggested that Ruth and I might come to her English class and speak to her 'senior' students, as part of her English teaching programme.

When we arrived, we were given a warm welcome by a large group of Chinese diplomats, some of whom had returned from their postings abroad to improve their English language skills.

I began to share with this interesting group about how we knew Carolyn, their teacher, and that we had been together in Afghanistan. Although my brief here is not to dwell on political issues, it was important to understand that these Chinese diplomats did not approve of the Soviet involvement in Afghanistan. There was a certain 'wavelength' of agreement on this massively significant international conflict, bearing in mind that Soviet soldiers had just been withdrawn from Afghanistan.

To my surprise, I found myself talking about matters close to my heart, from our personal experience.

'I'm a doctor.' I said, 'But I believe that we are more than "body and mind" ... we are also "soul and spirit". I wonder what you believe?'

I smiled, I even grinned at them. They smiled back! The atmosphere was not only alive, but warm and positive.

Then I found myself telling them the story about the 'Man

in the Mountains' whose eye had been healed, post-operatively, when we prayed in the name of Jesus.

It was almost astonishing to see how they received our words. There was real interest ... and the warm atmosphere remained. However, it was certainly reassuring and encouraging when Carolyn told us later that some of her students had said to her that they should have more classes like that!

That time in Beijing was only a few days before the events of Tiananmen Square, when there were student demonstrations, quickly subdued with the deployment of tanks and thousands killed or injured throughout the city.

Carolyn herself was obliged to leave China because of security concerns.

No. 1292, 50 Years On

Ruth and I travelled by train, overnight, to our next destination, Shanghai, city of my birth.

In Shanghai, we found the house where my family had lived when I was born. We had three very old and tiny black-and-white photos of our different homes in Shanghai, which we showed to our taxi-driver, with the old address. After some touring, we found one of the properties, located in what had been called the French Concession. The house had been No. 1292, Avenue Joffre. It had become Hueihai Road, but the same number was on the front of the house. No. 1292—after 50 years!

A delightful older Chinese couple invited us into the house when they heard our story. Our communications were a little awkward, but I'm sure they understood, particularly when we showed them our very old picture. Part of the house, on the ground floor, had been converted into a shop. They sold tea eggs.

THE UNION CHURCH AND HOSPITAL

As Ruth and I strolled along The Bund near the waterfront in Shanghai, we came to a street which curved beside a tributary of the Huangpu River.

'Ruth, this is the street where the Union Church was situated. My father played the organ here, and I sang in the choir.'

'Ruth! Look!' High up, behind a building with many offices, was the distinct structure of a western-type church.

We walked around the offices and found ourselves in front of the church. As we looked for the entrance, a man in a medical white coat greeted us enquiringly. 'I'm Dr Murray, and this is my wife, Ruth. When I was a boy, aged 9 and 10, I came to this church every Sunday. My father played the organ in the church.'

'Yes!' replied the gentleman, 'This used to be a church, but now it is a hospital.'

It became apparent that our new acquaintance was, in fact, the Director and Senior Physician of the hospital. He kindly offered to show us around the medical facility, but first we should meet the political officer appointed to the hospital. A small and serious Chinese official greeted us formally. We posed, all four of us, for formal photographs. Then our host, the Director, took us into the old church building, and we began our tour. Memories flooded back! A new floor had been constructed, level with the old balcony of the church. There, in full view, were the upper parts of the organ pipes.

I assured the Director that I would send him, regularly, the *Community Eye Health Journal*, for which I was Editor, on my return to the UK.

As Ruth and I were taking our leave of the Director, outside the hospital, he said to us, very quietly, 'My brother! My sister! I'm so excited to meet you. I'm a Christian!'

Part Nine

FAMILY MATTERS

SCHOOLS AND FAMILY INTERESTS

Our three kids have been a constant blessing to us. David and Andrew were both born in Glasgow, while Carrie was born in the US AID compound in Kabul, Afghanistan.

Ruth, being a musician, would concentrate on encouraging music, while I, particularly enjoying sport, would encourage their sporting activities.

AHLMAN ACADEMY

There was an excellent international school in Kabul, called Ahlman Academy, with around 100 children, and 26 nationalities. This was a perfect place of education for our three children growing up, to discover first-hand how to care for and relate to others from all over the world. Some, initially, were not English speakers. There was a delightful mixture of cultures and a very caring community, where every child made friends with, and looked after others. What a great start in life for David, Andrew, and Carrie, who learned from their early years to look out for anyone who might feel lonely or left out or in need of a friend.

Ruth taught music at Ahlman Academy while I worked at the NOOR Eye Institute, our modern 100-bed eye hospital.

MORE SINGING

What happened next with the kids' education, on returning back to Britain, was another wonderful example of God's care and provision. At first they went to Killermont Primary School in Bearsden, Glasgow.

At the time, there was a large and excellent youth choir in Glasgow, attached to the SNO (Scottish National Orchestra) and run by two amazing ladies. Not long after the kids joined Killermont School, one of these ladies came round headhunting for pupils who could sing and go on tour with Scottish Opera, including a performance in London's Dominion Theatre. David, aged 9, was picked and ended up having the time of his life with chaperones and first-class hotels, singing at different venues! *Tosca* (Puccini), *Werther* (Massenet) and *A Midsummer Night's Dream* (Britten) were three operas with Scottish Opera. After this experience, it was no more 'mince and tatties' for him! Both boys then sang in the Proms in Glasgow's Kelvin Hall, Carrie being a little small at the time.

DRUMLEY HOUSE SCHOOL (AYR)

The next exciting development was a very generous offer from the Headmaster of Drumley House Preparatory School, a boys' prep school in Ayr. He offered places for David and Andrew, half fees for each boy to weekly board, because of his keen interest in the humanitarian work we were doing in Afghanistan. Both boys loved the school and did extremely well there. David, being the older brother, became Head Boy and then was recommended to sit for an 'All Rounder Scholarship' at Bedford School, which was about one hour's drive north of London.

BEDFORD SCHOOLS

David had to sit through three gruelling days of exams in every possible subject in Bedford. Academics, Sport, Art, and Music were all on the agenda. Amazingly, he became the first Jack Carlton Scholar at Bedford School, with remission of all fees!

Andrew followed, winning an Academic Scholarship to Bedford, then Carrie a Bursary at nearby Clarendon School, the School Ruth had attended many years earlier.

FIGARO!

Andrew had a musical highlight in his teens, singing the lead part of Figaro in *Figaro's Wedding*, with the Bedfordshire Youth Opera. Most of his close family were in the audience and thoroughly enjoying the music, including David and Carrie, together with Ruth's Aunt Muriel, herself a music teacher.

HILARIOUS INTERLUDE WITH THE SPRINGBOKS

David, aged 19, was playing rugby for a Scottish Development XV against a touring South African Development XV in Musselburgh, near Edinburgh. The rain was pouring down.

David was called onto the pitch as a replacement soon after half-time. Ruth, who loves photos, moved from relative shelter into the pouring rain, right down to the side of the pitch, her camera at the ready. Next to her, with their South African jerseys and Springbok headgear (horns and all), was a group of very friendly South African supporters, who immediately engaged her in lively conversation.

'Who are you cheering for? What's his name?'

'David!'

'What's his number?'

'No. 18!'

Then, without a pause, he yelled across the pitch.

'David! Number 18! DO something! Your Mum's getting WET!'

WHAT A GOAL!

Carrie was a very keen all-rounder on the sports field, particularly in field hockey. She moved schools in her final two years to Monkton Combe School, in Bath.

Carrie (Club Captain of the School 1st XI), was playing against a touring Argentine Schoolgirls' side. Ruth, David and I were watching the match, along with Carrie's fine Headmaster and also her boyfriend (a prop forward in the School 1st XV).

Monkton Combe were attacking the Argentine goal. The ball was swept in front of goal and was met by Carrie, whose powerful shot saw the ball rocketing into the goal with incredible velocity! The Argentine girls wisely, and with speed, fell apart to allow the ball's flight to continue.

In our little watching group, the boyfriend was the first to speak. 'That's my girlfriend!'

Then David, Carrie's brother, declared, 'That's my sister!'

Then her father said, 'Those are my genes!'

A SCOTTISH MA

Let's go back to the early 80s and discover how Ruth found herself studying full-time at Glasgow University, for a Master of Arts degree.

I had really encouraged Ruth to attend evening classes at Glasgow University, which she did twice each week for the academic year. Her subjects were Sociology and History of Fine Art.

'Ruth, you should apply for a degree course at the University.' The advice from her teachers was very clear.

She applied to Glasgow University to study for a Scottish MA (Master of Arts).

Ruth was allowed to carry over two subjects from her *Diploma in Theology* (from LBC with London University). These were Philosophy of Religion and Church History.

Her chosen language was German. Other subjects included English, Sociology, and Human Biology.

The required subjects were completed in two years instead of the usual three years. Ruth's lecturer strongly recommended that she study for a further 'Honours' year, even asking Ruth if 'her husband realized her potential?'

She was not moved! She didn't have any desire to pursue an Honours degree. Honestly, I tried to leave her to make her own decision. But when she had decided, the next day I had breakfast in bed!

The graduation was in Wellington Church, opposite the University, as the renowned Bute Hall was not available. Ruth's parents, Rev and Mrs Henry Brash Bonsall, came north from Birmingham. I arranged a celebration lunch in Pollok House, on the Pollok Estate, asking the staff to arrange a suitable cake for the occasion. Towards the end of our pleasant meal, the swing doors of the kitchen swung open and the staff burst into the restaurant, the cake with candles held aloft, singing Cliff Richard's song, 'Congratulations and Celebrations!'

Subsequently, an intensive course on Teaching English as a Foreign Language (TEFL), in Edinburgh, was put to good use when Ruth was asked to head up a new department at Bedford School, teaching English to foreign pupils from a number of countries. She had Malaysian scholars, able German boys, some of whom were outstanding field hockey players, and other boys from Europe (e.g., Spain, Greece), Hong Kong, and China, even Brunei.

Before anything else, Ruth's main role has been to support and look after her husband and bring up our three children, which she has done so very well!

Written many years on, these notes and stories bear testimony to that!

RUNNING FOR REVIVAL

Ruth's parents were an amazing couple! I had first met the Reverend Henry Brash Bonsall and Mrs Bonsall at meetings in Central Halls, Westminster, in London, a few years before meeting their daughter.

'AN ABRAHAM KIND OF MAN'

What an example they were! Pa Bonsall died just after his 85th birthday. The year was 1990. He had continued as Founder Principal of his College in Birmingham until his 84th year! Ma Bonsall 'went to be with the Lord' at 79, in 1993.

Ruth wrote their story in *Running for Revival*, published in 2000.

Our son David wrote in *Running for Revival*, 'If I had an exam or an important rugby match, I knew that Grandma and Grandpa would have already prayed for me, before I got out of bed!'

Our son Andrew wrote that Grandpa was 'an Abraham kind of man'.

Our daughter, Carrie, wrote, 'A few nights before my exam ('A' Level: Church History and the Reformation) I had a dream. There was Grandpa in his long trench coat, striding briskly ahead of me on the same route to church. In my dream I was waving Grandpa's notes. "Grandpa! I'm using your notes. They're great!" He turned round with a twinkle and a smile. "I know – and it's going to be fine!" Then he faded out of sight.'

LONDON SCOTTISH VERSUS NEWCASTLE FALCONS

David was part of the new professional rugby union set-up in the UK and, of course, played for London Scottish. London Scottish was founded in 1878 and, in over 100 years, had more players capped by Scotland than any other Scottish team.

The rugby club needed a team doctor to cover home games at Richmond, south-west London, on Saturdays, and I was easily persuaded to take on the role. In 1996, with the advent of the professional era, I was asked to carry out a medical examination of each player in the rugby club.

One player, who had Canadian roots, a fine wing three-quarter, was taken through the process of the medical examination. During the routine procedure, I asked the question, 'Do you have a qualification to play for Scotland?'

He thought for a moment and then replied, 'My stepfather's name is "Hamish"! 'That's fine!' I responded. 'You're certainly eligible to play for Scotland!'

'BRAVEHEART' AND A 'STITCH-UP!'

For the game against Newcastle, London Scottish had a huge billboard on display, with David in his kilt and his face painted, as in *Braveheart*, the movie! The caption read,

WE ARE READY FOR YOU!'

It was certainly a lively game, although I can't remember the score, and there were injuries, actually almost entirely to Newcastle boys. Newcastle had a number of well-known internationals. One of these was a very fine winger, Tony

Underwood. (His brother, Rory, was also an England winger). Tony came into the treatment room with blood dripping from a vertical laceration of his forehead. It seemed that the studs of his team captain, Dean Ryan (also an English international, whose own wound I stitched after the game), had caught Tony's forehead during a typical loose scrum ('ruck')!

Tony was lying on the surgical table with drapes in place. 'I know you're a Scottish doctor, but please do a good job!' quipped my patient. The repartee was good humoured and characteristic amongst rugby players. England were playing Scotland the following week at Twickenham, the English national stadium.

With the help of our excellent nurse, I put in eleven sutures—I submit fairly neatly, as an eye surgeon. Tony Underwood was kind enough to report in the newspapers that the surgeon had done a good job!

Another Newcastle player I stitched in the same match was Doddie Weir, a fine Scottish international. This meant that Tony Underwood and Doddie Weir, both of Newcastle, would be in opposition to each other for the England versus Scotland game at Twickenham.

At the time of writing this section (Christmas 2019), Doddie Weir had just been awarded the Helen Rollason Award at the BBC Sports Personality of the Year Awards in Aberdeen. Doddie had shown such amazing drive and initiative, bravery, and good humour, in promoting his Foundation to encourage research into Motor Neurone Disease, which he had himself developed, the diagnosis made in 2016.

Doddie Weir, OBE, died on 26 November 2022.

ERIC LIDDELL ('CHARIOTS OF FIRE') WITH MURRAY'S FATHER IN CHINA

HARBOUR VIEW

GLASGOW & EDINBURGH V SOUTH AFRICA.
EXAMINING MY CAPTAIN'S TORN EAR!

Kochi matriarch (nomad)

A cry for help...

'SALAAM ALEKUM!'

GLASSES AFTER CATARACT SURGERY IN BAMIYAN

SETTING THE WORLD TO RIGHTS!

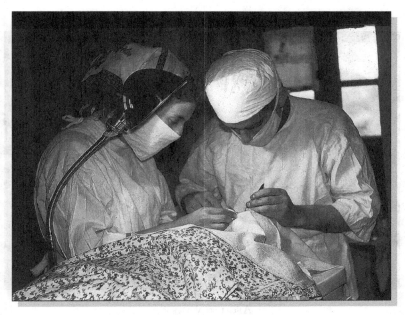

Cataract surgery in the Panjshir Valley.
Murray and Ruth team.

Eye camp clinic in Panjshir (60 patients that morning.)
Women seen separately

Afghan warrior

Presidential palace under fire. Aftermath
of coup d'etat, April 1978

The NOOR Eye Hospital, Kabul, Afghanistan...in winter snows

Three ophthalmologists (Murray, UK; Russell, NZ; Herb, USA) with our senior administrator (Albrecht, Germany)

Murray and Ruth. Snow in the Urals

Schoolgirls in Kabul

Our David

Part Ten

COMMUNITY EYE HEALTH

THE INTERNATIONAL CENTRE FOR EYE HEALTH, LONDON

The Professor in Glasgow, Wallace S. Foulds, first President of the Royal College of Ophthalmologists, had always been so supportive in my professional life and career, especially as I came and went to and from Afghanistan.

'Murray, with your ongoing interest in ophthalmology in the more disadvantaged areas and countries of the world, the Department and Centre you should consider is the new one, set up in London by Professor Barrie R. Jones, the International Centre for Eye Health.'

At the same time, my friend and mentor Dr Jock contacted me from the same International Centre for Eye Health (ICEH). 'Murray, would you consider coming to ICEH to speak with Professor Barrie Jones about an appointment here?'

I travelled to London, met with Professor Jones and Jock, and mentioned a project and vision I had for a Journal addressing the particular needs of health workers in deprived countries and regions worldwide.

Meanwhile, I and my family were still based in Scotland. My commitment professionally was as an ophthalmologist in Lanarkshire.

I did believe that the International Centre for Eye Health in London could be significant. But when? And how?

I resigned from the locum consultant post in Lanarkshire.

In the New Testament biblical account, the writer to the Hebrews records the following: 'By faith Abraham obeyed when he was called to go out to the place which he would receive as an

inheritance. And he went out, not knowing where he was going'
(Hebrews 11:8).

Please know that any personal similarity to Abraham only
relates to his obedience to God's directive!

BEDFORD

Bedford is a market town 60 miles north of London. David was
awarded a full, all-rounder scholarship at Bedford School, with
complete remission of all fees. Later, Andrew was awarded an
academic scholarship to Bedford School. Later still, Carrie was
awarded a bursary to Clarendon School, near Bedford.

It was interesting, to say the least. Usually, the father or
mother of a family has a new appointment, and the family
follows. But for us, the children were finding financial support
for excellent fee-paying schools in or near Bedford.

In the summer of 1986, we sold our house in Bearsden,
Glasgow; travelled south to Bedford; and bought a house there
within two days! There was a real miracle in this too!

A retired couple in Bedford told us later how they had come
to sell their house to us. They had no thought of selling the
house. The wife told us that God spoke to her while in their back
garden. 'There is a family looking for your house. Sell the house!'

We had the impression that this was not an everyday
experience. That is, to hear from God in this way.

This was startling for her husband, who had been a senior
policeman. But a few days later, he was reading the local
newspaper and saw the advert an estate agent had placed in the
paper on our behalf, with a list of certain specifications exactly
describing their house! He said to his wife, 'Don't you think it's
our house this family is looking for?'

They contacted the estate agent. And so it came about. There was no 'For Sale' notice involved or required.

But I still had no job! This is why I've sometimes referred to the example of Abraham. He went out, in obedience to God's directive, in the old English of the King James Version of the Bible, 'not knowing whither he was going!'

A VISION FOR A JOURNAL ON THE PREVENTION OF WORLD BLINDNESS

The new Professor at the International Centre for Eye Health (ICEH) was Gordon J. Johnson, who had been practising ophthalmology in Canada.

I shared with Gordon my thoughts about a Journal on the Prevention of World Blindness, which he very much took on board, committing himself to seeking funds for the proposed Journal. We were to become close colleagues over 16 years of working together in and from the International Centre for Eye Health.

CBM AND SIGHTSAVERS INTERNATIONAL

Gordon Johnson secured funding for my appointment to ICEH, which was supported by Christian Blind Mission (CBM International) and Sightsavers International (formerly Royal Commonwealth Society for the Blind).

These two outstanding international organizations, which have played hugely significant roles in pioneering and delivering programmes for the prevention of world blindness, have maintained their vital support of the *Community Eye Health Journal* throughout the 36 years of its existence.

Another key funder to *Community Eye Health,* in its early years, was Coca-Cola Europe.

EDITORS OF COMMUNITY EYE HEALTH

It was a privilege to be Editor of the Journal from Issue No.1 to Issue No.47. My excellent successors, Victoria Francis (Editor for 14 Issues) and Elmien Woolvardt (Editor for over 50 Issues) have carried the vision forward so very well!

PRINTED EDITION

Professor Johnson called *Community Eye Health* the 'flagship' of the International Centre for Eye Health. In 2018, paper copies of *Community Eye Health* had 23,000 readers in at least 136 countries worldwide, with English, French, Chinese, and Spanish editions available.

ONLINE EDITION

In 2015, 229,824 users from 220 countries and territories visited the websites for the International and French editions.

Many experts and authorities in the field of eye care and blindness prevention responded to invitations to write for the Journal. Health professionals, some of them former students at ICEH, wrote for the Journal, describing their programmes and experience in their home countries.

International organizations involved in healthcare and the prevention of world blindness were sending the Journal to health professionals they supported. The World Health Organization, CBM International, Sightsavers, Helen Keller International (USA), Fred Hollows Foundation (Australia), and others valued their association with the International Centre for Eye Health and the *Community Eye Health Journal*.

Other core supporters of *Community Eye Health* over the years have included the Conrad Hilton Foundation, ORBIS, Tijssen

Foundation, The Seva Foundation, International Trachoma Initiative, and the Brien Holden Vision Institute.

LONDON SCHOOL OF HYGIENE AND TROPICAL MEDICINE

In 2002, ICEH moved to the prestigious London School of Hygiene and Tropical Medicine, in central London.

In recent years, the International Centre for Eye Health has been led by co-Directors, Professor Allen Foster and Professor Clare Gilbert, both with large vision and focused energy and purpose.

The present Director of the International Centre for Eye Health is Matthew Burton, Professor of Global Eye Health and Wellcome Trust Senior Research Fellow.

All successful work requires teamwork. In this, we were positively blessed by our association with colleagues who had a heart for the needy and disadvantaged around the world. With that, they had outstanding gifts and knowledge which gave such reassurance to the Editor of the *Community Eye Health Journal*.

A JOURNAL: COMMUNITY EYE HEALTH

THE JOURNAL TEAM

The preparation of *Community Eye Health* was initially from a small office in ICEH, ably supported by my secretary, Faith. Then Professor Johnson secured funding for a purpose-designed portacabin with three offices and a library / reading area. There we developed our programme, a small but focused team in a portacabin on the edge of a building site, effectively between the Institute of Ophthalmology and Moorfields Eye Hospital. Yet from this spacious portacabin, teaching and educational materials for the prevention of blindness were to be distributed worldwide.

The excellent Journal team, based for some years in the portacabin, included those who were with us long term: Hugh Lugg (Design/DTP), Keren Fisher (Secretary), Sue Stevens (Nurse Adviser), Anita Shah (PA/Administrator), Ann Naughton (Finance), Pak Sang Lee (Photography), and Sally Parsley (Online Editions).

A tribute here to our longest serving team member, Anita Shah. Anita coped admirably with all three Editors, each for a number of years. Anita's diligence and experience, with resilience and good humour, facilitated the production of many Journals.

The First Edition of *Community Eye Health* was in 1988. The Editorial Committee of *Community Eye Health*, over the years, has included men and women who were and are recognized authorities in their field, and who mostly had a background in clinical ophthalmology and surgery.

EDITORIAL COMMITTEE, CONSULTING EDITORS AND JOURNAL TEAM

Let me list the names of our Editorial Committee and Consulting Editors for the arbitrarily chosen Issue No. 26, Volume 11, 1998.

COMMUNITY EYE HEALTH 1998; 11: 17–32

Editorial Committee: Dr Allen Foster, Dr Clare Gilbert, Professor Gordon J. Johnson, Dr Murray McGavin (Editor), Dr Darwin Minassian, Dr Ian Murdoch, Dr Richard Wormald, Dr Ellen Schwartz

Consulting Editors: Dr Harjinder Chana (Mozambique), Dr Parul Desai (UK), Dr Virgilio Galvis (Colombia), Professor M. Daud Khan (Pakistan), Professor Volker Klauss (Germany), Dr Susan Lewallen (Canada), Dr Donald McLaren (UK), Professor Detlef Prozesky (South Africa), Dr Angela Reidy (UK), Professor I. S. Roy (India), Dr Randolph Whitfield Jr (Kenya)

Nurse Adviser: Ms Susan Stevens

Administrative Director: Ms Ann Naughton

Editorial Secretary: Mrs Anita Shah

Photographer: Mr Pak Sang Lee

Online Edition: Ms Sally Parsley

HANDING OVER

In 2003, on reaching and completing Issue No. 47 of *Community Eye Health,* the time was right to hand on the role of Editor to new and capable hands. The event took place at the London School of Hygiene and Tropical Medicine. The attendees included staff and associates of ICEH, a WHO representative, and the Director of CBM International, the Rev Christian Garms.

As part of the proceedings, I was presented with a rugby ball which had been signed by many in the gathering and, probably, by those who were unable to attend. You see, they knew of my love of rugby and that I had played '100 years earlier!' Also, they knew of our son David, who had been in the England Schools rugby squad and then moved up in the world by captaining Scotland Under-21 rugby! They also shared our grief at the loss of David in a car accident when someone fell asleep at the wheel and crossed over into the path of the car David was in. (More of that so very sad event later.)

My comment on the occasion, while holding the oval ball, was to say that, despite reaching the 'nearly but not quite' lesser heights of a final Scottish rugby trial at Murrayfield, I was still waiting by the phone, hoping to receive the call telling me that I was to be 'capped' by Scotland! Without a pause, the articulate Professor Allen Foster commented, 'Well, Murray, the way Scotland are playing, you'll probably get the call!'

An encouraging comment during that occasion was offered by the Director of CBM, the Rev Christian Garms. He informed the company that his decision, years earlier, to support the *Community Eye Health Journal* was one of the first he made as the new Director of CBM and one of the best decisions he ever made! Bless him!

My successor was the very able health educator Victoria Francis, originally from South Africa. Victoria was Editor for 14 Issues of the Journal.

In 2007, Elmien Woolvardt, also from South Africa, was appointed Editor. Elmien has done a great work and as of the end of 2023 had taken the Journal to 120 Issues.

COMMUNITY EYE HEALTH: 100TH EDITION PROGRESS OVER 30 YEARS

To celebrate the 100th Issue of *Community Eye Health*, Ruth and I were invited to a special occasion and party at the London School of Hygiene and Tropical Medicine. The date was 10 January 2018.

The 100th Issue of *Community Eye Health* was given to us at the gathering:

Community Eye Health 2017; 30: 69–108

The front cover of the 100th Issue of this 40-page *Community Eye Health Journal* has the following headings:

Celebrating 30 Years and 100 Issues
*Four Editions *23,000 Readers *136 Countries Worldwide*
1988—2018: How Far Have We Come?

Editor: Elmien Woolvardt
Consulting Editor for Issue 100: Allen Foster
Editorial Administrator: Anita Shah
Editorial Committee: Nick Astbury, Matthew Burton, Sally Crook, Allen Foster, Clare Gilbert, Hannah Kuper, Fatima Kyari, Janet Marsden, Priya Morjaria, G V S Murthy, Daksha Patel, Noela Prasad, Babar Qureshi, Serge Resnikoff, Richard Wormald, David Yorston
Regional Consultants: Hannah Faal (AFR), Kovin Naidoo (AFR), Wanjiku Mathenge (AFR), Van Lansingh (AMR), Andrea Zin (AMR), Ian Murdoch (EUR), Janos Nemeth (EUR), G V S

Murthy (SEAR), R Thulsiraj (SEAR), Babar Qureshi (EMR), Mansur Rabiu (EMR), Leshan Tan (WPR), Hugh Taylor (WPR)

Proofreader: Caroline Thaung

Design: Lance Bellers

Address for Subscriptions:

Anita Shah, International Centre for Eye Health, London School of Hygiene and Tropical Medicine, Keppel Street, London WC1E 7HT

Email: admin@cehjournal.org

Online Edition and Newsletter: web@cehjournal.org

Back Issues (HTML and PDF): www.cehjournal.org

The Journal is available in English, French, Spanish and Chinese

Subscriptions: Readers in low and middle-income countries receive the Journal free of charge. Send your name, occupation and postal address to the following address:

Email: admin@cehjournal.org

To subscribe online, visit: www.cehjournal.org/subscribe

COMMENTS ON COMMUNITY EYE HEALTH

In her Editorial in 'Our Centenary Issue', Elmien Woolvaardt made some telling statements:

> Blindness, visual impairment and eye disease affect people everywhere. However, not everyone is equally at risk; even in wealthier countries it is always the poor who suffer most.

> The history of the *Community Eye Health Journal* is deeply entwined with that of global eye health. We are the only publication specifically

for eye care workers in low and middle-income countries, and we have been here since 1988.

Elmien also shared a comment from an optometrist in Nigeria: 'Without this Journal, I am in utter darkness!'

A statement was made by a respected colleague, Dr Daniel Etya'ale: 'When you get to the end of the road somewhere in the middle of Africa ... there you will find a clinic with a single ophthalmic nurse who only had her study notes of 20 years ago ... until she received the Journal!'

COMMUNITY EYE HEALTH
1997; 10: 49–64   LANDMINES

THE BLINDING EFFECTS OF LANDMINES

Looking back at many significant articles and publications, one publication in 1997 (Issue No. 23) was unique in the medical literature as the first publication on the blinding effects of landmines. We had articles from Afghanistan, Cambodia, and Mozambique.

It was the year when Princess Diana was killed in the horrendous car accident in Paris. Later, Ruth and I attended the National Prayer Breakfast in Westminster and were placed at the table of Professor, The Lord Alton. When he asked about our work, I showed him the latest Journal on Landmines. Lord Alton arranged for copies to go to the offices of Princess Diana, in view of their ongoing campaign, despite Diana's death, seeking to have international bans on this horrific form of warfare.

This ghastly, so-called passive form of waging war often leaves uncharted lethal debris—landmines! Civilians, and particularly children are the front-line victims of devastating explosions, even months and years later.

A sad memory I have is of holding the hand of a man, possibly in his 30s, who had both eyes almost destroyed by a landmine explosion. It was at the end of a short visit of some weeks back to NOOR in Kabul.

'Doktar Sahib, will I see again? Please help me!'

His right eye was destroyed, damaged beyond repair. His left eye had severe injuries. Some 'light perception' of his left eye with 'good projection' gave a glimmer of hope, if surgery were to be attempted.

Explaining to the patient that his right eye could not be saved, and telling him that surgery to his left eye should not be carried out immediately and would have an uncertain outcome, was so very difficult.

I was leaving Afghanistan in a couple of days. We felt that the eye should receive treatment for a few days, at least, to achieve a quieter eye, including local and systemic antibiotics. This might provide greater opportunity for a reasonable post-operative outcome. Sadly, I don't know the final outcome for this severely traumatized Afghan.

Why this preamble about my personal experience? It seemed good to give some personal background to the decision by our Editorial Board of *Community Eye Health* to have a Journal devoted to the Blinding Effects of Landmines. Thus, in 1997:

COMMUNITY EYE HEALTH
1997; 10: 49–64

Articles in this first publication on the blinding effects of landmines included the following.

1. 'Preventable Blindness and Anti-personnel Landmines' (Larry Schwab)

Antipersonnel landmines are used by military forces to deny opposing armies, civilians and refugees, mobility and territory. Landmines are rarely removed by those who place them.

2. 'Childhood Blindness due to Landmines' (Clare Gilbert)

In 1992, in a School for the Blind in Tirana, Albania, there were 70 pupils, 50 of whom were available for examination. 11 children had lost vision during childhood (30%), and 9 of these were boys who had been playing with landmines (24%). The added tragedy is that 3 of these blind boys had lost a hand and one boy had lost both hands.

3. 'VISA in Afghanistan' (D. C. Minassian and Briar Whitehead)

One agency in Afghanistan, the National Organisation for Ophthalmic Rehabilitation (NOOR)—a co-service with VISA— is doing outstanding work to save sight among Afghans. Its logo is one of the most well-known in the country, and its reputation is almost legendary.

4. 'Anti-personnel Mines: Information from British Red Cross' (1997)

1. There are an estimated 119 million active anti-personnel mines in 71 countries around the world.
2. On average, 24,000 people are killed or maimed by anti-personnel mines each year; that is about one person every 20 minutes.
3. In Angola, there is one amputee per 334 inhabitants, and in Cambodia there is one amputee per 384 (compared to a figure of one in 22,000 in the USA).

THE JOURNAL IN 2023

The quarterly *Community Eye Health Journal* was distributed free of charge to 132 countries.

There were 21,000 print copies. 10,000 journals were emailed. 2,500 used the app. CEHJ articles had 2 million views on PubMed.

INTERNATIONAL RESOURCE CENTRE FOR THE PREVENTION OF BLINDNESS: A MODEL FOR OTHERS

It was encouraging to see the development of our International Resource Centre in London, with its small but dedicated team which worked so well together.

From the early days, beginning in 1990, as part of the Institute of Ophthalmology, to the transfer to the London School of Hygiene and Tropical Medicine in 2002, the team was expanding its role and contributions towards the prevention of world blindness.

The main commitment of our team was to publish the *Community Eye Health Journal* approximately three times each year. Other teaching and educational materials were being prepared, including our teaching slides/texts briefly described in the next section.

In July 1993, it was my responsibility to organize a three-day World Health Organization Workshop on Teaching and Educational Materials for the Prevention of Blindness at Moorfields Eye Hospital, in London.

Then, in early 1994, as Eye Adviser to the British charity HelpAge International, I attended the Partnership Committee of International Non-Governmental Organizations, in Uruguay. A specific request by the Partnership Committee was to set up a Clearing House of Teaching and Educational Materials in the field of blindness prevention, which would be part of the commitment of the team at the International Resource Centre, London.

The International Resource Centre gathered information and provided resource material relating to countries, research, teaching materials, photography, and personnel needs in low- and middle-income countries.

It became apparent that different countries appreciated the model of the International Resource Centre in London and enquired about support and guidance in establishing their own centres in-country.

SUE STEVENS

Here I pay tribute to Sue Stevens, our Nurse Adviser, who travelled to different countries and advised on the establishment of a Resource Centre suitable for the particular country and region. More than that, back in our own International Resource Centre, Sue responded to requests for teaching and educational materials from all over the world.

Resource Centres were planned in-country and set up in the following strategic locations, each in association with our London team.

*Colombia *South Africa *Tanzania *Nigeria *India *Pakistan *Fiji

Perhaps the significance of these early Resource Centres was their encouragement to health professionals in developing their own programmes for the prevention of blindness.

TEACHING SLIDES AND TEXTS

This significant and effective training programme of Teaching Colour Slides and Texts was prepared in cooperation with colleagues at the International Centre for Eye Health. Each teaching set had 24 slides (with up to 50 photographs) and a handbook with a text.

Some teaching sets had an external author who is acknowledged below. The exceptions are the four sets where the texts were written by Sue Stevens, very much a key member of our team in the International Resource Centre.

Usually, the teaching slide sets and their development were used as part of our teaching of students studying for a Certificate or Diploma in Community Eye Health.

1. *Examination of the Eyes* (handbook, 36 pages)
2. *The Eye in Primary Health Care* (handbook, 37 pages)
3. *Cataract* (handbook, 28 pages)
4. *Prevention of Childhood Blindness* (handbook, 47 pages)
5. *Onchocerciasis (River Blindness)* (handbook, 41 pages)
6. *The Glaucomas* (handbook, 61 pages)
7. *Trachoma* (handbook, 50 pages)
8. *Leprosy and the Eye* (handbook, 42 pages; Author—Dr Margreet Hogeweg, The Netherlands)
9. *HIV / AIDS and the Eye* (handbook, 52 pages; Author—Dr Philippe Kestelyn, Belgium)
10. *Practical Ophthalmic Procedures*; Volumes 1, 2, 3, and 4 (Author—Ms Susan Stevens)

ECOLOGY WEEK

We called it Ecology Week. Perhaps it was my mistake to express interest in the proposed new one-week course at the International Centre for Eye Health! Our Head of Department and Director, Professor Gordon Johnson, responded, 'Will you organise and have oversight of the Ecology Week, Murray?'

It was certainly a fascinating and highly relevant subject and area of study! How does the environment impact our eye health and eye disease?

The week began with a lecture on the Greenhouse Effect, examining the effects on our climate of greenhouse gases, such as carbon dioxide and methane. Then we began to address the influence of the environment on the common blinding diseases worldwide. For example, the water supply to a community or communities has enormous effect on two of the more common blinding diseases.

One causal factor in the onset of cataract (the most common cause of blindness worldwide) is acute dehydration earlier in the life of the patient. Professor I. S. Roy of Calcutta, India, told me that he had seen the 'acute' onset of cataract during cholera epidemics in India.

Trachoma is one of the most common causes of blindness in our world. If children can be encouraged to wash their faces, the prevalence of trachoma is dramatically reduced. Also, many other general hygiene issues can be dealt with when there is a good water supply.

It was interesting to find myself suggesting to our students that the best 'ophthalmologist' for a community could well be the engineer who provided good and clean water. We invited a health professional to lecture to us on The Supply of Good Water for Communities.

One lecture I enjoyed giving, during the Ecology Week, which had a good response from our students, was called 'Customs, Cultures, Beliefs and Eye Disease'. Some cultural practices around the world can be harmful to general health and disease.

Children who have neonatal conjunctivitis, possibly due to *Neisseria gonnorrhoea*, may have had a variety of 'drops' put in the eye, including kerosene or even urine! In treating the child, the mother and her sexual partner should also receive treatment, which may have difficulties in many instances.

In Pakistan, Professor M. Daud Khan, a senior ophthalmologist in Peshawar, wrote of the children or young people who presented with a syringe needle having penetrated the eyeball and still stuck deeply into the eye.

The Professor explained that syringes, with the needle still attached, might be discarded at waste sites, or anywhere, only to be picked up by youngsters to use as water pistols. The kids, having fun, would leave the needle attached to the syringe and, when used as a water pistol, the needle would 'fly' with the water! There may not only be considerable trauma and damage to the eye itself, but also the introduction of infection into the eye, including the danger of HIV infection.

Professor Daud Khan instituted a campaign to inform the public of the great dangers of discarded syringes with potentially contaminated needles attached.

The lecture, 'Customs, Cultures, Beliefs and Eye Disease', also found a place for the story of the girl with 'hysterical' blindness and her response to prayer, which is reported earlier in this book of stories.

Part Eleven

INVITATIONS: MOSTLY TO DEVELOPING COUNTRIES

AFGHANISTAN 1981

In the autumn of 1981, an invitation was received from Dr R. T. Lienert FRCS, Project and Medical Director of NOOR, and Dr M. H. Sherzai, former President of the NOOR Project, to write a Seven-Year Plan for Ophthalmology in Afghanistan. This Plan was submitted at the end of a six-week visit.

TUNISIA 1982

In the Spring of 1982, a Swedish colleague, Lars Molin, who had been a senior administrator at NOOR in Afghanistan, invited me to visit Tunisia with him. We were to write a feasibility study on proposed Aid in Rehabilitation for the Disabled, including the Visually Disabled. Lars Molin, with his family, subsequently worked full-time in Tunisia.

SULTANATE OF OMAN 1984

At New Year 1984, Dr T J Thomson CBE, President of the Royal College of Physicians and Surgeons, Glasgow, asked me to visit Oman and write a Report on Ophthalmology in Oman.

INDIA 1987

In May 1987, Professor Gordon J. Johnson, International Centre for Eye Health, Institute of Ophthalmology, London, invited me to visit India with him. Professor Johnson's brief was to write

Protocol Agreements between the Government of India and the Overseas Development Administration, UK.

SOMALIA 1988

In September 1988, responding to a request from Professor Simon Franken, I visited Afgooye, near Mogadishu, to participate in the Eye Programme established by Christian Blind Mission, Germany.

PAKISTAN 1989

In February 1989, my wife and I visited former colleagues in the North-West Frontier Province following a request to examine Afghan children in the refugee camps. More than 700 children were seen.

CAMBODIA 1989

In November 1989, Southeast Asian Outreach asked me to visit Cambodia with a view to their potential involvement in an eye care programme in the country. This was the first visit by a western ophthalmologist after Pol Pot and the atrocities of the 'killing fields'. Our excellent interpreter, a woman probably in her 30s, told us that eleven members of her family were killed during the horrendous times under Pol Pot. Only three members of her family survived.

MOZAMBIQUE 1990

At the end of April and in early May 1990, at the request of HelpAge International, discussions were held with Ministry of Health officials in Maputo. A senior ophthalmologist from Mozambique successfully attended the 1990–1991 Course for the *Diploma in Community Eye Health* at the International Centre for Eye Health, London, and subsequently became Director of Eye Care Services in Mozambique.

When travelling to outlying clinics and hospitals, we had to fly. It was too dangerous to travel by road because of the ongoing civil war.

AN OLD PEOPLE'S HOME

A visit to an Old People's Home (*HelpAge International* was supporting this service) included being introduced to a fine couple who shared their own room and facilities. The wife was sitting on her bed, wearing a new pair of glasses, and open on her lap was her Bible. I asked my hosts to express to her that I was blessed to see her with her Bible and that I read my Bible also.

Then I turned towards the husband, who was sitting quietly in the semi-darkness, and was so disappointed to see the disease affecting his face. He had the clinical facial features of lepromatous leprosy. I advised the staff to arrange for full examination and institution of appropriate treatment.

NO AVAILABLE GLASSES

It was so interesting to join an Ophthalmic 'Tecnico' in his clinic and watch his good care of his many patients. One older woman clearly had presbyopia, the 'normal' ageing process affecting the lens of each eye. As the lens becomes less able to change shape for near vision, there is the need of glasses with convex / plus lenses for close vision, such as reading or sewing. The Tecnico examined his patient very competently. He placed new plus lenses in the trial frame for each eye. I was most impressed with the patient. With her lenses in place, she threaded a needle with remarkably steady hands. So all was well; her new prescription would transform her life!

But no! The Tecnico advised me that nothing further would happen. There were no glasses available to give to the old lady.

Some time later, back in the UK, I was asked to take part in the This Morning programme with Richard and Judy in the ITV studios at Liverpool docks. The personality on the programme was 'Percy Sugden' of the British TV soap production Coronation Street. This was an appeal by Boots Opticians and the Lions Clubs for unused spectacles, which would be checked for their lens powers and then sent out to developing countries.

I told the viewers about the old lady in Mozambique who was given lenses and threaded a needle with such steady hands but did not receive any glasses because none were available.

AFGHANISTAN 1991

In July 1991, I took part in an eye camp in Pul-i-Khumri, arranged by the NOOR Project in Afghanistan. It was disturbing to see so many patients with injuries and children with corneal scarring, probably due to old vitamin A deficiency, both consequences of the years of war. Approximately 16 rolls of film were taken for teaching purposes.

A MILITARY CONVOY

Reaching the planned situation of the eye camp was quite complicated. It involved flying from Kabul to Mazar-i-Sharif in the north, then travelling south by road, well over 100 miles to Pul-i-Khumri. Providentially, the young Governor of Mazar-i-Sharif Province was driving, in convoy, along the route from Mazar to Pul-i-Khumri. Limousines and armoured military protection vehicles, all appropriately manned with AK-47-wielding soldiers, carried us safely into central Afghanistan.

An explanation was provided by the Governor, who can't have been more than 30 years old.

'We are carrying a great deal of money!' advised the Governor, who had kindly invited me to share his limousine. 'In fact, it is around $30,000. That is why we need to have adequate protection, in case of any attacks by bandits or marauding militia!'

ANTHRAX

An unusual patient who presented at the eye camp was a middle-aged woman with anthrax. The infection was peri-orbital with florid inflammation and swelling. A small black eschar on her forehead revealed the likely site of 'inoculation' with the anthrax bacillus, probably carried by an insect bite.

These patients, and we saw them occasionally in Kabul, will often develop what we call a cicatricial ectropion—that is, scarring of the eyelid causing the eyelid to turn inside out. If this happens, we would later consider a skin graft, with skin taken from behind the ear and placed in the lower eyelid. This particular patient did not require a graft.

In giving illustrated talks in the UK or elsewhere, I would often show a picture of this poor woman and challenge my medical audience to give me a diagnosis! Of course, very few in the West have seen anthrax.

Then I would inform the audience that the woman had recovered quite remarkably well 'with prayer and antibiotics', in that order! For example, I shared this when speaking to the combined meeting of Senior Fellows of the Royal College of Surgeons of Edinburgh and the Royal College of Physicians of Edinburgh. No one challenged my conviction!

After the camp was over, I was invited by a very senior religious leader in the centuries-old Ismaili sect of Islam, to visit his home and dwellings in a valley near to Pul-i-Khumri. It was an honour to receive the invitation, as my host wanted me to examine himself and also the womenfolk of his household.

A SHEEP'S HEAD FOR BREAKFAST

An overnight stay and some sleep (somewhat disturbed by another male visitor who had recurrent episodes of sleep apnoea!) was followed by a communal breakfast. This was enjoyed, sitting on carpets, apart from having to stare into the eyes of a sheep's head which was situated directly in front of me, possibly as another honour. I had this strange apprehension that they might offer me a sheep's eye as a delicacy because I was an ophthalmologist!

Between 1991 and 1996, further visits were undertaken to Cambodia (1991 and 1992), Uruguay (1994), Taiwan (1994), Pakistan (1995), Sudan (1995), and Uganda (1996).

LIBYA 1997

In July 1997, at the request if the World Health Organization, I reviewed ophthalmic services in the country and advised on the development of the Centre for the Prevention of Eye Diseases and its programme.

A GIFT FROM GADDAFI

My host was the senior ophthalmologist in the country whose base and offices were in Tripoli. However, part of the plan and programme was to travel to Sirte, in the desert, where Muammar Gaddafi had established his seat of power and government.

I was to meet the Deputy Minister of Health. I met the Deputy Minister in the biggest office I have ever seen. An almost empty room of vast proportions, stretching about 40 yards to a desk with chairs at the far end was traversed successfully, followed by a formal and courteous discussion.

However, the incident I have in mind happened en route to Sirte, travelling in my host's own car, which he was driving. I was in the passenger seat. A military checkpoint appeared. My host and driver slowed the car, bringing it to a stop. An extremely officious soldier of uncertain rank summarily indicated to my host to get out of the car, waving his hands with a haughty expression!

My host began to steam! 'I'll sort him out!'

'Okay!' I murmured. 'It's your country.' My host was a big man, probably in every way. He beckoned to the soldier to go around to the back of the car. What on earth was he thinking of doing?

After a minute or so, my host and the soldier reappeared. The transformation in the military man was astonishing. He was bowing and scraping! The best word I can think of is 'obsequious'!

With a 'that sorted him!', my host climbed back into the driving seat. As we drove away, I asked, 'So what in the world did you do, then?'

'I took him round to the back of the car (I knew that!) and

showed him my number plate, and he immediately recognized that this car is a personal gift from Colonel Gaddafi!'

SAUDI ARABIA 1997

In November 1997, an invitation to speak at an International Nursing Education Symposium, King Khaled Eye Specialist Hospital, Riyadh, involved three one-hour presentations, two of which were at the Symposium. Around 400 delegates attended.

The invitation to speak in Riyadh was accepted, but with one request. Could I bring my wife with me if we travelled economy class, instead of flying on my own, first class? The response was positive.

We arrived in Riyadh and were taken to the King Khaled Eye Specialist Hospital. Ruth was given a beautifully embroidered black abaya, providing complete covering apart from her face and hands, to wear out in the centre of town and marketplace.

A WELCOME 'CUP OF TEA'

Amongst the welcoming group were some American expats who were working in the Hospital. 'When you've freshened up,' said one, 'Come up to my apartment for a cup of tea.' And so we did. On arrival, I was handed a glass of 'apple juice'. I like apple juice, but when I sipped the welcome drink, it was certainly not what I expected!

My brief was to speak about world blindness, the huge imbalance of eye care services around the world, and what was being done by the World Health Organization; the International Agency for Prevention of Blindness (IAPB); University Departments, such as our own International Centre for Eye

Health (ICEH), London and International NGOs, working with eye healthcare professionals, all seeking to combat the prevalence of preventable blindness worldwide.

AFGHANISTAN 2003

In October 2003, at the request of Christian Blind Mission, I visited ophthalmic centres in Afghanistan—Kabul, Jalalabad, Mazar-i-Sharif, Herat, and Kandahar—submitting a report recommending the establishment of a National Ophthalmic Resource and Information Centre.

This visit to Afghanistan required very careful planning, as I found myself on 16 different flights in 23 days.

A BRIEF STOPOVER IN LASHKARGAH

As we flew into Lashkargah, in south-west Afghanistan, by the desert of Helmand, the pilot of the small Bakhtar Airlines plane informed passengers who were disembarking to do it fast! He taxied to a stop, having turned the plane ready for take-off. A few passengers tumbled out at speed!

The reason for his anxiety and haste? We had already seen a warlike group of Afghans by the runway, most of them on horseback, coming at a gallop straight for our plane!

Thankfully, our pilot cleared the runway just in the nick of time!

RUSSIA 2004
AN INVITATION TO YEKATERINBURG

In October 2004, I was asked to present two papers at a specially arranged two-day conference in Yekaterinburg, The Urals. This invitation was extended by the Department of Ophthalmology, Veterans' Hospital, Yekaterinburg. This hospital was the largest of 57 Veterans' Hospitals in Russia.

Ruth was able to join me. Yekaterinberg is the fourth largest city in Russia. It has the striking golden-domed 'Church on Blood' built on the site of the Romanov executions of 1918.

For three well-attended days, there was considerable commitment, lecturing and discussing, with the main theme, 'World Blindness and its Prevention'. My translator was a delightful Tadzik girl who understood my 'slightly' Scottish accent very well! I recall being a little concerned that my main work abroad had been in Afghanistan! Thus, my illustrations and photographs were often of Afghan patients.

Many of these veterans in the hospitals had experienced much trauma, both physical and mental, while in Afghanistan. There had been the classical consequences of fighting and conflict, especially in distant lands.

Part Twelve

DAVID

DAVID

One Saturday morning, on 19 August 2000, our world was turned upside down. A policewoman, named Odette, came to our door at 71 Brickhill Drive, Bedford.

'I'm so sorry to tell you that your son, David, has been in a very serious car accident, on the A23, south of London.'

A phone call came from Mayday Hospital, in Croydon, south of London. It was a consultant anaesthetist. 'Your son David has been involved in a car accident. We are taking him to theatre now, but it's very unlikely that he will make it through surgery. I'm so sorry to bring you this news. We'll do all we can.'

'We know you will. Thank you for letting us know.'

Police cars, at least three, were lined up to take us, as fast as possible, from Bedford to south London, a distance of around 100 miles, but on some of the busiest roads in the UK. Our drivers drove furiously, sometimes through red lights, with sirens blaring, and linked us to the next car at appointed changeover places.

Carrie was with Ruth and myself in the police cars. Andrew was attending a wedding in Germany.

MAYDAY HOSPITAL

We arrived at the Mayday Hospital. There, waiting for us, was one of David's great friends, Ed Quibell. As he was driving to the Hospital, Ed had been playing a very special worship song, 'I love to be with You, beautiful God!' Ed was with us as we went through the next few traumatic minutes. Ed knew! In a real sense, he knew in spirit, before arriving at the Hospital, that David had gone.

We were shown into a room and asked to wait. A moment

or two later, a young lady doctor entered the room. Dr Rosalind van Every was so kind and compassionate.

'I'm so very sorry to tell you that David did not survive the operation. David's last words just before going to theatre were, "O Jesus! O Jesus!"'

Had Jesus Himself appeared to David? One day we will know. I hugged Ruth and Carrie. We followed Dr van Every upstairs to say our goodbyes to David. It was peaceful and heart-wrenching. We said that David looked as though he had just been in a rugby match.

Apparently, David had been sitting in the front passenger seat with his seat belt on. A man driving the opposite way along the A23 had fallen asleep and come across the highway, directly into the path of the car. Two girls were in the car with David. Sue was driving, and Maria was on the back seat. Both these special girls survived the impact, but with severe injuries. The driver of the other car and two passengers, an older lady and a young boy, all survived the accident without serious injury.

Ruth had brought David's donor card with her. It was an agonizing decision to make in the midst of uncertainty and impending grief. After gently telling us that David was no longer alive, Dr van Every asked us if David's corneae could be used for corneal grafts. We gave our permission.

Later, we heard that two young men had had sight restored through corneal grafts using David's corneae.

SOUTHWARK CATHEDRAL

Months later, we were invited by Simon Hughes, MP, a friend of David's, to a Service of Commemoration and Thanksgiving at Southwark Cathedral. The very large, 1,000-plus congregation that filled the church had many recipients of successful transplants and their relatives in attendance, but also the relatives and friends of those whose own loved ones had donated their organs, mostly because of their untimely deaths. It was so moving!

Names were all beautifully inscribed on our programme, but without any indication of who had given life, or sight, to whom.

QUERNMORE

The funeral service for David was in a little church at Quernmore, near Lancaster, a small village in the fields in north-west England. Ruth's parents are buried there.

After the service, Ruth and I travelled north with Andrew and Carrie for a few days in Glasgow. Andrew and Carrie were then living in Glasgow and attending a lively church which had been established by special American friends, Jake and Cherry Chadney.

Time passed. The police family liaison officer, Ian Edwards, was absolutely wonderful. We were to meet him some months later, at Croydon Crown Court, when a case was brought against the driver of the other car by the Crown Prosecution Service.

THANKSGIVING SERVICES

There were three Thanksgiving Services. The first was at Great Ormond Street Children's Hospital, where David had been involved in their fundraising programme. The second was at the Oasis Trust (Rev Steve Chalke), where David and his team had just launched XALT, a Christian internet company, only a few days before the accident. Steve Chalke and Simon Hughes, MP, wrote an obituary for *The Scotsman*. The third Thanksgiving Service was at David's own church in London, Holy Trinity Brompton.

The Thanksgiving Service at Holy Trinity Brompton was on

a Wednesday at lunchtime. There were over 800 people there, with a balcony of young friends from the four Harpur Trust Schools in Bedford. More pals (11 in all) were ushers, and other friends played their musical instruments on the platform. We heard a few years later that former school friends would meet in London on 19 August, the date of the accident, simply to remember David.

The Holy Trinity Brompton newspaper had a headline:

'A Young Man Loved By Many'.

Andrew and Carrie sang a duet, with Ruth playing the piano. I showed pictures and said a few words. David's three friends Rufus, Seb, and Jerry all spoke. David's Uncle Charlie, Rev Charles Bonsall, shared some personal thoughts. Rev Steve Chalke, a little ruefully, told us that David had said he would arrange for him to speak at HTB ... There were tears and laughter. The minister of HTB, Rev Sandy Millar, spoke on Lazarus and how Jesus raised him from the dead!

Such deep sadness, but with a quiet and reassuring peace, as we knew that our David was safe in the arms of Jesus.

There were international rugby players. Later I said that if you are hugged by a Scotland prop forward, you are really hugged!

One of David's special friends shared with us an amazing picture revealed to her just after the accident. The scene was a large and beautiful field of poppies. Standing in the middle of the field, she saw David with his hands raised to heaven, exclaiming, 'I knew it was true! I knew it was true!'

Sometime later, I was interviewed about my work by BBC Scotland. The interviewer also asked me about David. My final words in that interview, speaking about David, were 'We believe we'll see him again!'

Dr Rosalind van Every wrote to us on 27 October 2000: 'I cannot begin to imagine the sadness you must be going through. I myself cry every time I remember that morning in August - I don't know how I got through that weekend on call. It is obvious from what you have told me, and from what I have read that he was a fantastic young man, even in death he exuded something extraordinary. I will never forget his name ... or his face. I have been a doctor for 7 years, and seen over a hundred deaths, but David's was different. God took him at a crucial time. What does He mean?'

DIAMONDS

A year later, Ruth was walking in the centre of Bedford and met a good friend from our church there. Lyn asked Ruth, 'How are you?'

'Actually, not so good today, Lyn,' said Ruth. Lyn responded, 'Let me tell you something that I experienced during the service at HTB a year ago. While the service was going on, I suddenly pictured the Lord Jesus walking down the main aisle. Your David was walking right behind Jesus, over his right shoulder. They were having an animated conversation, and there were smiles, and even joy! Jesus was dressed in a flowing cloak with many folds. His hands were throwing diamonds from the folds of His cloak. The diamonds were landing amongst the crowd, and people were picking them up!'

HANSIE: 'YOUR DAVID IS LIKE DOMIE!'

One of our dearest friends while living in Glasgow was Hansie Douglas (Johanna Ruth Dobschiner), who wrote her powerful life story, *Selected to Live*. It became a bestseller, and a movie followed. In her life story, she loses most of her close family in

Amsterdam, who were taken by the Nazis. But Hansie hid herself in a coal bunker. She was later rescued by a fine young Dutch pastor, called 'Domie', who hid her 'underground' in occupied Holland. Domie rescued at least 200 young Dutch Jews before he was captured, tortured, and shot.

Hansie knew and loved our three children as they were growing up. One year after we lost our beloved David, at 28, she phoned us in our Edinburgh home with these amazing words: 'You know, Ruth, Domie rescued so many in his lifetime, but the truth is, he blessed more people after his death than during his life.'

'Your David is like Domie!'

Now, looking back over the years since we lost David, we can see it's true! What a blessing that is!

CROYDON CROWN COURT

A year on, there came the court case, with the accused being the driver of the other car. The charge was 'death by dangerous driving'.

The police wanted me to write a condemnation, or at least a strong letter, as the driver had driven his car after having little or no sleep before flying into Gatwick and then going straight to his car.

A sleep expert, in court, was unequivocal; the driver had fallen asleep more than once.

However, we, as a family, did not feel that we should write a letter of condemnation. We agreed that we would forgive the driver of the other car, who, in the court, was desperately sorry that this had happened.

Ruth and I attended the court proceedings in Croydon Crown Court on the second of three days. At lunchtime, the court adjourned, and to our surprise, the accused man actually walked between Ruth and myself. He bowed his head over his hands, held in a position of prayer. He had already expressed his great regret from the dock.

I squeezed his arm, in a sense, reassuringly. Unknown to me, on the other side, Ruth murmured words of forgiveness.

This was not easy or trite in any way. I sought out the family liaison officer and found him in his office. He agreed to write a letter for the judge, at my dictation. This was what Ruth, Andrew, Carrie, and I had agreed.

The family liaison officer wrote the words: 'While we miss our very dear son so very much, we choose to forgive [name given] for the loss of our son'. We asked the judge to recognize our request and consider leniency regarding a prison sentence. I was startled to witness this seasoned policeman and family liaison officer, writing with tears streaming down his face!

We finished the dictated letter. This special family liaison officer, with whom we still keep in touch, gripped my hand and then told me that he sometimes has people coming into his office 'spitting blood'!

Apparently, the judge read out our letter on the third day. He recognized the request we had made but said that the appropriate law and procedure should still apply, and a shortened prison sentence was given.

We recognized that the judge had made an appropriate and right decision, also taking into consideration our letter and its content.

Part Thirteen

MEETING THE QUEEN

QUEEN ELIZABETH

This very special meeting is reported here because it relates particularly to the production and distribution of the *Community Eye Health Journal*.

We were in Dallas, Texas, after the birth of twins Joshua and David to our daughter, Carrie, and Texan husband, Jeff. The year was 2009. The twins were born in Parkland Hospital, where President John F. Kennedy had been taken after his assassination in 1963.

An email advised that I was to attend an investiture in the United Kingdom to receive an MBE, awarded by a member of the Royal family.

On our return to the United Kingdom, arrangements were to be made as to the 'where and when' of the investiture. I recall making a phone call and being slightly thrown when the voice said, 'Buckingham Palace'!

The date was arranged for 13 July 2010 at Holyrood Palace, Edinburgh. We were delighted that it was to be the Queen who would be making the awards on that day. Ruth, Carrie and my sister, Margery, were there for the occasion. How very special to have my 'big sister' sharing in this family honour.

Andrew, unfortunately, was unable to join us due to a very important prior commitment.

When I spoke to officials in Buckingham Palace and explained that Andrew could not be with us, they said there was no problem ... and would my son Andrew like his invitation as a keepsake and memory of the day?

On the special day, as we walked into Holyrood Palace, a gentleman official enquired who I was and murmured, 'You are a recipient ... and I have an envelope for you. It has your son Andrew's invitation as a memory of the day.' Amongst the huge crowds milling around and within the Palace, this personal touch, with such courtesy, was truly amazing!

After receiving instructions in an anteroom, the 'recipients' filed through to the long room to be received in strict but relaxed order by Her Majesty, The Queen.

The question is often asked, 'What did the Queen say to you?' The Queen was straight to the point! 'What do you do?'

'I'm an ophthalmologist, Your Majesty! And the special country abroad, for us, is Afghanistan!'

'Afghanistan!'

'Yes, Ma'am! Our daughter was born there ...'

Her Majesty expressed her congratulations and pinned the medal on my lapel. Then an ungloved hand was stretched out to shake mine. It was the gracious signal that the brief time in her presence was at an end.

I backed up, bowed, and turned to the right.

'Dad!' said our daughter. 'You had a minute or so with the Queen, and you told her that I was born in Afghanistan!'

'Yes, Carrie' I responded. 'It's now well known in Royal circles!'

Part Fourteen

ICTHES WORLD CARE JOURNALS

ICTHES WORLD CARE: AROUND THE WORLD IN 10 YEARS

In the late 1990s, as a family, we considered setting up a charity to promote and distribute other medical journals addressing different areas of need, all based on the model and experience of *Community Eye Health*.

The name of the charity was 'ICTHES World Care'—that is, 'International Community Trust for Health and Educational Services'.

In 2001, soon after the loss of our David, we moved from Bedford to Edinburgh, mainly because Andrew and Carrie were in Scotland. I continued to commute to the International Centre for Eye Health in London for some days, every couple of weeks or so. One thing about editing a journal in this era of the internet, is that you can accomplish a great deal at home or on a train journey.

Our home in Edinburgh was 44 Murrayfield Avenue, very near to the famous Scottish national rugby stadium! Ruth wrote in one family newsletter that we were close enough to hear the cheers from Murrayfield! Andrew remarked, 'Or the groans!'

But we needed offices in Edinburgh. Our good friend Denis Robson was a senior official in Ethicon Ltd, part of Johnson & Johnson. Denis had previously arranged for his Company to contribute £30,000 to the work of the International Resource Centre in London, including the *Community Eye Health Journal*. In the short ceremony at the International Centre for Eye Health, when I received the £30,000 cheque, I expressed our gratitude, saying, 'This generous gift will contribute to the prevention of blindness worldwide.'

Denis gave us excellent offices to use in their Sighthill site in west Edinburgh, beside the offices of Scottish Business in the Community.

Trustees were appointed in Scotland. Our chairman was our great friend Nick Lunan who, with his wife, Ruth, had supported us in our former work in Afghanistan, particularly by their prayers. Amongst many other things, while we were abroad they kindly looked after our house in Bearsden, Glasgow, just around the corner from their own home.

Our aim was to produce a range of other medical journals for low and middle income countries worldwide.

Four journals were developed and published under the auspices of ICTHES World Care, although, sadly, *Repair & Reconstruction* only ran to two Issues.

Repair & Reconstruction: Two Issues on Burn Injury: 2001, 2002

Developing Mental Health: First published in 2003

Community Ear & Hearing Health: First published in 2004

Community Dermatology: First published in 2004

Our Trustees worked hard to supervise and establish the three ongoing publications, for which we were very grateful.

A FAMILY TEAM

Each of our three children, now in their 20s, at different times, made significant contributions in fundraising, editing, and proofreading.

David (26), a semi-professional rugby player with London Scottish, was a founding Trustee. He then moved into a fundraising role at Great Ormond Street Children's Hospital, London. In 2000, just months before we lost David, he ran the London Marathon to raise money for the Great Ormond Street Hospital Appeal.

But his most amazing contribution to our work was an incredible London evening, on 30 May 1998, in the Aquarium overlooking the River Thames. This party, called 'Deep C', was conceived and pulled off by David and nine other friends who had different resources, all in aid of ICTHES World Care. Invitations were sent out to 1,500 young guests from in and around London, each of whom was given a luminous armband (no gatecrashers allowed!) and kept in shape by scary-looking bouncers at different doors, while Ruth and I were upstairs showing slides of our work around the world. There were several floors at the Aquarium, each with luxurious sofas and six bands playing, while sharks slowly glided around menacingly behind glass windows! Unique, I would say, and a wonderful evening! The bouncers said that it was unusually peaceful!

Our other son, Andrew, who had just completed a four-year degree in International Relations and French at St Andrews University, came in to take over from David. He had never attempted fundraising in his life but spent four years working with us, and doing a great job. He had to learn all the ropes of fundraising and by the end of his time with us had brought in a significant grant from the Scottish government. There was great interest in our journals, perhaps particularly *Developing Mental Health*.

Finally came Carrie, our daughter. Occupational therapist and exceptional editor and proofreader, Carrie became part of the team, with Mum, Dad, and Andrew, joined in due course by a very special and supportive friend, Sally Collier.

We worked together as a team in Edinburgh (2001–2004).

Each of us would pool our thoughts, discuss, proofread, with Dad (Murray) having the final say!

These teaching journals—*Developing Mental Health (DMH)*, *Community Ear & Hearing Health (CEHH)*, and *Community Dermatology (CD)*—were of very good quality, written by experts and authorities in their respective fields, but with an appreciation of the cultural and particular needs in the developing world.

DEVELOPING MENTAL HEALTH

A number of senior consultant psychiatrists came to me with a request.

'Murray, we know the *Community Eye Health Journal* which you edit. We need a similar Journal in Mental Health.' The psychiatrists came up with a great name for the new Journal, primarily for developing countries.

Writing the Editorial in the first Issue, Professor Andrew Sims (former President of the Royal College of Psychiatrists) said, 'In trying to help and provide support for the most under-privileged group in society, the Editorial Board offers this service in the spirit of Christian service and concern. However, the content will not be "religious" but strictly practical, directed to the needs in our patients, and the authors will come from many different, and no religious traditions. For example, please see Dr Shakil J. Malik's significant article from Pakistan.'

In his Editorial, written in 2003, Professor Sims mentioned that learning disability is much more frequent in some developing countries than in the West, and that post-traumatic stress disorder (understandably) affected a substantial proportion of the whole population in Rwanda.

Officers for the first Issue:

Developing Mental Health 2003; 1: 1–16.

Editorial Board: Professor Andrew Sims (Chairman), Mr Simon Barrow, Dr Dominic Beer, Mr Chris Bocutt, Dr Marjorie Foyle, Dr Elizabeth Guinness, Dr Maureen Wilkinson

Developing Mental Health was handed on into the good hands of PRIME International.

COMMUNITY EAR AND HEARING HEALTH

Rev Christian Garms, Director of Christian Blind Mission International, had supported the *Community Eye Health Journal* from its very beginnings in 1988.

We were at a meeting of the Partnership Committee of the International Non-Governmental Organizations, taking place at the World Health Organization, Geneva, Switzerland.

'Murray, we need a journal on the prevention of world deafness, based on the example of *Community Eye Health*. Will you take this on?

It was such a vivid personal experience and invitation that I replied to Christian, 'You're right! This is exactly the vision—to expand into other fields.'

Community Ear and Hearing Health was first published in 2004. The Editorial Board appointed an individual Editor for each publication.

The Issue I have chosen had the following officers:

Community Ear and Hearing Health 2006; 3: 17—32

Editorial Board: Professor Jose M Acuin, Dr Piet van Hasselt, Dr Ian J Mackenzie (Editor for this Issue), Professor Valerie E Newton, Dr Beatriz C W Raymann, Dr Andrew W Smith
Regional Consultants: Professor Jose M Acuin (Philippines), Dr Juan Madriz (Costa Rica), Dr Beatriz C W Raymann (Brazil)
CEHH continued publication from the *International Centre for Evidence in Disability*, at the *London School of Hygiene and Tropical Medicine*.

COMMUNITY DERMATOLOGY

Dr Paul Buxton was a Consultant Dermatologist in Edinburgh. We were introduced to each other at the National Prayer Breakfast in Westminster, London.

The key to any new and innovative venture, particularly in a field of medicine which is not your own speciality, is to identify the person who would have the vision and purpose (and contacts) to carry the shared vision forward. Dr Paul Buxton became Editor of *Community Dermatology*.

The first Issue of *Community Dermatology* was in 2004. An Editorial Board and International Editors for *Community Dermatology* were agreed and established.

The publication I have chosen had the following officers:

Community Dermatology 2005; 2: 1–16

Editorial Board: Dr Beverley Adriaans, Dr Paul Buxton (Editor and Chair), Dr Neil Cox, Dr Claire Fuller, Dr Sam Gibbs, Dr Richard Goodwin, Dr Barbara Leppard, Dr Chris Lovell, Dr Michele Murdoch, Ms Rebecca Penzer, Dr Margaret Price, Dr Michael Waugh

International Editors: Professor Hennig Grossman (Tanzania), Professor Rod Hay (UK), Dr Don Lookingbill (USA), Professor Robin Marks (Australia), Professor Aldo Morrone (Italy), Professor Ben Naafs (The Netherlands), Professor Terence Ryan (UK), Professor Gail Todd (South Africa)

The *Community Skin Health Journal*, formerly known as *Community Dermatology*, is now an official Journal of the International Foundation for Dermatology.

THE CYPRUS CONNECTION

In due course, the Cyprus Connection allowed an increase in the circulation of the journals. The costs of both printing and airmail distribution were significantly less expensive than in the UK. Printed paper copies of DMH, CEHH, and CD at one time were sent out to over 200 countries worldwide.

CLOSURE

Sadly, there came a time when things changed, with differences of approach within our team, partly relating to Cyprus and the development of our work over there. While we, as a family, had been clear about our call to this strategic Mediterranean island, with its hugely cheaper costs of printing and airmailing journals worldwide, certain members of our team did not share our vision and made their views known. Also, significantly, there was no sign of the needed new funds to continue the work.

ICTHES World Care was closed down in 2009. It was really tough for us all, both team and Trustees. In the ensuing couple of years, these significant journals were handed on to the specialist teams that formed the Editorial Boards.

A very special 10 years!

Part Fifteen

ICTHES AND
THE CYPRUS
CONNECTION

ICTHES AND CYPRUS

Why Cyprus? How did we find ourselves directed to Cyprus? What was God's purpose, soon after the grief of losing David?

We had been planning for years to create an organization which would replicate the model of the *Community Eye Health Journal* in other medical fields. It was in the context of grief that we moved forward with this vision.

DAVE AND JULIE

Dave and Julie, who had been in Afghanistan, were now based in Cyprus. Right after David's accident, they came to Bedford UK, just to be with us. They suggested that we might go out to Cyprus as a family and stay for a time in their house there. The idea was to have family time and recover, as far as possible, in very pleasant and different surroundings.

Ruth, Andrew, Carrie, and I took up their very kind offer.

FRIENDS IN CYPRUS

During these times in Cyprus, we met so many marvellous folk, both Cypriots and expats from many countries, mostly associated with Larnaca Community Church, the New Life Fellowship in Nicosia, and a House Fellowship in Larnaca, led by a very special couple, Panayiotis and Fay Morphakis.

Another American couple, Tom and Teresa, were to be so important in this new phase of our family's lives. God brings people into our lives to bless us, encourage us, and advise us. So it was with Tom and Teresa.

Now in Cyprus, as Tom and Teresa were sharing with us, we began to discover what God was clearly saying to us, calling us to have a base on this delightful Mediterranean island.

John and Ann Smith have always been a special couple whom we met often—mostly in Cyprus but also in Canada, where they had their home, and in Scotland. John and Ann always encouraged us in our Christian faith and had significant 'words' for us. In September 2021, our dear John, the 'gentle giant', went into his Lord's nearer presence. Sadly, for the family and us, and very recently, Ann joined her husband in heaven.

Richard and Sue Fairhead kindly made their separate apartment available to us on our many visits, when tenants were in our own Cyprus home. They have been so helpful in bringing this present book towards completion.

STEPHEN, AND A BEAUTIFUL HOME IN KITI

We were introduced to a key person in our Cyprus adventure. Stephen Iacovou is a British Cypriot. He was an officer in the British Navy for some years, including the Falklands campaign.

Married to a Scots girl, who had been a very fine Scottish athlete, they have two sons, both of whom are outstanding footballers. Stephen was a financial consultant in Cyprus, later branching out into building houses.

Ruth and I began to consider a possible home in Cyprus. We were drawn to Kiti, near to Larnaca, a town and area with ancient roots, the original Kition. Kiti itself has a very old church, named Angeloktisti, which was built in the 11th century over the ruins of a 5th-century early Christian basilica. Of course, Cyprus is steeped in biblical history, particularly the apostle Paul's journeys. There is even a church to commemorate Lazarus, whom Jesus raised from the dead in Israel, but who eventually died in Cyprus.

Stephen identified and purchased a plot of land in Ayialousis

Street, Kiti. Tom and Teresa prayed over this plot of land which we dedicated to the Lord.

Together with Stephen, Ruth and I planned and designed two properties, semi-detached, each with a garden behind. Building commenced and continued over the next year or so. We received the keys for our Cyprus home in April 2004. Our own home in Cyprus initially became an office for ICTHES World Care, without any costs or expenses incurred by our charity, apart from occasional flight costs.

IMPORTANT CONTACTS

Meanwhile, Teresa was writing one of her excellent books and introduced us to her printer in Nicosia. Panicos Kamasia had his Square Dot offices in central Nicosia.

Panicos was to become a good friend who printed our journals to a very high standard. *Developing Mental Health*, *Community Ear and Hearing Health*, and *Community Dermatology* were produced at very competitive prices when compared with other publishers in the UK and Europe.

Panicos then introduced us to Chris Kythreotis, who had a mailing house in Nicosia. Chris airmailed our journals from Nicosia at amazingly reduced prices. These reduced costs were given by the Cyprus Post Office provided publications are printed in Cyprus.

Part Sixteen

LATER EVENTS
A WORLD IN NEED
FINDING THE HEALER

50ᵀᴴ ANNIVERSARY OF THE NOOR PROJECT

The year was 2006—fifty years since the NOOR Project was established in Afghanistan.

The main occasion and function, celebrating the 50 years of service, was in the Intercontinental Hotel ballroom in Kabul.

I had opportunity to share my deep gratitude to Afghanistan, pointing out that the years in the country stimulated thoughts of a journal of primary eye care for developing countries. This had resulted in the *Community Eye Health* publication, first published in 1988 and, in 2024, still being sent out worldwide.

A fundraising document written in 2017 emphasizes the ongoing enormous needs in eye care in Afghanistan 'About 500,000 people are blind in Afghanistan, that is, 1.5 to 2% of the population.'

The document continues: 'The NOOR Eye Care Programme was established in 1966. Since then, NOOR has partnered with the Government of Afghanistan to support eye care facilities and services and to train eye care professionals. NOOR now provides or supports most eye care services available in Afghanistan. NOOR operates referral hospitals in Kabul, Mazar-i-Sharif and Kandahar, provides logistical support to a Community Eye Hospital in Ghazni, and provides logistical support and financial oversight to the Ministry of Public Health's Central Polyclinic in Kabul and Herat Ophthalmic Centre, both of which continue to operate under NOOR protocols.'

AN OUTSTANDING LIFE CUT SHORT

There has been reference to Tom and Libby previously in this discourse. They were such valued and important team members at both the NOOR Eye Institute in Kabul and the Herat Ophthalmic Centre in the north-west of the country. Tom's energy and commitment was almost legendary. A good man to have in a crisis, and any other time as well. This quiet American had shown extraordinary bravery when 'under fire', rescuing wounded Afghans with gunshot injuries.

Tom, with Libby, made enormous contributions to the care of the visually impaired, and more than that, their service over 30 years was characterized by their love for the people of Afghanistan.

Then, in August 2010, tragedy struck. When returning from leading an eye camp in Nuristan, eastern Afghanistan, Tom and nine other team members were ambushed and shot by a marauding band, whose origin has remained in question. There were six Americans, two Afghans, one British doctor, and one German. Two other Afghans were allowed to go free.

There was worldwide condemnation of these foul murders.

Tom himself, and certainly Libby, his wife, would never want or look for any accolades. Their lives were given in service to people in need for over 30 years. For them it was simply getting on with the task in hand, without fanfare or fuss.

Tom Little was recognized as the 2010 International Optometrist of the Year by the World Council of Optometrists.

President Barack Obama presented Libby with the 2010 Presidential Medal of Freedom in honour of Tom's outstanding life of service.

COMMUNION, A PROMISE, AND A NIGHT ATTACK

Of course, violence doesn't only happen in war-torn countries.

It was getting late on a freezing Friday evening in January 2011. Ruth and I decided that we would take communion together, just the two of us.

We were alone in our flat, on the top floor of West Hurlet House, near Glasgow, a stately home built for the Earl of Glasgow in the mid-19th century. In fact, we were entirely alone in this very large 30-room property, as all friends who had lived on the two floors below us were no longer there. The house was in the process of being sold. It was very cold!

It was 10.30 p.m. Ruth prepared the bread and wine, and we sat together in our sitting room. We decided to read the Scripture from Isaiah chapter 54, specifically verse 17. My Bible just happened to be lying open at the very same Isaiah 54. I read the Scripture:

> No weapon formed against you will prosper
> And every tongue which rises against you in judgement
> You shall condemn.
> This is the heritage of the servants of the Lord,
> And their righteousness is from Me

We concluded our special service and went to bed.

Four hours later, at about 2.30 a.m. on that Saturday morning, we were abruptly woken from deep sleep by the most horrendous shouting and crashing! We realized that someone was smashing our wood-and-glass partition and door at the top of the stairs into our flat!

Our bedroom door was right beside that front door. We both leapt out of our big double bed. The doors were near to Ruth's side of the bed. She didn't hesitate!

Within seconds, we were both at our front door, yelling back at the intruder, 'What on earth do you think you're doing?'

Ruth shouted, 'In the Name of Jesus, GET OUT!'

He was a young man, only 17 years old, we learned later, with 32 recorded convictions.

Perhaps he had expected a doddery old couple who would panic? Had our experiences in Afghanistan helped us? Frankly, I was encouraged by our immediate reaction!

He was wielding an axe in one hand, which he was smashing into our door. In the other hand, he had a large kitchen knife, which he kept stabbing through the smashed glass and wood of our front door.

Ruth shot into our study and phoned the police. 'We're very busy right now!' said the police telephone operator. 'Is it urgent?'

Ruth responded, 'Can you hear that shouting and crashing? My husband's out there!'

Meanwhile, the young man was yelling at me. 'I'm goin' tae stab youse!'

Then he slightly changed his tone. I thought he was saying, 'Gie me *more* keys!' I realized that, in fact, he was saying 'Gie me yer *motor* keys!' That was 'Glaswegian' for my car keys. Then he said, 'Gie me the keys ... and I'll go!'

We had two cars: one a Toyota Avensis, off the road—and unfortunately, I had stopped the insurance—the other a Toyota Corolla, in good nick.

I was gazing down at the two sets of keys, trying to decide

which car keys to give him. Our attacker was exasperated! 'What are you doing?' he screamed!

'I'm deciding which keys to give to you.' I gave him the 'dud' Avensis keys, even though I knew the car had only been starting, uncertainly, with jump leads.

Thankfully, looking back, the car did start for him.

He must have passed the police car, which came at speed up the long drive to the stately home, within minutes. A mile or so from our place, our assailant crashed the car, which was written off! He escaped!

The CID came later that Saturday morning. The detective said that he had a good idea who had done this—a boy addicted to alcohol and drugs. The next day, Sunday, we met detectives briefly, and Ruth confidently chose one boy out of 24 mug shots shown to us. The following Tuesday, this same young man was arrested.

There were court proceedings some months later, and a prison sentence followed, but, because of his age, he was subsequently released again. How often had that happened? Looking back, we realize how God had protected us. 'No weapon formed against you will prosper' (Isaiah 54:17).

However, this was not the end of the story for this deeply troubled young man. About two years after our experience at West Hurlet House, the same young man (aged 19) broke into a home in Crookston, Glasgow, only a mile or so from our former home, and attacked an older couple. The wife came downstairs to help her husband and was stabbed multiple times by the assailant. She later died. Her husband survived.

WAS IT AN ANGEL?

In 2001, our son Andrew was driving our car along Allison Street on the south side of Glasgow. In the car was Ruth; our daughter, Carrie; and myself.

Our route took us across a very busy main road, Pollokshaws Road. The crossing had traffic lights, and as we approached, the lights were clearly on green in our favour. Andrew drove steadily up to the crossing. The lights were still at a steady green.

Suddenly, he rammed on his brakes! A bent old man was shuffling slowly and deliberately right across our path. He was looking straight ahead with the obvious intent of crossing our path to get to the other side. The lights, for him, would be absolute red!

We came to an immediate halt! The man progressed in front of us, apparently utterly oblivious to our presence. We waited in moderate frustration as he completed his course, when suddenly the sound, then appearance of a black car roared into our vision, from the right!

The car rocketed down Pollokshaws Road, and over the crossing, careering through the red lights, to disappear at considerable speed and noise towards Glasgow city centre.

Had we progressed, with the green lights beckoning us on, we would have been hit amidships, and surely no one could have survived!

The old man reached the safety of the kerb, having stopped us abruptly in the process.

The extraordinary timing of the incident made us all wonder whether God had caused the old man (dangerously and inappropriately) to cross the road as we were approaching—or whether he might even have been an angel!

A WORLD IN NEED

Our world remains in great need. Despite so many enjoyable and fulfilling experiences described in this book, there are also stark reminders of the trauma and sadness of a world in desperate need of peace and healing.

Finding the Healing Place—or, more accurately, 'The Healer'—should surely be the hope and even anticipation of us all.

FINDING THE HEALER

THE HEALER .

This very personal story of my and our lives has the theme referenced in the title 'in search of The Healing Place'. However, it is beyond that, in the finding of 'The Healer', that I respectfully want to direct our final thoughts.

I submit that the only person in human history who is uniquely qualified to be this Healer is Jesus. He is able to bring justice, peace, reconciliation, restored relationships, and community with physical, emotional, and spiritual healing.

He died on a cruel cross! That is historical fact. It was an act of love and of choice! The Healer submitted to sacrifice so that we might be healed!

This is my experience and conviction. I recommend Him to you.

Part Seventeen

SCRIPTURE VERSES
ON HEALING

SCRIPTURE VERSES ON HEALING AND DELIVERANCE

On either side of the river was the tree of life, which bore twelve fruits, each tree yielding its fruit every month. The leaves of the tree were for the healing of the nations. (Revelation 22:2)

He was wounded for our transgressions; He was bruised for our iniquities; the chastisement for our peace was upon Him, and by His stripes we are healed. (Isaiah 53:5)

The Spirit of the Lord God is upon Me, because the Lord has anointed Me to preach good tidings to the poor, He has sent Me to heal the broken-hearted, to proclaim liberty to the captives, and the opening of the prison to those who are bound. (Isaiah 61:1)

Bless the Lord, O my soul ... Who forgives all your iniquities, Who heals all your diseases ... so that your youth is renewed like the eagle's. (Psalm 103: 1, 3, 5)

Jesus Christ is the same yesterday, today and forever. (Hebrews 13:8)

When evening had come, they brought to Him many who were demon-possessed ... and He cast out the spirits with a word, and healed all who were sick. (Matthew 8:16)

Then great multitudes came to Him, having with them the lame, blind, mute, maimed and many others; and they laid them down at Jesus' feet, and He healed them. (Matthew 15:30)

When the men of that place recognised Him, they brought to Him all who were sick ... and begged Him that they might only touch the hem of His garment ... and as many as touched it were made perfectly well. (Matthew 14:35–36)

For assuredly, I say to you, whoever says to this mountain, 'Be removed and be cast into the sea' and does not doubt in his heart, but believes that those things he says will be done, he will have whatever he says. Therefore, I say to you, whatever things you ask when you pray, believe that you receive them, and you will have them. (Mark 11:23–24)

With men it is impossible, but not with God; for with God all things are possible. (Mark 10:27)

These signs will follow those who believe; in My name they will cast out demons; they will speak with new tongues; they will take up serpents; and if they drink anything deadly, it will by no means hurt them; they will lay hands on the sick, and they will recover. (Mark 16:17–18)

Most assuredly, I say to you, he who believes in Me, the works that I do, he will do also; and greater works than these he will do, because I go to My Father. And whatever you ask in My name, that I will do, that the Father may be glorified in the Son. If you ask anything in My name I will do it. (John 14:12–14)

EPILOGUE: STOP PRESS!

During times of preparing and proofreading the text of this book, throughout 2021, 2022, 2023 and 2024, we have been experiencing an extraordinary worldwide pandemic due to the coronavirus, Covid–19.

Jesus spoke of 'pestilences' in the last days before His return to earth, His Second Coming. This could fairly be translated as 'epidemics' or 'pandemics'.

In all that is happening to us on the world scene, is God trying to get our attention? I believe so!

Are we witnessing the fulfilment of Bible prophecy?

While attempting to write our story, it suddenly and unexpectedly seemed irresponsible of me to complete this book without any reference to the times we are in and the urgency of the hour.

I recommend the reading of the words of Jesus in Matthew, chapter 24, of the New Testament.

The disciples of Jesus asked Him, 'Tell us, when will these things be? And what will be the sign of Your coming, and of the end of the age?' (Matthew 24:3).

Jesus answers: 'You will hear of wars and rumours of wars. See that you are not troubled; for all these things must come to pass, but the end is not yet. For nation will rise against nation, and kingdom against kingdom. And there will be famines, pestilences, and earthquakes in various places' (Matthew 24:6–7).

Jesus continues: 'This gospel of the kingdom will be preached in all the world as a witness to all the nations, and then the end will come' (Matthew 24:14).

Further He says: 'Then the sign of the Son of Man will appear in heaven, and then all the tribes of the earth will mourn, and they will see the Son of Man coming on the clouds of heaven with power and great glory' (Matthew 24:30).

ABOUT THE AUTHOR

Murray was born in Shanghai, but grew up in Scotland...with a very early calling (aged 12) to be a doctor and practise abroad, wherever he was needed!

A long medical training, specialising in 'eyes' and the prevention of blindness, led to a post as Director of the NOOR Eye Institute in Kabul, Afghanistan. Afghan staff numbered 130 plus, with an international team of 25 – 30. NOOR was a superb, well-equipped 100-bed eye hospital, serving thousands of needy patients from all over the country, and also former members of the royal family...in the midst of a Soviet take-over!

Murray had many friends around the world who believed in the power of prayer and faithfully prayed for him and his family. Miracles were to follow!

Later, an appointment to the International Centre for Eye Health, London, established the *Journal of Community Eye Health*, for which Murray was Founder Editor. First published in 1988, copies are distributed worldwide, with health professionals in many countries now reading the Journal online.

Murray also travelled on short term consultancies, working with international organisations, such as the World Health Organization, Sightsavers, Tearfund and CBM International.

His book majors on medical adventures, prayer, and occasions where Murray had to work as a diplomat in testing situations. Unexpected challenges for an eye doctor from Scotland!

Printed in the United States
by Baker & Taylor Publisher Services

Printed in the United States
by Baker & Taylor Publisher Services